D0744955

A History of Force

A History of Force

Exploring the worldwide movement against habits of coercion, bloodshed, and mayhem

James L. Payne

Lytton Publishing Company
Sandpoint, Idaho

ISBN: 0915728176

OCLC 53973401

Lytton Publishing Company
Founded in 1975
Box 1212
Sandpoint, Idaho 83864
www.lyttonpublishing.com

Preface

Many years ago, at the age of seventeen, I spent a year in England attending a boarding school in London. It gave me a chance to visit historic sites and ancient monuments on free afternoons and weekends. For an American who had hardly ever seen a building that had been erected before 1900, touring England was like entering a fairy tale with its knights, castles, and peasant villages of thatched cottages. Or, rather, the experience was one of discovering that the fairy tales were real, that the events and personages of history from across the Atlantic, so far-off as to seem imaginary, were literally yesterday's news.

This feeling of shocking realism hit me most forcefully on my visit to the Tower of London, where I saw—and touched—the wooden chopping block that was used to cut off Anne Boleyn's head. What a shudder I felt! Until that moment, I had treated the account of how King Henry VIII had executed his wives Anne Boleyn and Catherine Howard as a fictitious tale, on a par with stories about dragons and trolls from the Brothers Grimm. Now I felt its reality, and it deeply distressed me. That anyone would cut off the head of a living soul was horrible enough, that the victim was a beautiful woman made it worse, and that this woman was innocent by modern standards made the deed still more appalling.

I was not alone in feeling revulsion at the murders of Henry VIII and at similar acts of bloodshed of yesteryear. Most people in modern society feel the same way. My reaction was simply a reflection of my culture. However, what was clear to me, as I stood in front of that cherrywood chopping block, was that people in Henry VIII's day did not share this cultural orientation. The killing of Anne Boleyn was not a murder committed in a back alley by one depraved individual. It was carried out by a famous king, apparently well respected in his own time, and it was carried out in this public and official place with the approval of hundreds of public officials. The people of that age obviously were not horrified by it as we are today. They were human beings with arms and legs and powers of speech, but in their attitude toward suffering and bloodshed they were, from our perspective, strikingly alien. They accepted and even took pleasure in violence that today appalls us.

How widespread is this shift in attitudes toward the use of force? This is the question this book sets out to answer. My survey of coercive customs and practices around the world shows that England has not been unique, but is part of a seemingly universal pattern: a tendency toward a decline in the use of force appears to be at work in all human communities.

This is a broad generalization, of course, one that begs for elucidation and expansion. As I progressed with this study, it became increasingly clear that I was raising more questions than I was able to answer. The use of force may be declining, but how fast? Is the rate of decline the same for different cultures? Can it affect one use of force and not others? How do we account for departures from the trend, cases where the use of force increased, at least for a time? And what is the locus of the shift against force? Does it reside in culture, or institutions, or citizen attitudes, or leadership attitudes? The subject of force is a large puzzle with many pieces still missing.

Then there is the matter of policies and strategies. Is there something we can do to hasten the decline in the use of force? Or is this process beyond deliberate human control? I say a few words on this subject in the last chapter, but I feel they must be rather tentative. After all, how can one prescribe an intervention when the process is but dimly understood?

Yet frustrating as these many unanswered questions may be, we should not let them obscure the larger picture. We may not fully grasp how or why a change is taking place, but we can still mark the change. Understandably, we are upset by the scenes of shocking violence that the media bring into our homes on a daily basis, and our first impulse is to assume that bloodshed and destruction are about to engulf civilization. But if we step back a bit and consider the behavior of our ancestors, as I was prompted to do that day at the Tower of London, it becomes clear that, in its halting, complicated way, the world is transcending the violent habits of the past. From this fact, I believe we are entitled to draw a serene, if guarded, optimism about the future of the human race.

Sandpoint, Idaho
July 2003

Contents

I

The History We Can't Stand

We seem to have a history of everything. I just searched an Internet site of used books for titles containing "history of" and the search returned 845,000 volumes, covering a bewildering variety of subjects. There's a history of British native ponies, a history of celibacy, a history of the canoe, a history of the sauna, and a history of the First Presbyterian Church of Orlando, Florida. There's even a history of history. Humankind, it seems, has a powerful and ubiquitous need to uncover the background, development, and trends of every subject under the sun.

Except one. There is no history of force. There is no account of the background, development, and trends of man's use of physical action against his fellow man. Of course, there are treatments of subcategories of this topic: histories of war, histories of capital punishment, histories of torture, histories of taxation, and so on. But each of these specific uses of force is considered in a compartmentalized fashion, as if it had no relationship to any other use of force. No one has thought it fitting to look at the general willingness to inflict physical harm, to make a survey of how this impulse varies from age to age and from place to place.

When you stop to think about it, this omission is really quite remarkable. For sheer drama, force is the great attention-getting subject of the human race, as a perusal of newspapers, television, novels, and movies amply documents. "If it bleeds, it leads" is the operative principle in mass media. In principle, then, a history of force ought to have more appeal than a history of almost any other subject.

Force is not just a gripping topic, however; it also plays a central role in the evolution of modern institutions. Indeed, one could say that the advance of civilization has depended on humankind's ability to reduce the use of force—and that communities that continue to be relatively uncivilized are so because force looms so large in their culture. Consider the arrangement we call democracy. What does this system require? The first answer is a relatively low use of force. Democracy cannot exist where rulers routinely murder their opponents, where opposition leaders routinely try to murder rulers, and where parties and factions are constantly starting wars when they don't get what they want. This is what went on almost everywhere in the world centuries ago, for the most part accounting for why there was no democracy. And it still goes on in a number of places today, again precluding democracy.

Given how closely democracy depends on a reduction in the use of force, we might suppose that scholars would have carefully tracked the decline in the tendency to use force over time. We might have expected to find scores of studies linking the declining pace of civil wars, revolutions, revolts, military coups, riots, and political executions to the evolution of modern political institutions. But, no, we do not find any books on this subject—not even, so far as I can tell, a single journal article.

The use of force is linked to another topic of vital interest: economic prosperity. Again, the connection seems obvious and elementary. What kind of economy can a community have in the midst of perpetual civil war? How can production increase if mobs of workers are burning down factories? What happens to the transportation of goods in a land where gangs of robbers threaten every road? What happens to prosperity when soldiers seize farms and factories? A reduced use of force is obviously a necessary condition for prosperity.

Yet, strangely, this theme appears to be almost entirely ignored. Generations of scholars have pondered the subject of economic development, and we now have a very long list of possible factors contributing to it: technology, deep-water ports, roads, a stable currency, an educated labor force, mineral resources, population, population density, arable land, savings, investment, and so on. Yet missing from this list is the obvious requirement of a reduction in the use of force. Somehow the point has been overlooked that prosperity cannot develop in an atmosphere of seizing, burning, smashing, and killing.

For forty years, the great historians Will Durant and Ariel Durant worked on the most comprehensive history of civilization ever published. Their ten massive volumes—astute, engrossing, and fact-filled—cover the span of human experience from the ancient empires of Persia and China to the French Revolution. After they completed their immense work, they summarized their general conclusions about the progress of civilization in a volume entitled *The Lessons of History*. In it they identified more than a dozen "precious achievements" that the human race has made in its long and difficult evolution, including fire, language, writing, song, agriculture, and social organization. It's an excellent list, of course, but it involves a striking omission. The Durants say nothing about the amazing decline in the use of force, about how the progress of civilization has depended on setting aside the vicious, bloody habits of yesteryear. It is as if a farmer, summarizing the principles of growing crops after forty years of experience, never mentioned the role of rainfall.

We have, then, a subject that is interesting and dramatic, one that plays a decisive role in political and economic progress and, indeed, in the progress of civilization itself. Yet the world has not recognized it as a topic of inquiry. There is no history of force. Why not?

Is it because the topic is too broad? The subject of force is indeed a sweeping one, a point I have felt acutely as I worked on this volume. How I wished that a team of researchers would take over the task, a body of scholars commanding all the languages and all the history of all the societies of the world that could compile a proper encyclopedia of this vast subject. Yet the fact that the subject is broad hardly explains why it is not discussed, for many other broad topics attract scholarly interest. People write books on the history of ideas, the history of art, the history of religion, even the history of civilization and the history of the world. So the complexity of the subject doesn't explain why it is avoided. There's some deeper resistance going on in the case of force.

An Embarrassing Contradiction

The reason why we avoid contemplating the history of force is that this topic involves a complex embarrassment. Like sex, force is a subject on which we have strong positive and negative opinions at the same time. To escape the disconcerting feeling of being wrong no matter what we say, we avoid the subject. Let's look into how this conflict comes about.

"How do you feel," asks the pollster, "about the practice of doing physical harm to human beings? Do you approve or disapprove?" If the question is put to us in this general form, what is our opinion about the use of force? Because we are members of the human race in the twenty-first century and sympathize with our fellow humans, at least in the abstract, our first impulse is to say we disapprove. With horror and revulsion, we point to wars, genocides, tortures, and mutilations. Furthermore, the historical record indicates—and this book confirms—that the use of force is tending to decline. The worst excesses belong to "barbaric" and "primitive" cultures, and modernization—despite certain shocking exceptions—brings with it a more humane approach. So we think we know where we stand. Taking the general, historical point of view, we conclude that the use of force is wrong, that both history and the angels are on the side of avoiding its use.

But then we turn our attention to the particulars of daily governance, and we discover an opposite perspective: we think the use of force is right! Society employs the threat of inflicting harm on person and property in thousands of circumstances in order to accomplish, or to attempt to accomplish, what we consider to be good objectives. Our libraries, art museums, schools, and universities rely on the implicit threat of violence embedded in the tax system. The shadow of force lies heavily over most trades and professions, from plumbing to surgery, in the form of government licensing regulations. If we fail to heed these rules, government agents will seize our property or even drag us off to jail. Most of the products we use, from headlights to hairsprays, are regulated through the threats of physical action against the person and property of those who fail to obey the relevant dictates.

There are, of course, many disagreements about whether a particular use of force is wise or needed, but it is practically impossible to argue that they all are unnecessary. Those who deplore the idea of using the tax system to subsidize farmers are keen to rely on it to subsidize symphonies. Those who think regulating barbers is absurd insist that stockbrokers be regulated. Those who say it was folly to use force to ban alcoholic beverages are eager to fight a war on drugs. Those who deplore capital punishment still want people to go to jail for murder. All of us, in different ways and for different reasons, embrace the use of force. We can't imagine doing without it altogether.

We have, then, two opposite conclusions about force: that it is evil and barbaric, but also that it is wise and necessary. How can we resolve this contradiction? A sophisticated solution would adopt a two-level perspective. We might say that force in general is unsound, but that it is excusable on a temporary basis for this or that purpose until we figure out—or evolve to—a nonviolent way of handling the problem. One says, in effect, that using force is like living in caves: it's an unhealthy idea in general but understandable if you haven't developed anything better.

This kind of complexity is not suitable for public opinion, however. The mass mind thinks along simple lines, and a practice is either right or wrong. It is either right or wrong to raise funds through taxation, for example. The public cannot accept the view that it is a harmful, inefficient arrangement, but all right to continue it for a few more years until voluntary systems of fund-raising can take over.

Furthermore, systems using force demand legitimization. The officials involved—tax collectors, politicians, judges, police officers—will not be content with the idea that they are engaging in a crude, unhealthy activity that can be excused only as a temporary expedient given the primitive state of human development. Who would spend his life in such a career believing his actions are thus tainted? Those who use force—and those who benefit from its use—need to believe that their enterprise is noble. They need to believe that even in the most highly developed civilization there should be school taxes, drug wars, and building codes.

The ambivalence about the use of force is not new. When Moses came down from Mount Sinai, one of God's commandments on the stone tablets he carried was "Thou shalt not kill." When Moses found the Hebrews worshiping the golden calf, he recruited the sons of Levi to massacre the idol worshipers, some three thousand being slain according to the account in Exodus. Obviously, there were (at least) two distinct kinds of killing in this culture: a private slaying for personal motives, or murder, which was considered wrong, and public slayings for those considered guilty of idolatry, which were considered not just right but divinely ordained. Anyone who discussed both phenomena under one heading—writing "A History of Killing," let us say—would confuse and anger his audience because this focus would suggest a degree of equivalence between the right kind of killing and the wrong kind.

Thus, we see why societies are not comfortable with general discussions about the use of force: no society can accept the idea that its major institutions are primitive, tainted, or temporary. That is why there has been no history of force. I undertook this study to satisfy my own curiosity about where civilization has come from and where it is headed. I have made it available for those who might share this curiosity. Tracing changes in the use of force has been an invigorating exercise, one that has left me with a deeper understanding of history and, especially, with a new appreciation for the mysterious, unexpected way that human institutions evolve. I hope I have been able to communicate something of this excitement to my readers.

2

The History We Can't Believe

One objection to the study of force, as I explained in chapter 1, is that it makes us uneasy, for it seems to equate the "bad" uses of force that we deplore with the "good" uses of force that we endorse. To avoid this moral confusion, we avoid the subject. But this confusion is not the only problem with the subject. There is a second obstacle that is perhaps even more potent: we find it difficult to believe the facts that this historical study reveals!

As far as we can tell from the historical record, we live in a much more peaceful world than has ever existed. Humans are less vicious, less inclined to inflict physical injury than they used to be. Within this broad picture there are of course deviations and exceptions, cases where certain regimes and cultures have exhibited temporary increases in violence. But these exceptions cannot obscure the larger pattern. As the following chapters show, the evidence for a decline in the use of force is massive, so broad and so obvious as to make the point something of a self-evident truth.

But, for most people, the observation seems to be wrong—and not merely wrong, but irresponsibly wrong and irritatingly wrong. Swayed by a number of fallacies and distortions, they are convinced that, compared to the past, we live in particularly vicious, bloody times. They therefore are disposed to reject out of hand any study that purports to find the opposite. Even if you can get them to look at some of the evidence and to agree that the facts do indeed indicate a dramatic decline, they are convinced against their will, so to speak. In their minds there remains a bedrock of contrary conviction that will continually reassert itself. For example, they will demand still more data to support the conclusion that force has declined—never noticing that they have no data to support their conviction that it has not declined!

I have wrestled with this problem long enough to know that on the subject of trends in the use of force, the average person is in the grip of a firm prejudice. What is left to the scholar is to try to understand and analyze the causes of this mental block. The fallacies and misconceptions that keep modern observers from reaching sound conclusions about trends in the use of force are formidable biases. They can be grouped into three categories: (1) the fallacy of presentism, (2) the distortions of activism, and (3) the distortions produced by the sampling bias of the media.

The Power of Now

Human beings are inevitably self-centered. We think that we are important and that the times we live in are important. Combine this bias with the fact that most people pay little attention to the study of history, and the result is the fallacy of presentism: the tendency to assume that events of the present are larger, more important, or more shocking than events of the past. With regard to the use of force, presentism underlies an impulse to suppose that modern violence is worse than violence in the past.

The television viewer who watches a news story about a multiple killing in a local restaurant is quite likely to shake his head and say, "What is the world coming to?" By this question, he implies that the violence just reported exceeds, to a worrisome degree, the violence of yesteryear. How did he reach this conclusion? If we ask him what he knows about killings in the distant past, he will concede that he has not made a study of the subject, that he is uninformed about the nature and frequency of murders in times past. He has fallen victim to presentism. He assumes that the killings that loom so large in his consciousness must be worse than killings about which he knows nothing.

The best corrective for presentism is, obviously, to start

collecting information about what actually happened in the past. Take the matter of homicide. It happens that someone recorded the number of murders in Yorkshire, England, in the year 1348. There were eighty-eight deaths, a figure that indicates, as criminologist Christopher Hibbert has calculated, a murder rate more than seventy times the modern statistic: "If murders were committed on this scale now," comments Hibbert, "there could not be less than ten thousand murders a year in England and Wales, instead of an average of about a hundred and forty."[1] Instead of worrying about a supposed rising tide of violence, our television viewer should be relieved that he doesn't live in 1348.

The bias of presentism is not confined to casual observers. Scholars also have a tendency to assume that in those times and places about which they know little, episodes of violence were relatively minor compared to those of the present. A typical illustration of this error is found in a comprehensive sociological study of war published in 1986 and entitled *War in International Society*. At the beginning of the book, the author announces that he is excluding from his survey any past wars in Asia and Africa on the grounds that these conflicts were between tribes, not between recognized states, and that information about these tribal conflicts "is in any case inadequate to provide a proper record or basis for comparison." Yet in his concluding chapter, he forgets this disclaimer: "In the Middle East, Africa and Asia, war has probably been more frequent, and certainly more costly, in the last 40 years than for centuries past."[2] How could the author be so sure ("certainly") that modern war in Africa is more costly than wars of earlier times? He himself declares that the information to make such a comparison is missing. The fallacy of presentism fills the gap: he assumes that the modern events he knows about are larger and more frightening than past events of which he is not aware.

Contributing to the fallacy of presentism is the failure to focus on *rates* of violence when comparing the present with the past. At the beginning of human history, there were only a small number of people in the world. If the number of murders were twice as high today, it would be absurd to say that killing had "doubled." The relevant statistic is the homicide rate—that is, the number of murders compared to the size of the relevant population. World population has increased enormously in recent times; just since 1800 it has sextupled. Therefore, to make valid statements about the intensity of violence in the form of riots, genocide, or war, one must compare the number of casualties to the size of the population involved.

To illustrate, the total number of deaths on the Union side in the Civil War was 364,511, and the number of Americans killed in World War II was 405,399. The raw numbers show an absolute increase, suggesting that twentieth-century war was more costly. But the population of the United States increased sixfold over the period between these wars. As a result, the death rate in the Civil War was actually more than five times higher than that in World War II: 1.6 percent of the population died fighting in the Civil War, compared to 0.3 percent in World War II. If you were an American of military age, which century would you rather live in?

The classic example of presentism is the oft-heard declaration that the twentieth century was the most violent in history.[3] This claim has been repeated so often that it is now considered a truism, but it has no scientific basis. After all, there are some forty centuries of history involving thousands of human communities scattered all around the globe. Almost all of the information about bloodshed in these forty centuries has been lost or was never recorded. The readiness to accept the claim about the twentieth century being the most violent clearly documents the strange, irrational power of presentism. We are so impressed by the violence of our own time that we unconsciously assume it must be worse than that of unknown times and places.

The Vested Interest in Perceiving a Violent World

The human race is a problem-solving species, eager to right wrongs and anxious to stamp out bad behavior. This disposition toward activism powerfully influences the way we perceive the world. The first step in any effort to change things for the better is to emphasize the wrong in order to attract attention and support. There is but a small degree of difference between emphasizing a wrong and exaggerating it, and this fine line is routinely crossed in just about every campaign of reform the world has ever seen. As a practical matter, activism implies exaggeration. If a fire is burning in one part of town and you want citizens to turn out to fight it, it makes sense to claim that this fire is very large and might even threaten the entire town. If you report that the fire is relatively small and will probably go out on its own—which may well be the truth—fewer firefighters will show up.

In the modern world, violence is the fire that everyone deplores. We want to see less of it, and this activist stance leads to exaggerated statements about how violence is "growing" and about how it therefore represents an "increasing" threat. An observer who tries to point out that violence is declining goes very much against the grain. He seems to lack moral concern. Take the statement about the twentieth century being "the most violent in history." Although it has the appearance of a factual statement, it is not really intended as such. It is the speaker's way of communicating an activist attitude—namely, that he is shocked by and deplores the violence of that period and hopes it never happens again. Listeners agree with this emotional point by agreeing with the speaker's irresponsible statement: yes, they say, nodding their heads, the twentieth century was the worst. Anyone who disagrees with the factual claim seems insensitive, implying that the wars and genocides of the twentieth century weren't all that bad and that we shouldn't worry about a repetition of these events. This person will be excused from the party.

This tendency to exaggerate is multiplied for organizations that play a role in dealing with or reporting violence. A military organization, for example, has a vested interest in exaggerating foreign threats. Generals are loath to report that the danger of foreign aggression is diminishing, for such a report would suggest the desirability of a reduction in military spending. Ironically, peace organizations obey the same imperative: if they report that the world is getting more peaceful, they make their mission seem less necessary, and donations to them will slack off.

Over the years, I have collected many examples of the way violence is exaggerated for organizational purposes. For example, in June 1999 my local newspaper carried an Associated Press story with the headline, "Armed Conflicts Are Increasing Around World, Institute Says." The basis of the story by the Associated Press was a press release from the Stockholm International Peace Research Institute (SIPRI), which makes a yearly compilation of wars in progress. The institute had just released its 1998 figures, which showed twenty-seven wars, up from twenty-five in 1997. "Clearly," the SIPRI official was quoted as saying, "1998 shows a worse picture in terms of armed conflicts around the world." This statistic, the story concluded, "paints a gloomy picture of global security on the eve of a new millennium."[4]

As it happens, the institute and the Associated Press were combining forces to paint a biased picture. The institute's own data show that the total number of armed conflicts was running at thirty-five to thirty-six a year in the mid-1980s, when it began the tabulation, and peaked at thirty-seven in 1990.[5] Since then, the number of wars has declined dramatically, touching an all-time low of twenty-five in 1997. The 1998 figure was up slightly but still way below the peak at the beginning of the decade. Thus, the headline reporting the SIPRI data should have been, "Armed Conflicts in Decline." Such a story was not expedient, however, for it would contradict the mission of a peace institute, which cultivates both antimilitary sentiment and donations by painting a picture of growing violence.

We see the same pattern repeated time after time, whether the subject be the rate of criminal executions, violence in the schools, genocide, or the size of military forces.[6] The data may show declines, in many cases steep declines, but the spirit of advocacy keeps commentators from focusing on this fact. In order to criticize these uses of force and to mount a campaign against them, activists claim worrisome increases.

Sampling Bias and the Mass Media

Among the many social changes wrought by modern communications, perhaps none is so striking as our newfound ability to learn about and react quickly to violence. In an earlier age, cities, countries, and even civilizations could be swallowed up in bloodshed without other parts of the world even knowing about it. Today, tragedies in the farthest corner of the globe are comprehensively reported. One notes, for example, that the Library of Congress catalog already lists fifty-one entries on the Rwanda genocide, an episode that occurred in 1996 in an obscure corner of the world. To take another illustration of the intensity of modern record keeping, a recent book on the "troubles" of Northern Ireland lists the names and circumstances of death of all 3,637 victims of the political infighting since 1970.[7]

The increasing scope of reporting on violence creates a serious problem of "sampling bias": the increase in *information* has led to a perception that violence itself has increased. Consider how editors and producers in news organizations decide to allocate their information-gathering resources. They do not place their cameras randomly around the world. If they did, they would merely capture boring pictures of people peacefully walking around cities, towns, and villages. Instead, these news organizations send their reporters and camera operators wherever there are scenes of violence because they know they need this footage to interest their audience. As a result, viewers will gain the impression of an extremely violent world, regardless of the actual trend.

Suppose that 1 million people are being killed in riots, wars, and genocides around the world in one specific time period. Camera operators will obtain scores of scenes of violence and fill the airwaves with them. Now suppose that several generations later the rate of killing falls to *one-tenth* the previous level: a dramatic decline, one that ought to be headline news. Owing to the selection bias of news media, however, the public will never suspect this change. The camera operators and reporters are still able to find plenty of images of violence, for in this relatively peaceful world 100,000 people are still dying. Furthermore, the increasing ease of transportation will enable news personnel to get quickly to more places, thus increasing the coverage of strife and giving the impression that violence is increasing!

Sampling bias also affects scholars who attempt to study trends in the use of force. Because there is so much more information about recent violence, their tabulations will exaggerate the extent of modern bloodshed compared to that of the past. For example, in 1960, the statistician Lewis F. Richardson compiled data on the cost of war over the past two centuries to see if there was any trend. He didn't find any overall pattern, but that was because his information about wars in the nineteenth century was highly incomplete. Richardson himself was aware of this distortion: he noted, for example, that he excluded from his tabulations some 80 revolutions in nineteenth-century Latin America, and 477 wars and revolts in nineteenth-century China owing to the lack of data about them.[8] Many of these wars in China were stupendous bloodlettings that cost millions of lives, as one can estimate from the abrupt declines in population following the upheavals. For example, as a result of the fighting and massacres of the Nanking revolt of 1853–64, the population of the province fell by 70 percent.[9] The exclusion of hundreds, even thousands, of nineteenth-century wars from his tabulation caused Richardson to miss the finding that the war death rate was declining. (The distortion of activism was probably at work here: Richardson was a devout Quaker who wanted to emphasize the horror of war. It would have detracted from his message to find that the world was getting more peaceful.)

Sampling bias and the media's economically driven compulsion to emphasize violence have created a popular perception about trends in worldwide violence that is utterly at variance with the facts. Soaked in the wall-to-wall coverage of violence, the public believes that we live in an increasingly bloody and dangerous world. The truth is that, compared with the past, we live in an astonishingly peaceful one.

Librarian Matthew White has compiled comprehensive statistics on world violence in the twentieth century that illustrate the overall trend in genocide and other types of killing. Using data from dozens of reference books and studies, he calculated death totals from all known wars and genocides as well as deaths in other types of political repressions for each quarter of the twentieth century. Then he expressed these deaths as a fraction of the world population in that period. His results, shown in figure 2.1, indicate that the war casualty rate in the world has been falling dramatically in modern times.

Figure 2.1

Trends in World Violence, 1900–2000

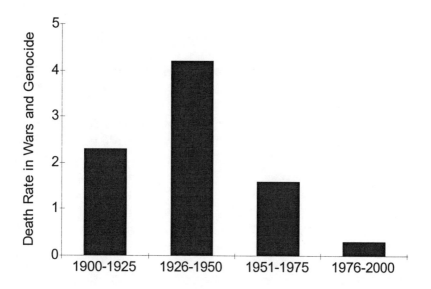

Note: The death rate is the percentage of world population killed in the quarter century. To obtain a yearly death rate, the figures would be divided by 25.
Source: Matthew White, *Historical Atlas of the Twentieth Century*. Available at: http://users.erols.com/mwhite28/20centry.htm. Accessed March 21, 2001.

And it is still falling! One way to illustrate this point is to calculate the number of lives that war and genocide would be claiming each year if the pace of killing of earlier times were being maintained. White's data indicate that if the war death rate of the 1900–1925 period were maintained today, we would see 5,520,000 deaths a year. The actual number of deaths in the twenty-five or so war zones in the world in recent years has been running at less than 50,000.[10] In other words, the rate of killing today is less than 1/100th the pace of a century ago!

Even if the future should suddenly fulfill our worst fears about possible episodes of violence, it would still have to be described as relatively peaceful. Suppose, for example, that terrorists set off a nuclear weapon that kills twice the 50,000 that died in the Hiroshima blast. And suppose that in the same year India and Pakistan plunge into war and bomb each other's cities with a total of ten double-Hiroshima nuclear blasts. All this mayhem would produce 1,100,000 deaths. Now further suppose that in every succeeding year, other terrorist actions and other nuclear wars continue at this same pace of killing, producing 1,100,000 deaths each year. This pattern would represent appalling and deplorable violence, to be sure, but it would still reflect progress, for it would leave the world with a yearly level of killing less one-fifth the rate of a century ago!

In 2001, two foreign policy experts, Robert S. McNamara and James G. Blight, wrote a book on the problem of world violence and on what should be done about it. McNamara is a former secretary of defense and also president of the World Bank, and Blight is a professor of international relations at Brown University—credentials that should have kept them from straying too far from the truth. Yet, in opening their discussion, they make a colossal error, declaring that "throughout the post–Cold War period, brutal war and communal killing on an alarming scale have increased."[11] Significantly, they did not feel it necessary to present any trend data to support their claim. Although the facts indicate that there was something on the order of a *99 percent decline* in world violence in the post–Cold War period compared to the early part of the twentieth century, they "knew," without even looking, that it was increasing!

As I said, the information indicating a decline in the use of force is massive and obvious, but it is difficult to get a public in the iron grip of presentism, advocacy, and media distortion to believe it.

Out of Sight, Out of Mind

In addition to the three distorting effects just discussed, there is another reason why people disbelieve the idea that the use of force is declining: we take the changes for granted. Certain coercive customs and practices disappeared so long ago in our culture that we don't register them as changes.

A simple illustration would be the custom of human sacrifice. This was an extreme use of force involving the kidnapping and slaying of human beings. The practice of human sacrifice was extremely widespread in the ancient world. In Mesopotamia and Egypt, when rulers died, their entourage of wives, concubines, and servants were slain with them. In Wales, Germany, and Japan, primitive peoples practiced foundation sacrifices, slaying victims to commemorate the construction of castles and temples. In Carthage and Palestine, they engaged in child sacrifice, hurling screaming children into fiery pits. All this was socially approved violence. If you asked the man in the street what he thought about it, he would have said it was necessary for the well-being of the community. Attitudes now have totally reversed. Human sacrifice is seen as appallingly evil, and politicians and religious leaders would never think of engaging in it. The disappearance of this custom, then, constitutes a dramatic instance of the decline in the use of force, but it is one the public does not notice as such.

Another example is slavery. Slavery is state-sanctioned and state-enforced kidnapping. Human beings are captured in wars or raids, and this "kidnapping" is made permanent by the application of physical punishments in cases of defiance—whipping the recaptured slave, for example, or even hanging him as an example. This vast, brutal application of force used to be universal around the world. Aristotle declared it to be an inevitable feature of human society. Today it has virtually disappeared, and this change represents a dramatic decline in the use of force that is seldom remarked upon today.

We also obscure the movement away from the use of force through our use of terms that hide the role of force. One example is the term *freedom*. Traditionally, this has been used to refer to declines in the state's various uses of force. For example, in England in Henry VIII's time, government officials burned an average of 3.25 heretics per year.[12] In England today, they don't burn any heretics, and the practice is so remote from current values that it would be a joke to suggest they reintroduce the practice. Here, then, is a clear instance of a decline in a particular use of force, but the public doesn't notice it as such because we use different language to describe the change from earlier practices. Instead of saying there has been a decline in the use of force to regulate religious practice and belief, we say that we now enjoy "religious freedom."

In practical terms, a political freedom is the ability to do something without this activity being blocked or punished by government officials using physical force. Thus, freedom of religion means that force is not used against those with disapproved religious beliefs. Freedom of the press means that writers and printers are not beaten, jailed, or hanged for what they write and publish. Freedom of assembly means that people can meet together to form a labor union or a political group without this meeting being broken up by police officers wielding clubs, and so on. Thus, the observation that modern societies enjoy many freedoms not available in the distant past is another way of referring to many dramatic declines in the use of force. The word *liberty* is often used as a synonym for *freedom*, referring to areas of behavior no longer subject to government's use of force. The Statue of Liberty symbolizes a country where the force of the state is lightly used.

Another term that hides many important declines in the use of force is *right* or *civil right*. In ancient times, rulers and their armed officials could use force against citizens in any way they pleased: beat them up, seize their lands, throw them in jail, slay them. What we call the "rule of law" and the associated citizen "rights" represent the evolution of a system for restraining the use of state force. The right to property meant that government officials could not simply seize your cow or your farm because they wanted it. They were restrained by procedures (due process) that recognized the citizen's ownership of property. The right to life meant that government officials could not kill you on a whim or because they wanted to settle a personal score with you. They had to observe many limits, limits that we now recognize as rights in criminal procedure: the right to a trial, the right to an attorney, the right to face accusers, and so on. These restrictions are all ways of limiting the ability of government officials to use physical force. They make it more difficult for police and prosecutors to put you in jail or put you to death.

Although traditionally a *right* referred to a restriction on government's use of force, in modern times a whole new usage of the term has emerged that reverses this meaning. In modern discourse—or perhaps I should say in modern demagogy—a *right* is something the public wants without having to pay for it. Thus, the "right" to education refers to the idea that education should be provided free of charge. The same is true for the "right" to medical care or the "right" to food or to housing. In practice, the way these "free" goods are supplied is through the taxing power of government. Therefore, the advocacy of these modern "rights" implies an expansion of the state's use of force, at least to the degree that tax levels are increased.

See the confusion that results! If a person says he is for increasing "rights," he can mean either that he favors a *limitation* of the state's use of force or that he favors an *increase* in the state's use of force, depending on the particular case. When it comes to the use of force, our language is often obscure and indirect, covering up what is involved. Perhaps this is because, as pointed out in chapter 1, force is something about which we are embarrassed. We have found ways of talking around the subject without directly naming it. This pattern of semantic evasion and euphemism often hides critical declines in the use of force.

Our perceptions about trends in violence in the world, then, are affected by numerous biases and misconceptions. Once these distorting biases are cleared away, it becomes rather obvious that the human race is turning away from force-based practices. This evolution is by no means complete, of course, and there are many ups and downs in the trend. Some societies are far ahead of others in this evolution, and all societies still endorse many practices based on force. Furthermore, the use of force by deviants—which we call crime—is deplorably common. My purpose in pointing to the progress we have made is not, as the reader might fear, to make us complacent about force. If this book has a prescriptive message, it is the opposite one. It is that we have become too comfortable with the violent practices that still prevail. We have lost sight of the achievements made, and as a result we are confused and apathetic about continuing the task of emancipating ourselves from the use of force.

3

What History Is Up To

This exploration of historical trends and practices reveals that a broad decline in the use of force has been taking place in the world. Before we examine the specifics of this decline, it would be useful to discuss it in general terms and develop an explanation for it. What accounts for the trend against the use of force?

The best way to answer this question is to trace out the implications of the definition of *force*. In popular speech, we use the word *force* to cover any situation where an action seems strongly motivated. At the bridge table, a player may say, "When George led the queen, I was forced to cover with the king." The meaning given to *force* in this book is much more restrictive: *deliberate physical action against the person or possessions of another*. Thus, *force* here always refers to physical force. It refers to concrete, physical actions such as cutting, piercing, restraining, and taking, as carried out by physical implements such as hands, clubs, swords, bullets, and bombs. In general, my use of the term *force* refers to those acts that would be called crimes of violence if carried out by a private party, such as murder, robbery, arson, kidnapping, and rape. In this book, I use *violence* as a synonym for *force*.

Although there is a distinction between using force and threatening to use it, in most contexts the distinction is an unimportant one. Both can be called a use of force. A robber who physically extracts your wallet from your pocket while holding you down on the ground has used force, but so has a robber who has obtained your wallet by threatening to push a knife into your stomach if you don't give it to him.

It is important to distinguish force—physical force—from the many other ways in which human beings try to control each other's behavior. When George led the queen at the card table, he did not pull a gun on his opponent and say, "Play the king or I will kill you." Therefore, he did not "force" him to play the king in the sense of the term employed here. The opponent played the king motivated by a desire to play successfully within the rules of the card game, not by fear of physical harm.

There are many situations in life where circumstances strongly compel a certain action but do not involve the use of force. We might hear, for example, that an employer "forces" waitresses to wear a particular uniform. Does this usage conform to our definition? Almost certainly not. The employer who requires uniforms is threatening to discharge—that is, not pay—the employee who fails to conform to his wishes. Refusing to buy something from someone is not an act of physical aggression. (Every shopper does it to thousands of merchants every day.) The use of the term *force* would be correct only if the employer drew a gun and threatened the waitresses with bodily injury if they decline to wear the uniform.

What if a waitress could get no other job and might therefore starve if she were discharged? The threat of being fired would certainly strongly compel her to wear the uniform, but she still would not be forced. The definition of *force* does not hinge on the possible consequences of an action. It pertains to the nature of the action itself—namely, deliberate physical injury or threat of injury to the person or his possessions. A woman might drive her lover to take his life by refusing to marry him. People might be tempted to say in this case that "she killed him," but her action is not a use of force, not a crime of violence. All she did was say "no." A person who refuses to give bread to a starving man is not using force, even though his refusal might result in the man's death.

Human beings can harm each other in many ways that do not involve the use of force. Sometimes, in an effort to emphasize their points, writers transplant the language of physical force to these other spheres. They speak of "cultural violence" or "verbal violence" or "economic force" or "psychological force." In each case, the writer may well be pointing to some kind of wrong, some kind of harmful control, but it is not force in the sense of direct physical injury or restraint.

Government Does It Too

Another aspect of the definition of *force* that needs to be clarified concerns the status of the actors. In our conception, it makes no difference *who* uses physical means against another, whether it be an individual, a group such as a gang or lynch mob, or the agents of a socially approved unit such as a government. It is still force. This may seem an obvious issue, but in practice the confusion between private and governmental uses of force gives rise to many distracting arguments.

The source of this confusion is the fact that, as I pointed out in chapter 1, all societies have both socially approved uses of force and disapproved uses. This distinction, although perhaps clear enough to the reader of this page, is difficult to maintain in mass communications. Cultures want things in black and white: something is either wrong or right. Because force in the form of violent crime by individuals obviously has to be wrong, modern societies are led to disapprove of force in general. We say killing is wrong, robbery is wrong, and kidnapping is wrong. But this generalized disapproval leaves no room for the socially approved uses of force, specifically the ways that governments kill people or rob them or kidnap them.

The common way to escape this dilemma is to attempt to redefine government's uses of force as not "really" force. We see this confusion clouding the modern interpretation of taxation, for example. Taxation is, simply, government's extracting funds by force or by threat of force. In other words, in physical terms, it is robbery. However, because taxation is a socially approved activity, we don't use the negative-sounding term *robbery* to refer to it. We have an entirely different term—*taxation*—and try to make ourselves believe that it is in no way related to that criminal act. Indeed, many people, especially Internal Revenue Service officials who are embarrassed about their role, say that taxation does not involve force at all, that it is "voluntary."

This kind of confusion needs to be transcended if we are to have any clarity about historical developments in the use of force. We can debate whether a certain use of force is socially desirable, but this debate should not obscure the fact that it is still force. Governments can and do use force just as much as private individuals. Indeed, down through the centuries, they have been the greatest users, so to eliminate their actions from the study of force would be to set aside most of the data.

What's Wrong with Force?

Making a distinction between force and the other ways human beings try to influence each other is important not just for semantic clarity. It is essential in order to understand what history has been up to for the past several thousand years. There is no trend, so far as I can discern, against the emotional control of some people by others or against the exercise of economic power or against the wielding of cultural influence. The historical trend is against the use of force— physical force. Why has this type of force been singled out?

The broad answer, I believe, is that the use of physical force involves more harm more consistently than other methods of influence—social, economic, psychological, or intellectual. This difference stems from the fact that it is physical, that its user can depend on Isaac Newton's reliable laws about the behavior of mass and energy in causing pain. All other methods of trying to hurt human beings have an indirect and merely probabilistic effect.

Suppose an employer wishes to harm one of his employees. He is so angry with that employee that he wishes him dead. He therefore decides to use his economic power to its fullest extent: he discharges the employee, hoping that this will cause the fired worker to starve to death. This is bad behavior on the employer's part, without a doubt, but the action is not with certainty harmful. The discharged worker can get another job—possibly even a better one—or find income from some other source. Because of all the other alternatives, it is most unlikely that the worker will starve to death. Thus, economic power is limited in its capacity to do harm. Not so with force as defined here. By putting a bullet through the worker's body, the employer can kill him with certainty.

The same point applies to verbal power. Language can be used in many wounding ways, but its harm is both limited and uncertain. An insult, for example, may not wound at all. The hearer may laugh it off. There is no way to laugh off a knife in the ribs. What our fathers told us about schoolmates who taunted us was right. It is sticks and stones that break our bones. Perhaps it's too strong to say that "words can never hurt me," but even when they do hurt, their injury is normally much less than that caused by violence. Ask yourself: Would your rather be insulted or shot?

One reason we are poorly equipped to recognize the line between force and other kinds of harm is that religion, which traditionally has been the main source of ethical standards, almost entirely ignores the harm of using force. It dwells, instead, on many lesser wrongs and sins. For example, in the Bible, in both Old and New Testament, one will find only a handful of references to the wrongs of killing, robbing, and raping. Misbehavior like adultery and thinking bad thoughts are mentioned much more frequently. What accounts for the slighting of the wrong of force by religious authorities? One answer is that in earlier times, religious leaders used force to impose their doctrinal views and to punish unbelievers. This made them reluctant to condemn force. After just burning heretics at the stake, a sermon on how wrong it is to kill would be out of place.

Another part of the explanation is that religion sets its sights on perfection. It lumps all the different wrongs together as instances of falling short, or committing sin, that is, transgressing against God or the divine order. Thus, religions do not rank or rate misdeeds according to their degree of injury. For example, the Buddhist preaches the doctrine of "do no harm." It would undermine the transcendental character of this principle to analyze and discuss degrees of harm, saying, for example, that killing a mouse is four times as bad as killing a fly, and that killing a man is sixty-four times as bad as killing a mouse. Instead, all these acts of transgression against the living universe are viewed as equally wrong. Other religions take a similar absolute view of wrongdoing. They posit an infinite universe of sinful deeds—including sinful thoughts—and religious leaders have been loath to rank these wrongs according to their relative harm. As a result, the simple point that violence is a greater wrong than others is overlooked.

Another reason why religion downplays the evil of force is that the point is considered so obvious that it doesn't need to be dwelt upon. Most parents agree with this point. They spend far more time telling their children to say "please" and "thank you" than reminding them not to kill other children. Of course they consider killing a far greater wrong, but it seems obvious that the child already understands this.

For all these reasons, religions fail to emphasize that using force represents a level of wrong greater than other kinds of transgressions. Consider the story of the Good Samaritan. It dwells on the behavior of the Samaritan who gave aid to a traveler who had been beaten and robbed on the road to Damascus. It contrasts his helpful behavior with that of the priest and Levite who passed by the injured traveler without rendering aid. The moral of the story is "render aid to needy strangers." Notice how the real evildoers in the story are not even criticized. They are the robbers who used force, who caused the injury without which there would have been no need for any help. The first moral of the story ought to be "robbing and beating people is wrong," and the account should have severely condemned the vicious robbers. The priest and Levite didn't do as well as they should have done in the situation, but they come off rather well compared to the robbers.

Putting First Things First

If philosophers had sat down at the beginning of history and decided which evil would be the most important one for the human race to overcome, they surely would have picked the use of physical force. It's not that there aren't other kinds of wrongs and injuries, sins both of commission and omission. But this one stands out as the most important problem to be solved.

It also stands out as being the most *preventable.* It is easy to see and apply the rule that would eliminate the use of force from human affairs: don't initiate physical action against another person or his property. It is much more difficult to arrive at a rule to control the other kinds of harm that humans may do to each other. How would we control verbal abuse, for example? It's not good enough to say, "Don't make insults." People can be offended by words in the form of literary reviews, well-intentioned advice, and the truth. Similarly, how do we prevent economic power from leading to injury? We can't just say, "Don't sell," or "Don't buy," or "Don't fire employees." People may cause some kind of injury with their economic decisions in an infinite variety of circumstances (which is why the effort to define economic crimes is always arbitrary and convoluted).

Or take affairs of the heart. Problems involving love, romance, and sexual relationships certainly cause much woe, but by what rule can they be regulated to prevent this harm? No one should ever fall in love? Boy must never be allowed to meet girl? This is not to say that nothing could ever be done in this field. Dear Abby and Dr. Laura represent a useful beginning. But we are far from even imagining how to arrange matters in this complex and subtle terrain so that no one ever gets hurt.

I think our philosophers at the beginning of history would have grasped this point. They would realize that it makes most sense, in the attempt to improve the lot of human beings, to tackle an obvious, easily preventable harm. Later, when we get really good at righting wrongs and have the genie of force more or less completely in the bottle, we can tackle more obscure and intractable sufferings. Our philosophers would reach the conclusion, then, that from the standpoint of overall human progress, the reduction in the use of force ought to be considered the first priority.

Our philosophers are imaginary, however. Real philosophers almost never think along these lines, nor do moralists, prophets, preachers, or politicians. Worldly thinkers and doers do not make the reduction in the use of force the focus of morality or policy because, as noted previously, like everyone else, they are highly ambivalent about it. Yes, they condemn certain uses of force in certain contexts, but in other contexts they want to use force to accomplish their ends and to uphold their ideals and values. And so this policy—striving to bring about a general reduction in the use of force—remains an orphan in the world of ideas, unendorsed by any significant group, movement, or party.[1]

How then has the human race made progress in reducing the role of force in its affairs? If no party or ruler has consciously pursued this objective, how has it been achieved? One is almost tempted to answer that "History" is the protagonist in this drama. This is not quite fair, of course. Human beings, through their actions and inactions, have brought about the shift. But they have not consciously or directly attempted to reduce the use of force. They simply have tried to make things more sensible or less painful or more efficient, and, time after time, such goals happened to coincide with a reduction of force.

Perhaps an analogy will help clarify this subtle process. Let us suppose that at some point human beings made all their furniture out of straw. Straw was abundant, and they lacked the imagination or ability to make furniture out of any other material. From an analytical, objective point of view, we can see that straw is a poor material for furniture because it has no strength. However, the human beings involved lack this perspective. They believe that furniture has to be made out of straw. That's the way it always has been, they say, and the way it always will be.

Yet in individual instances, the users discover problems with the straw furniture. They discard a straw table because it has collapsed, deciding that it is easier to eat sitting on the floor. Later, someone brings in a plank of wood, which serves as a slightly better table than the floor. Later they support this plank on some logs, which works even better. Eventually they have a wooden table. They refuse to generalize from this experience, however. They still have straw beds, straw chairs, straw bookcases, and so on, and will not listen to the suggestion that straw in general is a bad idea for furniture. But one by one the other straw items of furniture prove dysfunctional and are discarded and replaced, so that in the end little straw furniture remains.

The movement away from coercive institutions has followed this pattern. The human race is unable to take an analytical, objective view of force, unable to apprehend the general principle that force is unhealthy and harmful. But on a case-by-case basis, force-based practices have been discarded because they were seen to be harmful or inappropriate.

As I have mentioned, this evolution has not taken place at an equal pace around the world. It began earlier in some parts of the world than others, and has proceeded faster in some places compared to others. The result is that societies differ considerably on this dimension. In some places, one finds a strongly force-oriented culture where force is widely used, officially and unofficially, to control behavior and punish transgressions, and inhabitants accept, and even approve of, many public and private uses of force. In another region, one might find a less force-oriented culture where coercive practices found elsewhere have been abandoned, or are applied less frequently. In their attitudes and opinions, the inhabitants of this less force-oriented culture show a degree of hesitation or skepticism about many uses of force.

What accounts for these variations in the orientation toward force? Why do some communities come to reject a certain use of force before others? Why, for example, does a community abandon human sacrifice when it does? Or, why does one country stop arresting writers and printers long before another country? As we shall see as we explore such points, there are no simple answers. However, two broad explanatory variables do emerge: increasing wealth and increasing communication. When people grow richer, so that they are better fed, healthier, and more comfortable, they come to value their own lives, and the lives of others, more highly. I expand on this theme later; for the moment, I simply note that economic advancement appears to be one broad condition that has fostered a decline in the use of force.

Communication is important in the reduction in the use of force because it enables objective third parties to draw conclusions about the harm of violent practices. The participants in a war, for example, are steeped in subjective hatreds, ambitions, and the desire for revenge. Therefore, to them, war seems a necessary, desirable institution. Far-off observers, untouched by these hatreds and ambitions, are more likely to see the folly and tragedy of the war and thus to begin to learn the lesson that war is unwise. Hence, the development of communication—written language, libraries, universities, printing, and organs of mass communication—plays a significant role in the decline in the use of force. It facilitates the creation of a reflective public opinion that can assess and evaluate the role of force.

These explanatory ideas will take us only so far, however. There is certainly not any one-to-one correspondence between prosperity and communication, on the one hand, and the decline in the use of force, on the other. Many ancient empires were relatively prosperous, yet were strongly force-oriented societies. Furthermore, the movement away from force is not a smooth and consistent one. A culture may go for many centuries with little change in its orientation, and then, in the space of a few decades, it may discard key violent practices. And there are cases of backsliding, when a coercive practice that has been seemingly rejected is momentarily readopted.

The routes whereby uses of force are abandoned are often quite unexpected, even mysterious—so mysterious that one is sometimes tempted to allude to a higher power at work. Time and again one encounters violent practices so rooted and so self-reinforcing that it seems almost magical that they were overcome. One is reduced to pointing to "History" to explain how this immensely beneficial policy—a reduction in the use of force—has been gradually imposed on a human race that has neither consciously sought it nor agreed with it.

4

The First Step away from Force: Overcoming Human Sacrifice

Around two thousand years ago, at the height of the Roman Empire, the present-day area of Germany was inhabited by a number of tribes whose practices shocked the more civilized Romans. The Roman historian Tacitus has given us a detailed account of these peoples, reporting, with a mixture of titillation and disapproval, their grisly practices. These tribes had made warfare a way of life. They did little tilling and raising of crops, Tacitus reported, because they believed it "stupid and spiritless . . . to acquire by their sweat what they can gain by their blood." Javelins and shields were everyday attire. "Without being armed," Tacitus reported, "they transact nothing, whether of public or private concernment."

Several of the tribes, notably the Cattans, practiced a revealing custom. "As soon as they arrive to maturity of years, they let their hair and beards continue to grow, nor till they have slain an enemy do they ever lay aside this form of countenance by vow sacred to valour. Over the blood and spoil of a foe they make bare their face." In other words, for males of this tribe, there was not just an expectation that they would kill other human beings, but a requirement! Killing was, as Tacitus put it, a "debt and duty contracted by their birth." Thus, long hair in males—which has had so many different meanings through history—was in this culture a sign of cowardice. Naturally, youngsters were eager to get into battle to be rid of it. The custom marks quite a gap between ancient and modern culture. German youth of today may be rowdy and even violent on occasion, but they are not brought up believing that their birthright requires them to slay other human beings.

In completing his account of these tribes' bloody customs, Tacitus comes to the most alarming of all: human sacrifice. It was practiced by the Semnones, the largest subtribe of the Suevians. "At a stated time of the year, all the several people descended from the same stock assemble by their deputies in a wood consecrated by the idolatries of there forefathers, and by superstitious awe in times of old. There, by publicly sacrificing a man," Tacitus continues, "they begin the horrible solemnity of their barbarous worship."[1]

His reaction is the attitude of all civilized peoples to the practice of human sacrifice. This custom is one of the most shocking uses of force, and it appears that it is the first violent practice that a community sets aside as it evolves toward a more pacific culture. An understanding of this practice and the reasons why it is abandoned provide important insights into the historical process of overcoming violence.

Varieties of Human Sacrifice

In sorting through the sacrificial practices of ancient societies, one encounters an almost overwhelming complexity and variety. Victims were slain in so many different ways and for so many reasons that one almost despairs of arriving at a useful way to classify the customs. The first problem one faces is that in ancient societies religion and ritual surrounded all important activities, which means that all public killings were religious sacrifices in one sense or another. But to classify all slayings as cases of human sacrifice would confuse analysis. Many of these killings correspond to modern uses of force, being different only in that they employed religious ritual. For example, ancient peoples would execute criminals in religious ceremonies that made the victim a sacrifice to a god. But such killings served a distinctly human end—punishing and eliminating wrongdoers—and this is the same as the aim of modern executions.

It is worth making a distinction, then, between *functional sacrifices* and *pure sacrifices*. The functional sacrifice is a killing that serves social purposes, such as ridding society of a wrongdoer or implementing human motives of revenge or fear. The pure sacrifice is a killing that seems to have no other justification than to please a god. The victims of a pure sacrifice are quite blameless. The slayers have no motive for killing the victims except their assumption that the god desires a slaying.

Most of the official killings in primitive societies can be considered functional sacrifices. They include executions for wrongdoing, executions for heresy (heresy angers the human believers in the religion), and killings in connection with war, such as the slaying of prisoners or the extermination of captured peoples. Another type of functional sacrifice is the political killing—that is, slayings undertaken by rulers to eliminate rivals or to prove their power and inspire fear. For example, in the African region that later became Ghana, nineteenth-century Ashanti rulers would single out tribal members for slaying in a religious ceremony as a way of terrorizing subjects. When the English attempted to put a stop to the practice in 1848, one Ashanti king was reported to have said, "If I were to abolish human sacrifice, I should deprive myself of one of the most effectual means of keeping the people in subjection."[2] In other places—Benin, Dahomey, Hawaii—this aim of terrorizing people into submission accounted for many "sacrifices." These political killings have close parallels in modern European history, except that when tyrants such as Hitler and Stalin killed opponents and detractors, they didn't bother with religious ritual.

It wasn't only kings who sought to maintain their power by using the sacrifice apparatus. Priests and others could also get back at personal enemies by accusing them of transgressing against the gods. For this reason, we have to be cautious in interpreting any sacrifice in which adults were the victims. Sometimes these killings were pure sacrifices, but they might also have been functional sacrifices, instances in which a person or faction was eliminating rivals. By the same token, we can generally assume that the ritual slaying of children constitutes a case of a pure sacrifice because an ordinary child would not represent a threat to anyone. (The slaying of newborn infants might be credited as a population-control practice, but this explanation isn't plausible for children reared for some years.)

One type of slaying that perhaps falls in the gray area between functional and pure is the burial sacrifice: killing people as part of the funeral services of an important person. Some of the earliest recorded instances of this type of slaying have turned up in archeological studies of the kingdom of Ur, dating from around 2800 B.C. Excavations of royal tombs reveal that dozens of servants and court officials were buried alive with the dead king, including soldiers, musicians, and women of the court. The practice of burying servants with their royal masters was followed in many other places as well, including Egypt, China, and South America.[3] A variant of this practice is the well-known custom of suttee, carried out in India even until the early part of the twentieth century, wherein the wife of the deceased is burned to death on the funeral pyre as part of the funeral rites. In general, burial sacrifices are not cases of pure sacrifice. A lavish funeral is something people want for themselves. Killing people at a burial is a way to demonstrate the status and power of the deceased and of his successors.

From Moab to Mexico

Confining our attention to cases of pure human sacrifice, we find that the practice was widespread in ancient times. Early legends of many different cultures refer to human sacrifice as a socially approved practice. One Greek legend concerns the first-born son of King Aeolus of Athamas (Phrixus) who was about to be sacrificed in the hopes of ending a drought when he was rescued by a ram. In another Greek legend, Iphigenia was sacrificed by her father Agamemnon in the hopes of raising a good wind for his fleet. Hindu legends also tell of kings who promise to sacrifice their sons to the gods.[4] A Druid legend from Wales tells how the attempt to build a fortress was repeatedly foiled as the building materials disappeared at night. The priests instructed the leader to find a child whose father was unknown, slay him, and sprinkle his blood on the ground where the fortress was to be built.[5]

Another type of ancient slaying is the foundation sacrifice: burying human victims in the foundations of important new buildings such as palaces, temples, bridges, and forts. It was practiced in many parts of the world, including China, India, Japan, Germany, and Wales.

The foundation sacrifice was addressed to placating a god and could hardly serve any human function. In his comprehensive survey of human sacrifice, Nigel Davies explains the logic: "A new building is. . . a form of intrusion on the domain of the local spirit, whose anger may be aroused and who therefore has to be appeased."[6] Of course, if criminals or prisoners were used in a foundation sacrifice—which sometimes was the case—then the deed would have a double purpose, human and god oriented. But if children were used for the sacrifice—which was common—then it was a clear case of pure sacrifice: the death of the humans served only to appease a god's supposed demands and was of no benefit to anyone participating in the slaying.

The Bible alludes to child sacrifice in numerous places. There is, of course, the famous story of Abraham and Isaac, recounted in the Book of Genesis, where the sacrifice was called off at the last minute. In Leviticus 18:21, child sacrifice is directly prohibited: "You shall not give any of your children to devote them by fire to Molech, and so profane the name of your God." This passage suggests there were competing religions in the region and that the worship of the Hebrew Yahweh may have been an evolution from earlier religions that did practice child sacrifice. Hence, the Hebrews could be tempted to backslide into this custom.[7] In 2 Kings 23:10, there is a report of a period of religious tightening up under King Josiah, who attempted to purge practices that were creeping into Hebrew worship, including the worship of Baal and male prostitution. One place that was slated for forceful cleansing was the Topheth (sacrificial arena) in "the valley of the sons of Hinnom." The aim was to stop the practice of child sacrifice: "that no one might burn his son or his daughter as an offering to Molech."[8]

A case of child sacrifice is reported during a war between the Hebrews and the Moabites. After losing a number of battles, the Moabites had retreated to their city, where they were besieged by the Hebrews and unable to break out. The writer reports that in these desperate straits, the king of Moab "took his eldest son who was to reign in his stead, and offered him for a burnt offering upon the wall." Significantly, the chronicler reports that this tactic worked, for in the next sentence he says, "And there came great wrath upon Israel and they withdrew from him [Moab's city] and returned to their own land" (2 Kings 3:21–27). Even though the Hebrews considered human sacrifice wrong, they apparently still believed that it was effective—a point that explains their tendency to backslide into it.

By the time of the Babylonian exile (585 B.C.), child sacrifice had been eliminated from the Hebrew community,[9] but reports from around the Mediterranean indicate that it was still performed in a number of other places after that time. In Carthage, it was apparently quite common.[10] Once, during the third century B.C., when the city was under siege by an army from Syracuse, the Carthaginians sacrificed two hundred children, reportedly of the noblest families.[11] Before a battle with Alexander the Great in 335 B.C., the Illyrians, a tribe to the north of Greece, sacrificed three boys, three maidens, and three black rams— apparently a regular custom before battle.[12]

In Rome, it appears that the practice of human sacrifice was dying out by the third century B.C.—dying but not dead. In 226 B.C., when Hannibal and his allied Gaelic tribes were sweeping toward a defenseless Rome, the population of the capital panicked. In this moment of hysteria, the Senate authorized human sacrifice to appease the gods. They made a rather stingy offering, however. Instead of killing the flower of Roman manhood, the Senate ordered four slaves—two Greeks and two Gauls—to be buried alive.[13] (The sacrifice might be said to have worked: Hannibal never advanced on Rome!) Later, in 97 B.C., Rome passed a law against human sacrifice, indicating that the custom had ceased to be official, but perhaps also suggesting that it was still being done privately on occasion.[14] In Ireland, according to historian Thomas Cahill, human sacrifice was practiced as late as A.D. 400. This custom, he says, was expunged by St. Patrick.[15]

In Europe and the Mediterranean region, human sacrifice was abandoned well more than a millennium ago. However, as explorers and colonizers from that region traveled abroad, they encountered human sacrifice in the newly discovered cultures. In the sixteenth century, Spanish explorers found human sacrifice being practiced in both Central and South America. The most notorious were the Aztecs of the Mexico-Guatemala region, who seemed to have made human sacrifice into a veritable industry. Sacrificing took place on an almost year-round basis, as different gods were worshiped in their different months. For the most part, the victims were captives taken in war, but they should not be viewed as ordinary prisoners of war being slain in anger. Wars were undertaken *primarily in order to capture victims for sacrifice.* Care was taken not to kill opponents in battle, so they could be delivered, with credit, to the priest-executioners. The prisoners were treated with honor, even danced with, before being sent off to be tortured and slain.[16]

For some ceremonies, children were used as sacrificial victims. For the sacrifice to the "Smoking Mirror God," an unblemished youth was chosen, feted like a god for a year, and then, after an elaborate ritual, slain the usual Aztec way, by cutting the heart from his living body. To appease the rain gods, children were sacrificed on seven different altars.

In the Andean region of South America, there is much evidence of the rather recent practice of child sacrifice. In the sixteenth century, the Spanish priest Cristobal de Molina interviewed Inca priests in the Cuzco region of Peru and concluded that a vast system of sacrifice had been in operation. The victims typically were ten-year-old children of noble birth and without physical blemish. Hundreds of such children were slain each year, often buried in sacred spots high in the mountains. Recently discovered bodies of children buried in extremely high, almost inaccessible mountaintops confirm Molina's account.[17]

In the nineteenth century, as the British began to learn about the social life of the subject peoples in their new empire, they discovered numerous sacrificial customs in many parts of Asia and Africa. Perhaps the most startling was the human sacrifice practiced by the Khonds of Orissa in southeastern India. These people sacrificed men annually to the earth goddess Tari Pennu to ensure good crops. What made the custom unusual was that the victims, called Meriahs, were born and bred as sacrifice victims. These men were even given lands and wives—with whom they had children who, in turn, were raised to be sacrificed. Victims were commonly dispatched by hacking the flesh from their living bodies and scattering it on the fields. British administrators stopped the practice in the mid–nineteenth century.[18]

Explaining the Decline of Human Sacrifice

For every word that has been written about the facts of human sacrifice, ten have been penned on theories about it. Given the variety of the myths, legends, rites, and artifacts involved in human sacrifice, there is almost no limit to the specialists drawn into this field. In one fashion or another, human sacrifice touches on every social science, from archeology to psychology. In spite of the great depth and complexity of the many discussions of human sacrifice, however, they have paid little attention to the most obvious question of all: Why did this practice disappear? What in humans' social or technological development led to the demise of human sacrifice?

Some might reject the premise of this question and contend that human sacrifice did not die out in any permanent, predictable way. It is a cultural option, not to be seen as "primitive" and not confined to any stage of cultural development. The practice can come and go, and it just happens to be in eclipse today because of the ascendancy of a culture—the Judeo-Christian—that happens to be opposed to it. This position is supported by the fact that suppression by Christian imperialists accounts for the demise of human sacrifice in many third-world places. One could suppose that without outside intervention, the Khonds in India and the Aztecs in Mexico, for example, might have continued their sacrificial practices indefinitely, never "evolving" to anything else.

On balance, however, the idea that the decline in human sacrifice is an accident seems untenable. For one thing, it appears that the practice died out in a number of places rather independently. The Hebrews rejected it by around 600 B.C. In most of the Greek islands, human sacrifice was abandoned by the second century B.C., if not long before that.[19] The Romans, as noted, dropped the custom by around 100 B.C. On the other side of the world, it appears that in both Japan and China the custom was transcended approximately two thousand years ago.[20] Another argument in favor of the developmental view is the absence of any significant return to the practice. Once human sacrifice is given up, it does not return in any significant way, suggesting that it is not a variable custom, like a style of clothing, which can come, go, and come again.

In attempting to explain the demise of human sacrifice, we need to remind ourselves that its victims were truly innocent. As noted earlier, other kinds of religious killings existed—and have persisted until recent times—but they served a social purpose. Societies that gave up human sacrifice continued to wage religious wars and to torture and slay religious heretics. These acts—religious wars and persecutions—served the human function of protecting and extending the perpetrators' own faith or served other human impulses such as lust, greed, or fear. Human sacrifice—of the pure kind we have been examining—does not serve any such function. The victim has not contradicted any religious doctrine; he has not stolen anything or harmed anyone. He is being killed out of no human motive except that the slayers believe it will please a god.

By modern standards, such a belief amounts to a monstrous superstition, which suggests that the decline of human sacrifice is connected with the rise of rationalism and the scientific approach to the world. It's a plausible theory, but the dates are wrong. Superstition continued to hold powerful sway for many centuries after the practice of human sacrifice passed away. For example, human beings were tortured and killed for being witches in relatively recent times all over western Europe and even in Salem, Massachusetts. Just like human sacrifice, these killings were based on superstition—that is, they were justified by imaginings, not by scientific evidence. The difference is that the slayings of witches enabled the slayers to vent their anger, hate, and fear. Thus, they served a social function. In a pure human sacrifice, the slayers are not angry at or fearful of the victims. The victims represent no threat to them, real or imagined.

To explain human sacrifice, then, we have to ask why people would kill an innocent, nonthreatening human being. One necessary condition for this practice, it seems, is a very low appreciation of human life. This low valuation of life would seem to be a typical condition in primitive societies where life spans were short and where sickness, pain, and death were constant companions. Even in the modern world, this condition of "the cheapness of life" still persists in primitive places. In the 1950s, John Goddard, an American traveler in the Nile region of the Sudan, observed the surprising lack of concern about death among the primitive peoples there. He found them "fatalistically resigned to tragedy and sudden death, accepting it as a foreordained destiny over which they have no control. When a Niolite is killed by a hippo during a hunt," he continues, "or snatched away by a crocodile while fishing, his friends and relatives might even joke about the calamity, regarding it as a comical happening, much as a modern might look at someone slipping on a banana peel and taking a pratfall. Certainly they wouldn't hesitate to return to the scene of the death to continue the same activity."[21]

This low appreciation of human life would seem to be one pillar of the sacrifice system. When people begin to value human life more highly, they are more likely to object to slayings. An episode in early Japan illustrates the transition away from human sacrifice as a result of a growing concern for the victims. In the year 2 B.C., in the funeral service for the emperor's brother, members of his personal retinue were buried alive with him, a typical burial sacrifice. However, it is reported that the victims didn't die for several days and "wept and wailed at night." Many listeners, including the emperor, apparently were affected by this suffering, and it was concluded that burial sacrifice was a bad custom. For the funeral service for the empress five years later, the emperor had clay images made to put in the tomb instead of humans, which became the custom thereafter.[22] In effect, the emperor shortchanged the gods because spending human lives had become too dear.

Even where human sacrifice was practiced, there was often a tendency to use less-valued human beings, especially prisoners of war and slaves. When children were used, they were often the children of strangers or orphans (as in the case of the Druid sacrifice mentioned earlier)—that is, children less valued by members of the community.

Beyond Sadistic Gods

A second issue involved in human sacrifice, one quite apart from the value humans put on their own lives and that of others, involves the conception of the deity, the beliefs about what gods like and dislike. In order for a human sacrifice to make any sense, the slayers must believe that the human suffering involved pleases the god being addressed. The idea of a sacrifice is that one is giving the gods something they like so that they will look with favor upon one's community and give it good crops or victory in battle. A human sacrifice, whatever its complexities of theology and ritual, therefore presupposes a sadistic god, a deity that gets pleasure from witnessing the suffering and death of human beings.

In this connection, it is worth noting that most sacrificial practices involve some form of torture or at least a death more frightening and painful than usual. In the Middle East, in Canaan, Carthage, and elsewhere, the children were put to death by throwing them into the Topheth, a fiery furnace. Drums were beaten during the ceremony so that, it was said, the fathers could not hear the screams of their perishing children.[23] In Mexico, one sacrificial ritual involved throwing victims into a fire and removing them before death so that their still-beating hearts could be cut out. Another Aztec ritual required that the bound victim make a hopeless struggle against attackers who slew him in the end. The Dayaks of Borneo sacrificed slaves by inflicting thousands of small cuts with needles and sharpened bamboo sticks until death finally ensued. Within the entire field, it is extremely rare to find a report of a sacrificial practice where the victim was killed mercifully. This pattern of vicious deaths suggests the primitive peoples believed in gods who obtained positive satisfaction from human pain, blood, and gore.

How did primitive peoples reach the conclusion that their gods were sadistic? Perhaps, to some degree, it was an inference from the world as they experienced it. Their primitive world was full of dangers, suffering, and nasty surprises, including plagues, famines, and wars. It would be natural for them to ask, What kind of god would create such a world? A plausible answer was: a sadistic god, a god who liked to see humans bleed and suffer. Consistent with this theory, we find many gods of ancient peoples described as hostile, vicious characters. One example is the Indian god Kali, to whom sacrifices were made in early times and who was the patron of the Thugs, a sect of professional murderers. Kali was a vicious god, an enemy of the human race. A garland of human heads sat atop her grotesque head; human corpses hung as pendants from her ears; and blood trickled from the corners of her mouth.[24] The Aztec god, Quetzalcoatl, is another example of a god hostile to human interests—a point conveyed by the representations of him as a strikingly ugly creature.

A conception of evil-intentioned gods, then, might justify human sacrifice. The way to please a god who desired human destruction would be to destroy human beings. Under this theory, human sacrifice would be a function of the harshness of life. As social and economic life improved—owing to such things as urbanization or a better system of agriculture or the pacifying effects of empire—this conception of god would change. As life became less dangerous and less painful, people would be less disposed to conclude that the gods who ran the world were evil-minded.

The easing conditions of human existence would probably be coupled with a changing perspective on sadism. Sadism involves the taking of pleasure from seeing pain and suffering inflicted on living organisms, including human beings. From the standpoint of social progress, sadism is not a functional attitude. It's difficult to feel close to neighbors when you know they would enjoy seeing you roasted alive or get a thrill from seeing your heart cut out! Although sadism is not a socially healthy attitude, it is part of the human endowment. Human beings do have a fascination with gore, and the evidence is that in the most primitive societies this impulse was given full rein and probably even praised. In such societies, people probably assumed that their gods obtained the same unalloyed delight from suffering and bloodshed as they did.

An alternate reading of the Abraham and Isaac story reveals how the practice of human sacrifice requires the assumption of a god delighting in slaughter. The story has God commanding Abraham to slay his own son, Isaac, and Abraham obeying. The fact that God calls off the sacrifice at the last second does not change the fact that Abraham *was* going to slay his son to please God. By modern standards, the story is extremely unflattering to Abraham. What would we think today of a man who was willing to murder his own son because, he claimed, he was obeying God's command? Most of us reject the notion of a violent, vicious God, so we would view Abraham as a psychopath or a devil worshiper.

Those who originally told and retold this tale in biblical times obviously did not share this view. They assumed that it pleased the God of their time to see bloodshed, that the death of a child was a customary demand for this god to make, and that therefore Abraham was acting reasonably in carrying out this supposed command.

It seems likely that at a certain stage in the intellectual and ethical development of a community, people come to the realization that sadism is an unwholesome impulse. This is not to say that they completely condemn or prohibit it. It continues as a popular vice like gambling or getting drunk: an activity widely indulged and openly permitted—but still seen as a vice, reflecting some degree of weakness, a shortcoming on the part of those who indulge. Therefore, a god—a supreme being—would be seen as someone beyond this kind of pleasure.

We see this perspective in an early debate on human sacrifice reported to have taken place in the Greek province of Boeotia in 371 B.C. Motivated by a dream, the king considered making a human sacrifice to assure victory in an important battle. His councilors argued against it, saying "that such a barbarous and impious obligation could not be pleasing to any Supreme Beings . . . that it was absurd to imagine any divinities and powers delighting in slaughter and sacrifice of men."[25] The same point is made in the Abraham and Isaac story. God's calling off the sacrifice is interpreted as meaning that his sympathy for human beings now outweighs the pleasure he might take from witnessing their suffering.

At bottom, the practice of human sacrifice reflects a culture where viewing the pain and suffering of others is an occasion of highly regarded pleasure, untainted by feelings of guilt or embarrassment.

Human sacrifice dies out when a culture develops a hesitation about gratifying sadistic desires and attributes this same reluctance to its deities. The rise of this inhibition against sadism seems to be an important precondition for moving away from many other violent practices.

5

With the Edge of the Sword:
The Changing View of Genocide

The mass slaying of groups of people—genocide—has received enormous attention in the twentieth century. Hundreds of books have been written about the killings that have taken place in recent times: Hitler's slaying of Jews, Stalin's massacres of the Kulaks, the slaughter of Armenians in Turkey, the slayings done by the communist Khmer Rouge in Cambodia, killings in Rwanda, and so on. One tabulation finds that just since World War II, there have been forty-four episodes of genocide in the world.[1] Strangely, there seem to be no books on the history of genocide, no books that study mass slayings of long ago in the Roman Empire or in Carolingian France or Mogul India. The paucity of information about other ages may suggest that genocide is something new, a practice that has arisen in the twentieth century. Indeed, some modern authors seem to have reached this conclusion. One entitles his book *Century of Genocide.* Another title advances the same idea: *Mass Hate: The Global Rise of Genocide and Terror.*[2]

A closer look shows that this impression is far from accurate, however. Mass slaughter of human beings has been a common practice from time immemorial. The accounts of ancient and medieval times are studded with mass killings. The practice appears to have been universal, spanning every part of the globe, from India to Europe, from China to the Americas. There is, therefore, nothing unusual about the genocide of modern times. Whether there was more or less genocide, in a statistical sense, in the twentieth century is difficult to determine. To decide such a question, we would have to introduce a number of controls. One problem is there are more people in the world, so that the same amount of killing would represent a declining genocide rate. Another problem is that twentieth-century systems of record keeping and communication mean that we know about virtually all modern cases of genocide. The lack of such systems in earlier times means that we have little information about most genocides of past ages.

Because of these complications, it may never be possible to make quantitative comparisons with earlier times. What is clear, however, is that there has been a significant change in attitudes, that is, in how genocide is viewed. Today, the mass slaughter of human beings is widely considered to be wrong. This attitude represents a dramatic break with the past.

When Genocide Was God's Will

To see the changed view of genocide, one need look no further than the Old Testament. Here numerous cases of genocide are reported; what is more significant, they are reported *approvingly.* The bloodshed begins as the Hebrews, liberated from Egypt, move toward the promised land under the direction of Moses. Their first encounter, which can be dated roughly around 1300 B.C., takes place against a people in the Negeb, led by King Arad. The Hebrews pray to their God, saying, "If thou wilt indeed give this people into my hand, then I will utterly destroy their cities." Their wish is granted. "And the Lord hearkened to the voice of Israel, and gave over the Canaanites; and they utterly destroyed them and their cities" (Numbers 21:3).

A little later the Hebrews—still under the leadership of Moses—gave the same treatment to the Amorites under King Sihon and then to the people of Bashan under King Og: "So they slew him, and his sons, and all his people, until there was not one survivor left to him" (Numbers 21:35).

One must naturally exercise a certain degree of caution in using ancient sources such as the Bible. Such documents contain a great deal of legend and exaggeration along with descriptions of historical events. However, when we use these materials, historical accuracy is not our main concern. We are interested in the attitude toward genocide, which is displayed whether the ancient writer is referring to an actual genocide, an exaggeration, or an entirely fictitious episode.

It is abundantly clear that the writers and the culture of which they were a part endorsed the genocides of the Hebrews. The writers are not apologetic about the slayings; to the contrary, they are proud, even boastful. They do not report the slayings as aberrations excused by the heat of battle or by the failure of a military commander to control his troops. The slayings are holy deeds, approved by God, and the genocides are an act of worship. At the battle of Jericho, Joshua tells his warriors, "Shout, for the Lord has given you the city. And the city and all that is within it shall be devoted to the Lord for destruction" (Joshua 6:16–17). When the walls fall down, after the famous blowing of the trumpets, the Hebrews carry out the divine command: "Then they utterly destroyed all in the city, both men and women, young and old, oxen, sheep, and asses, with the edge of the sword" (Joshua 6:21).

Facing the city of Ai, the Lord instructs Joshua: "Stretch out the javelin that is in your hand toward Ai, for I will give it into your hand" (Joshua 8:18). Joshua took the city and slaughtered all twelve thousand inhabitants. It was a deliberate, purposeful extermination: "For Joshua did not draw back his hand, with which he stretched out the javelin, until he had utterly destroyed all the inhabitants of Ai. Only the cattle and the spoil of that city Israel took as their booty, according to the word of the Lord which he commanded Joshua" (Joshua 8:26–27).

The pattern of Joshua's conquest is drearily repetitious. City after city—Makedah, Libnah, Lachisch, Horam, Eglon, Hebron, Debrir—is taken and then "smote with the edge of the sword, and every person in it utterly destroyed." This systematic extermination of whole peoples receives the Lord's approval and is, in fact, actively facilitated by Him (Joshua 11:20).

The Hebrews weren't the only ones practicing genocide in the name of their god. Their opponents followed the same approach. A stone monument erected by King Mesha of Moab around the ninth century B.C. tells of destroying Hebrew cities and slaying all the inhabitants as an act of devotion to his god, Ashtar-Chemosh.[3] The early Muslims had the same positive view of genocide. They did not see it as an ugly deed, something to be ashamed of, but rather as something to boast about. When Muslim tribes made their conquests of the Indian subcontinent, the new rulers routinely slaughtered the defeated peoples, and the Muslim court historians proudly detailed this bloodshed in their chronicles.[4]

In China, we find the same pattern of socially endorsed genocide. Historical observations of population changes suggest that China may have been the world leader in massacre. In civil wars, which have been very numerous in China from ancient to modern times, it was common practice to massacre people in the defeated region, sometimes by scores of millions. The result was that districts would be depopulated by 60, 70, or even 90 percent. Rulers were not ashamed of this bloody practice, but openly embraced it. For example, in 1644 the emperor Chang Hsien-chung ordered a massacre in the Great Western Kingdom and erected a stone monument celebrating it.[5]

The Pros and Cons of Genocide

In its ancient heyday, genocide was supported by the "best" people, by the forward-looking, community-minded leaders. If there was opposition to it, it came from those who were considered self-centered and morally negligent. The reason for this lineup of opinion was that, in the context of the time, genocide seemed to be a policy that served the long-run good of the community and to have a number of strong arguments in its favor.

The first argument was economic. The human race has always faced the problem of scarce resources, the problem of there not being enough land, water, trees, game, or minerals to go around. It always appears, at first glance, that sooner or later something will have to be done to prevent a catastrophic imbalance between the supply of resources and the demand human beings have for them.

The view that such catastrophe is inevitable, we now know, is largely a fallacy. Human beings are infinitely creative and able to adapt to scarcity—not without some initial inconvenience and suffering, of course, but without catastrophe. However, it would be surprising that ancient peoples realized this. Even today, the "scarcity fear" leads many well-educated people to propound extreme solutions to the world's supposed "overpopulation" problem. To the ancients' way of thinking, their tribe was in deadly competition with neighboring peoples for resources. The solution would be to annihilate the neighbors and thus permanently and completely take over their resources. Genocide seemed to make good economic sense from the viewpoint of the long-run prosperity of the entire tribe.

A second argument in favor of genocide was that it seemed to make good military sense. If a defeated people were allowed to live, they might at some future date become strong again and start another war—and even win it. And then, of course, they could be expected to exterminate the tribe that initially defeated them. The way to put an end to this danger for good would be to slay every man, woman, and child of the defeated enemy.

This policy has a problem, one that most ancient leaders were not sophisticated enough to notice. It assumes that genocides are complete, that—as the Old Testament claims in case after case of genocide—every last man, woman, and child of the alien people is slain. These reports of complete annihilation seem to be exaggerations and wishful thinking. In practice, genocides were rarely complete. The enemy people would scatter in towns and villages and hide in the hills, and the soldiers who were supposed to slay them would often be tired, lazy, and unwilling to track them all down.

Thus, the policy of annihilation was one of those political ideas that is supposed to work in theory, but does not work in practice. An army slays only some members of the defeated enemy group and leaves many survivors to regroup and avenge the slaying of their comrades. Therefore, genocide feeds a process of perpetual feuding that is, of course, harmful to the long-run interests of the tribe. But, as noted previously, it would have taken extremely sophisticated minds to grasp this point. The ordinary leader would have supposed that genocide was a permanent solution to his tribe's security problems.

A Sin <u>Not</u> to Kill

Perhaps the most compelling argument in favor of genocide was the moral one. An alien tribe had a religion and culture that differed from that of the conquerors. If these people were defeated but allowed to live, members of the victorious tribe might pick up their customs. Intermarriage would likely take place. The only way to keep religion and culture pure was to slay all members of the defeated community.

Through history, this "purification" argument for genocide seems to have been the most important one. It certainly was the main one in Old Testament times. There were many different religions in the Palestine region, and the leaders of each sect had reason to be concerned about their followers' taking up alien practices. The history of the Hebrews during the centuries after the Exodus illustrates this problem. As the Bible reports, they were constantly backsliding into the religious practices of surrounding peoples—to the dismay of their priests and prophets. Exterminating these neighboring peoples probably seemed an obvious "final solution" to the problem of religious diversity. This is why we find the highest religious leaders—Moses, Joshua, Samuel—urging genocide in the name of the Lord.

Although community leaders advocated genocide, the "sinners," the common folk, tended to resist or ignore the command to slay aliens. They were moved not by lofty arguments about ethnic and religious purity or by the supposed long-run health of the community. They had immediate, personal motives that tended to go against genocide. To begin with, the ordinary impulse of compassion led some to be merciful, at least under some circumstances. Slaying enemy soldiers in the heat of battle is perhaps instinctive, but slaughtering babies and children is probably not. And if the soldiers had had some personal, human interaction with the captives—as traders, prostitutes, or guides and interpreters—slaying them would have been difficult. Furthermore, captured prisoners can be made into slaves who wait on soldiers and do the heaviest, most disagreeable labor, and captured women and girls can gratify soldiers' sexual desires.

Such practical considerations led to a tension on the subject of genocide. The leaders urged it as a religious necessity ordered by God, yet the soldiers and the people sometimes failed to carry out the desired slayings. For example, in Joshua's campaigns, we learn that one defeated people were spared annihilation, the Hivites from the town of Gibeon. How did the Hivites escape? The official story is that they tricked Joshua into believing that they lived far away and therefore were no threat to the Hebrews. They begged Joshua for a covenant, a promise to spare them, which he gave. Therefore, the story goes, when Joshua found out the Hivites lived nearby, he couldn't slay them without breaking his promise (Joshua 9).

It's an implausible tale, one that assumes that Joshua and his men wouldn't have known the Hivites were neighbors and, furthermore, that Joshua carelessly made sacred covenants with perfect strangers. What seems to have happened is the Hivites—probably not a very warlike people—ingratiated themselves with the Hebrews by mingling with them, trading with them, and generally making themselves useful. They are reported giving the Hebrews bread and wine and offering to be their servants. "So the [Hebrew] men partook of their provisions, *and did not ask direction of the Lord* " (Joshua 9:14, emphasis added). In other words, the soldiers were won over on human terms and forgot the official religious policy of genocide.

This idea that it is a sin to show mercy to alien peoples runs through all the Old Testament conquest stories. When the Hebrews defeated the Midianites, they slew all adult males, but this wasn't enough slaughter for Moses. "Have you let all the women live?" he angrily asked the officers of the army (Numbers 31:15). The Midianites had led the Hebrews into the worship of Baal, so a more complete extermination was called for. "Now therefore, kill every male among the little ones," demanded Moses, "and kill every woman who has known man by lying with him" (Numbers 31:17). Moses saw that it was wise, however, to compromise his religious principles to the extent of letting the soldiers rape the virgins. "But all the young girls who have not known man by lying with him, keep alive for yourselves" (Numbers 31:18).

Several centuries later we see the same pattern in an episode that occurred in the time of the prophet Samuel. The Hebrew king Saul had been instructed by God, speaking through the prophet Samuel, to make war on the Amalekites and to "utterly destroy all that they have, [to] kill both man and woman, infant and suckling, ox and sheep, camel and ass" (1 Samuel 15:3). When Saul defeated the Amalekites, he spared the life of their king, Agag. Samuel was angry at this show of mercy and berated Saul for disobeying God's command to slay all captured people. Samuel then ordered that the prisoner Agag be brought out, and with his sword "Samuel hewed Agag in pieces before the Lord" (1 Samuel 15:33).

Other early religions show the same pattern where violence is demanded by the god in contradiction to the human impulses toward compassion. In the *Bhagavad-Gita,* one of the basic documents of the Hindu religion dating from around 400 B.C., we find a revealing argument between the god Krishna and the mortal Arjuna on the subject of war. Prince Arjuna is about to lead his forces in combat against an opposing faction of his own family relations. However, he is "overwhelmed with compassion" at the idea of having to kill family members, including his own grandfather and also his former tutor. "I do not see how any good can come from killing my own kinsman in this battle," he tells Krishna.[6] Krishna scorns these pacifist sentiments as "impurities" that lead to "infamy." It is clear, says Krishna, that duty lies in slaughter: "There is no better engagement for you than fighting on religious principles; and so there is no need for hesitation."[7]

It is interesting to note the changing role of the soul in connection with the use of violence. In modern times, the argument has been that because human beings have souls—an immortal spark of god—they are precious. Inflicting physical harm on them is therefore a kind of blasphemy, an attack on the divine. The ancients also believed in the soul, but for them its existence *justified* slaying. Because the soul was immortal, you could do any terrible, violent thing to the body and not affect it. Krishna makes this point to Arjuna: "The soul can never be cut to pieces by any weapon, nor burned by fire, nor moistened by water, nor withered by the wind." Therefore, Arjuna should take up his task of killing without hesitation: "You are mourning for what is not worthy of grief."[8]

The Road away from Genocide

At the dawn of history, then, genocide was backed by every argument—economic, moral, and religious. Slaying masses of human beings was seen as a necessary and farsighted policy, an activity to be proud of, something to boast about, and certainly nothing to feel ashamed about. Tracing the change in perspectives on genocide from early times to the present would require a major historical survey, a task clearly beyond the scope of this book. All I can attempt here is a brief overview of this evolution, especially as it applies to the West.

The first rejections of the pro-genocide view apparently took place on the practical, informal plane. Even in ancient times, the realization that human beings have a creative, productive potential often deflected the thrust toward genocide. Captured people could be taken as slaves—as happened to the Hivites who, the Bible reports, became "hewers of wood and drawers of water" for the Hebrews. Another less violent and more economically productive way of treating defeated communities was to have them pay tribute. We find an early instance of this in the period of the Hebrew kings, where the king of Moab is reported to have to pay an annual tribute of one hundred thousand sheep and the wool from an equal number of sheep to the king of Israel (2 Kings 3:4). People in many cultures began to appreciate the advantage of extracting such wealth from conquered peoples, instead of leaving a pile of dead bodies. By the time of the Roman Empire, it had become the norm to take slaves and demand tribute rather than to slay conquered peoples.

In Asia, the Muslim imperialists made the same shift in approach. By the thirteenth and fourteenth century, they came to favor slavery and the extraction of tribute over the previous habit of making a wholesale slaughter of weaker peoples.[9]

Though there may have been some lessening in the practice of genocide by medieval times, there is little sign that it was criticized or condemned. A few writers, such as Desiderius Erasmus (1517) and Hugo Grotius (1625) wrote against the bloodiness of war and indiscriminate slaying. But most people, including elites, viewed the mass slaying of ethnic or religious opponents as an acceptable practice. For an indication of thinking on the subject in the seventeenth century, consider England's treatment of the Irish at the time of Oliver Cromwell.

Since the twelfth century, Ireland had been the object of English invasion and conquest. Century after century, it was the scene of lamentable atrocities as the English pursued a policy of violent subjugation. In 1642–46, the English plunged into their own civil war, giving Ireland a few years of independence. Once the English civil war was over, however, and the victorious Puritans under Oliver Cromwell took up the reins of government, the English moved to reestablish control of Ireland. In 1649, Cromwell landed in Ireland with an army of seventeen thousand and attacked the city of Drogheda. When he took the city, his army indiscriminately slew the defeated forces.

Cromwell felt no need to hide or disguise the slaughter. He frankly described the killing in his report to the English Parliament. "It has pleased God to bless our endeavour at Drogheda," he wrote. "The enemy were about 3,000 strong in the town. I believe we put to the sword the whole number." Noncombatants were also slain, including a large number of women and children who had fled to St. Peter's Church in a vain search for safety. In words chillingly reminiscent of the book of Joshua, Cromwell praised the Drogheda massacre as a "mercy," the "glory" of which belonged "to God alone." Later in the year, the English Parliament unanimously declared in a motion "That the House does approve of the execution done at Drogheda as an act of both justice to them and mercy to others who may be warned by it."[10]

It seems clear, then, that at this time few believed there was anything wrong with massacring alien peoples if it seemed to serve one's political or religious purposes—or just because one felt like it. In the Irish city of Wexford, where Cromwell's troops slaughtered several thousand inhabitants, Cromwell commented, "I thought it not right or good to restrain off the soldiers from their right of pillage, or from doing execution on the enemy."[11]

Even in the late eighteenth century, we find the same open, boastful attitude toward genocide. The bloody French Revolution of 1789 and its aftermath gave the world numerous examples of horrible exterminations. In 1794, a rag-tag group of peasants rose up against the revolutionary government in the Vendee region. When General Westermann led the government army to suppress the revolt, his forces exterminated scores of thousands of men, women, and children in the region. To kill large numbers of people quickly, the army adopted a mechanized system of mass slaughter that utilized shallow slave ships, the *noyades*. Prisoners were loaded on them and locked in; the boats were briefly pressed below the water to drown all aboard; then they were refloated for the next load.

Like Cromwell, Westermann openly boasted of his deeds to the French Convention in his report: "The Vendee is no more. . . . According to your orders, I have trampled their children beneath our horses' feet; I have massacred their women, so they will no longer give birth to brigands. I do not have a single prisoner to reproach me. I have exterminated them all."[12]

The Emergence of the Modern View

The episodes of slaughter happening all over Europe—all over the world—were at this time still being treated as an acceptable phase of war (not so acceptable, of course, if it was done *to you!*). It is difficult to say when a more humane perspective became the view of the majority, or at least the dominant view of the elites that led public opinion. In English-speaking lands, a shift occurred in the last half of the nineteenth century. Elites became uneasy about massacres that soldiers and mobs carried out. Such massacres were no longer officially approved, but neither were they officially censured or their perpetrators punished. For example, the United States has a long history of genocide against American Indian groups going back to Puritan times. The nineteenth century saw perhaps half a dozen larger massacres— involving a hundred or so American Indians each time—but these massacres raised questions and concerns. One example was the 1864 slaying of 130 Cheyenne at Sand Creek, Colorado, by citizen and military forces. The massacre provoked army and congressional investigations, but no one was punished.[13]

In forging and holding their overseas empires, the European

colonial powers engaged in military struggles that often ended in massacres of the defeated indigenous forces. A dramatic example of the pattern occurred after the Indian (Sepoy) Mutiny of 1857. After the British forces gained the upper hand against the rebels, who had massacred groups of English, they massacred in turn. For example, when British troops retook Dehli, they massacred large numbers of Indians, including many bystanders. Although in some quarters these slayings were viewed as justified, some British leaders, such as governorgeneral Lord Charles John Canning, argued against the "rabid and indiscriminant vindictiveness" on the grounds that it would cause later resentment.[14] By the end of the century, the British had grown more sensitive on the atrocity issue. During the Boer War in South Africa (1899–1902), there were widespread protests in England against the brutal treatment of the Boer civilian population by the British army.

In the early twentieth century, this sensitivity was to provide the key to the independence of Ireland. During World War I, while Britain was fighting Germany, the Irish had gained a considerable degree of independence, and a nationwide election in 1918 had established an Irish Constituent Assembly. In 1920, the British moved to reestablish control, introducing regular forces into Ireland and organizing an irregular pro-British force known as the "Black and Tans." In their effort to establish order and subdue the Irish revolutionaries, these pro-British forces burned towns, villages, and factories and slew innocent men, women, and children.

News of the atrocities provoked massive opposition within Britain. The archbishop of Canterbury condemned British policy, as did former cabinet ministers and retired generals. The British Labour Party sent a commission to Ireland to investigate, which concluded that "Things are being done in Ireland, in the name of Britain, which must make her name stink in the nostrils of the whole world."[15] In marked contrast to the days of Cromwell, when rulers were openly proud of massacres in Ireland, British officials in the House of Commons at this time denied that the government was following any policy of reprisal against the Irish. The pressure of public opinion on the atrocity issue quickly led the Lloyd George government to conclude that Ireland could not be held by force and soon arranged terms for granting independence to it (more specifically, to the twenty-six southern counties).

This same reluctance to be involved in genocide-like repression lay behind Britain's moves to shed its overseas empire. In India, Mahatma Gandhi led nonviolent protests to pressure the British to grant independence. Rather than attempt a bloody suppression of this movement, the British eventually acceded to the demand (independence took effect in 1947). Perhaps Britain was somewhat ahead of other Western countries in the evolution of public opinion. For example, in attempting to hold Algeria when major rebellion broke out there in 1954, France was willing to wage a costly, atrocity-filled war for four years before granting Algeria independence.

The killings half a century ago in the Soviet Union and Germany further illustrate how recent the change in attitudes on genocide has been. At the time, thinking in these countries (both of which had strong traditions of glorifying state power) was rather ambiguous on the subject of how far a government should go in using force against undesirable groups. Those who controlled the dictatorships in these countries undoubtedly reflected an extreme, pro-violence perspective, but they were not clearly countered by a public opinion opposed to mass killings.

A consensus against genocide did not emerge in the West until after World War II. Indeed, the term *genocide* itself was not coined until 1944. It is only in the past half-century that mass killing has become a subject for analysis and debate, and a phenomenon scholars and activists have sought to study, theorize about, and, especially, prevent. One sign of this increased interest is the flood of books on genocide. The Library of Congress catalog contains 349 items on the subject, all published since 1945. Under the subject heading *atrocities*—the term the Library of Congress used to refer to mass killings before *genocide* became current—we find the same pattern of very recent interest. Of the 2,667 items under *atrocities,* 83 percent were published since 1940, and 99.6 percent were published since 1910.

Another indication of the modern interest in and disapproval of genocide has been the development of the United Nations Convention on the Prevention and Punishment of the Crime of Genocide. This international convention, first drafted in 1948, makes genocide a crime in international law. The U.S. government signed the convention in 1988, and 172 countries have now adhered to the convention. The legal approach to controlling genocide has weaknesses involving both the definition of genocide and the enforcement of punishment against violators, but they should not obscure the change the convention itself represents in world opinion.

The shift in public opinion on the subject of genocide is so strong today that, at least in modern Western countries, everyone condemns it. One notices, for example, that though there are some modern admirers of the Nazis, few of them praise Hitler for slaying millions of Jews. Instead, influenced by the modern sentiment against genocide, they claim the killings have been exaggerated—or even that they never took place at all. It seems likely that any future social or political movement in the West, even one with unsettling and deviant ideas, will incorporate the point that genocide is not an acceptable way to implement its aims.

Of course, the entire world has not caught up with the West. There are some Middle Eastern countries where both government and opposition forces view mass slayings as an acceptable tactic. In many African countries, genocide is all too common, especially in the heat of ethnic strife. But even in those places where genocide occurs, we see a sense of embarrassment, a need on the part of perpetrators to deny, disguise, or minimize their action. Public opinion against the mass slaying of human beings is now global. That is the real news about genocide in the twentieth century.

6

Conquer Thy Neighbor:
New Ideas about Empire, War,
and Military Forces

Until recent times, the history of the world was the history of conquest. Practically everyone believed that one's tribe or nation should expand its control over territory, which made imperialism as natural as drawing breath. Small countries expected to grow larger, and larger countries expected to become empires. Hardly anyone argued that seeking to subjugate neighbors was immoral or unethical; hardly anyone pointed out that it could be foolish and self-defeating. The result, all over the world, was war in an unending cycle of conquest, rebellion, and reconquest.

These violent processes shaped the institutions of the world. They put military forces in first place as the most important agency of the state. Military figures were glorified; martial virtues were cultivated; and the making of war commanded the attention and energy of national leaders. As Niccolo Machiavelli put it in *The Prince* (written in 1513), "A prince should therefore have no other aim or thought, nor take up any other thing for his study, but war and its organization and discipline. . . . The chief cause of the loss of states is the contempt of this art, and the way to acquire them is to be well-versed in the same."[1]

Government itself was conceived of mainly as an agency for making war. In the minds of the ancients, government's role in conquering and in defending against conquest justified its brutal policies of subjugation and taxation. We see this orientation in the Bible's explanation of the origin of government. The Hebrew people came to the prophet Samuel and begged him to create a king. Samuel resisted the demand, saying that it amounted to a rejection of God and that a king would oppress them with taxation. However, the people refused to listen. "We will have a king over us," they said, "that we may be like all the nations, and that our king may govern us and go out before us and fight our battles" (1 Samuel 8:19–20).

The main job of rulers, their route to fame and glory, was conquest. The career of Charlemagne, the famous king of the Franks from A.D. 768 to 814, illustrates the pattern. In forty-six years of rule, he made fifty-four military campaigns.[2] Louis XIV of France expressed this attitude frankly in a letter he wrote in 1688: "Self-aggrandizement is the most worthy and agreeable of sovereigns' occupations."[3] Practically every spring, Louis would begin another military campaign to increase the size of France. The process of aggrandizement led to four major wars during his reign, not to mention countless revolts and skirmishes, and left a country dreadfully impoverished by the taxation necessary to fund the military forces.[4] One notes, however, that Louis XIV is considered a "great" king—in fact, France's greatest!

This is one of the most revealing indicators of the human hankering for military conquest: those who did it were labeled "great." Even today, this bias lingers in our history books and public monuments. What makes Alexander the Great great? Did he write an inspiring book of literature or cure a disease? Nothing so useful or constructive as that. His claim to fame is that he subjugated more countries than most rulers were able to conquer.

I recall visiting Napoleon's tomb at the Hotel des invalids in Paris as a boy many years ago and being awed by its size and lavishness. At the time, I did not know who Napoleon was or why the tomb builders had worshiped him. I later learned that Napoleon's claim to greatness was military. He was a stupendous aggressor, an energetic general who knew how to organize and motivate troops, and whose hallmark was that he repeatedly overextended himself. The French followed him on a fifteen-year binge of conquest. After forty major battles, Napoleon ended up defeated and exiled, his mark on history being a "sea of blood," as one historian puts it.[5] In his last two campaigns alone, in 1813 and 1814, he lost more than a million French soldiers.[6] By modern standards, erecting a monument to Napoleon would be rather like glorifying a plague or an earthquake. That the French adored such an aggressor illustrates how popular imperialism used to be.

Just as Europe had its ruinous wars lasting thirty, sixty, and a hundred years, so the North American colonies had their own interminable wars of conquest and reconquest. The French and Indian Wars, which lasted seventy-four years (1689–1763), were a protracted struggle between England and France over domination of eastern North America, fought mainly by American Indians for the French and by colonists for the English. The casualty rate in this conflict was probably higher than in any war the United States has seen since. Thomas Hutchinson, the governor of the Massachusetts colony, estimated that between five and six thousand Boston males died in the first forty years of this conflict—a staggering number given that the population of Boston at that time was only approximately fifteen thousand.[7]

Two centuries later, in the 1890s, Americans still thought wars of conquest were a natural and necessary part of life. Eyeing Cuba—then weakly held by Spain—U.S. senators argued in favor of a war of aggression to take it. "We certainly ought to have the island in order to round out our possessions," said Senator Frye of Maine. "If we cannot buy it I, for one, should like an opportunity to acquire it by conquest." Senator Cullom of Illinois declaimed that "It's time some one woke up and realized the necessity of annexing some property—we want all this northern hemisphere." As historian Barbara Tuchman comments, "It was not, in 1895, necessary to disguise aggressiveness as something else."[8] The hunger for conquest led to the Spanish-American War and the U.S. acquisition of Cuba, Puerto Rico, and the Philippines.

Nor was the appeal of arms confined to civilized peoples. In most primitive societies, warfare has been a major occupation, often the dominant activity that establishes the status of leaders. Among many American Indian tribes, for example, bravery in war was the basis of the chiefs' authority. Meriwether Lewis, of the famed Lewis and Clark expedition, discovered this point when he tried to preach to the Hidatsa tribe the advantages of giving up warfare and turning to trapping, agriculture, and trading. A young brave asked him how, without war, their tribes would get new chiefs when the old ones died, for, he added, "the nation could not exist without chiefs."[9]

The Illogic of Imperialism

Why did it take the human race so long to reject the idea that conquering neighbors was a worthwhile policy? To some extent, the problem was ignorance. At first glance, force seems an effective way to accomplish one's goals. If someone has resources one needs, why not attack and take them? For millennia, this logic prevailed.

It was a false logic, however. Though plundering may seem profitable at first, it generally works to the detriment of those who attempt it. The problem is that the people being plundered tend to resist, and their resistance makes plundering a costly and ultimately wasteful effort. In the Highlands of Scotland, for example, cattle raiding was a way of life even as late as the eighteenth century. Warriors from one clan would capture cattle from neighbors and demand payment to return them. (The term *blackmail* comes from this custom, *mail* being the term for tribute and black being the color of the cattle.) Of course, the other clans would do the same thing; the result was that, as one historian reports, "at any given moment the average chief had half his warriors out stealing his neighbor's cattle, and the other half recovering the cattle his neighbors had stolen from him."[10] With the men literally wasting their time in raids and skirmishes, the whole community would have starved but for the meager crops raised by the women on tiny plots of land. The inefficiency of this plundering lifestyle left the Highland peoples desperately poor, living in mud and stone huts at a bare subsistence level.

Inefficiency and waste also overtakes nations and empires that follow a policy of international plundering known as *imperialism*—that is, trying to take over countries in order to reap their resources. Suppose, for example, that England wants copper from some foreign land. The imperialist would advocate invading that land, making it a colony, and taking the copper. It all seems so simple.

Further analysis reveals the many costs of this scheme. It costs something to raise an army to invade the country and make it a colony, and still more to maintain the army and police forces needed to keep the colony in subjugation. Furthermore, the copper isn't going to leap out of the ground. Workers will be needed to mine it. If they are recruited at gunpoint, as slaves, then soldiers will be needed to capture them and keep them prisoner. And even slaves require some expenditure on food and shelter. Furthermore, slave workers, being motivated by threats of force, will be uncooperative and relatively unproductive. In the end, the copper acquired through military conquest will by no means be cheap.

These kinds of economic arguments were made with increasing vigor in the eighteenth and nineteenth centuries, especially in England. Pamphleteers such as Richard Cobden and John Bright exposed the nation to the theory of free trade. They pointed out that through voluntary exchange, England could acquire what it needed from abroad more cheaply than through military conquest and occupation. A country that wants copper from abroad can simply buy it for less than the cost of conquering and administering colonies. Toward the end of the nineteenth century, socialists also took up this theme. In his popular 1902 work *Imperialism,* the economist J. A. Hobson persuasively demonstrated that although the British Empire may have provided a playground for the British military and diplomatic elite, this playground was an economic drain for the country as a whole. In 1910, British journalist Norman Angell wrote an immensely popular book on the folly of conquest, *The Great Illusion.* He pointed out that given the economic interdependence in the modern world, even a victorious aggressor would wind up an economic loser, destroying his own markets and suppliers. The idea that a nation could benefit through conquest was an illusion.

The Fatal Flaw of Pacifism

Although the growing understanding of the economic issues played a role in the decline of imperialism, it was not the only factor. Perhaps even more important was a growing distaste for violence.

Maintaining an empire requires a great deal of bloodshed. In ancient times, the ruthlessness needed for empire was not lacking. Nations were willing to sacrifice generations of their young men to establish an empire. Imperial tax collectors were willing to raze entire cities to punish tax evasion. Imperial governors were willing to slay thousands of captured rebels to intimidate other subjects into obedience. As cultures began to develop sensitivity toward human suffering—suffering of their own soldiers and taxpayers as well as that of subject peoples—the appeal of conquest began to diminish.

This cultural evolution against force unfortunately did not take place equally in all parts of the world. Some countries would get ahead of others in turning against war. Its philosophers would decry war, its young men would lose their taste for military arts, and its generals would grow reluctant to seek out battles. The consequence of these trends, however, was that more-warlike neighbors would overrun and annihilate this pacific community. One of the earliest examples of this pattern is Carthage, which was destroyed by the Romans in the second century B.C. Carthage was an important and successful trading nation in ancient times. It had been sparring with Rome since around 500 B.C. Major, prolonged conflicts—the three Punic Wars—broke out beginning in 246 B.C.

Carthage's underlying problem was that it was not a militaristic society. Grown rich and complacent after many centuries of successful trade, it had no tradition of warfare and soldiering. It relied mainly on mercenaries and on alliances with tribes hostile to Rome. The Romans, on the other hand, were—in this era—a militaristic people. They raised huge citizen armies, their senators fought and died in battle, and their merchants donated entire fleets of ships to the cause of conquest.[11] Thus, despite some moments of victory (notably Hannibal's famous campaign across the Alps with elephants), the Carthaginians steadily lost ground to the Romans. At the end of the Second Punic War, in 201 B.C., Carthage was willing to accept subservient status. It signed a treaty giving up its warships, promising to pay an indemnity, and agreeing not to make war, even in self-defense, without Rome's permission.[12] As we might say today, the rulers of Carthage decided to "give peace a chance."

The policy might have worked in our time, two thousand years later, when most countries have no interest in attacking their neighbors. Canada and Mexico don't fear invasion from the United States; Belgium and Luxembourg don't fear invasion by France; and so forth. But this was the second century B.C., and most peoples, including the Romans, believed in conquering their neighbors. Rome had no intention of peacefully coexisting with Carthage. The leading senator of the era, Cato, ended all his speeches, on whatever subject, with the refrain, "And besides, Carthage must be destroyed."

In 150 B.C., Rome's fleet sailed against a nearly defenseless Carthage. Carthaginian representatives rushed to Rome to offer terms of surrender. The Roman Senate promised that if Carthage sent three hundred children of the noblest families as hostages, Rome would respect the territorial integrity of Carthage. Weeping, Carthaginian mothers surrendered the child hostages, only to discover that the Roman Senate's promise was a lie. Even while the Senate was promising the emissaries of Carthage that it would spare the city in exchange for the hostages, it was secretly ordering the destruction of that city. The Carthaginians made a last-ditch effort to defend their nearly disarmed city but were overpowered. At the Senate's instructions, the Roman commander razed the city and sowed salt on the land. The handful of survivors of this city of half a million were taken into slavery. It was a chilling lesson on the danger of deemphasizing the use of force in a violent world.

The same lesson was taught on the other side of the world by the Muslim conquests of India, which began in A.D. 664. The Indian communities of the age were wealthy, and they had developed a rich tradition of art and architecture. Like the Carthaginians, however, they had allowed military arts and virtues to decline. The dominant religious philosophies emphasized nonviolence. The first principle of Buddhism was "Let not one kill any living thing."[13] Jainism, another popular Indian sect of the first millennium, went even further, espousing the doctrine of *ahimsa*—the principle of avoiding injury to anything alive. The good Jain would screen his lamp to prevent insects from flying into its flame. Although a minor sect in India today, it did influence the Indian leader Mohandas K. Gandhi, who developed the modern doctrine of nonviolent resistance to authority.[14]

Gandhi succeeded with his version of *ahimsa* because he had to contend with the more tolerant British. The Indians' opponents of more than a thousand years ago were entirely different. They were "barbarians" from the north who had embraced the creed of Islam. The practice of this religion had been set by the Prophet Mohammed—a warlord and the leader of a Bedouin band that subsisted on raiding caravans—in a culture where fighting was a regular way of life. Thereafter, Islam became the religion of the already violent tribes of Scythians, Huns, and Afghans to the north and west of India. They swept down across India, massacring inhabitants, confiscating wealth, and setting up their own violent regimes. In Delhi in the twelfth century, the Sultan Muhammad bin Tughlak killed so many Hindus that, in the proud words of his Muslim historian, "there was constantly in front of his royal pavilion and his Civil Court a mound of dead bodies and a heap of corpses." His successor, Firoz Shah, invaded Bengal and offered a reward for every Hindu head, ending up paying for approximately 180,000 of them.[15] It's the kind of statistic that makes a Jainist stop and consider.

A Common Culture Against War

It is easy to see, then, why the emphasis on conquest and plunder prevailed for so long. The pattern seemed impossible to escape. If a culture came to downplay military conquest as unhealthy or immoral, it neglected military arts, which in turn made it ripe for conquest by a more bellicose community. As a result, its more pacific outlook was lost. And when the invaders lost their appetite for war and conquest, more militaristic neighbors, in turn, overcame them.

It's not entirely clear how cultures escaped this vicious cycle. Perhaps the key to the shift was the rise of communication between national communities. Communication enabled the more pacific cultures to transmit something of their values, theories, and experiences to new aggressors and in this way to temper the aggressors' militarism. Such a common culture appears to have emerged in western Europe in late medieval times, facilitated by the development of printing, common church institutions, and the lingua franca of Latin. Scholars and theologians developed a critical view of war that spread to the elites in a number of countries. One of the leaders in this movement was the Dutch scholar Desiderius Erasmus, whose antiwar tract, *Complaint of Peace,* appeared in 1517.

A number of other churchmen made similar arguments against war and violence, including St. Francis of Assisi. With the publication of *The Law of War and Peace* in 1625, the Dutch jurist Hugo Grotius laid down the principles of international law, which became a recognized system for limiting nations' use of military force. The effect of all this shared communication about war and limiting war finally began to bear fruit in nineteenth-century Europe. Some nations, such as Holland and Sweden, dropped out of great-power military competition, and most of the others grew increasingly reluctant to turn to war. The result, for the first time in history, was that peace became the typical state of international relations. World War I (1914–18) represented the turning point in this trend. Prior to that time, the antiwar forces—though numerous and growing—were in a minority. Ideas about the nobility of war and its invigorating virtues were still dominant, even in western Europe. At the outset of World War I, the mood was one of exhilaration, even jubilation. After the conflict itself, however, war lost its heroic appeal.[16] It was not, it appears, the cost and pointlessness of the war that caused a general turning against the institution of war. Many previous wars had also been costly and pointless, yet the human beings involved learned nothing from them. A cultural and attitudinal shift against war had been gaining strength all along; World War I marked the tip point in this trend—at least in the economically developed world. After 1918, in the established countries—in Scandinavia, Europe, North and South America—majority opinion repudiated wars of conquest.

Though the emphasis on militarism and aggression was fading, it did not disappear in one stroke. Some leaders and some factions still valued war and saw military aggression as a positive activity. This was the problem of the twentieth century. Elites with an unusually militaristic ideology took control of three large nations, Germany, Japan, and Russia. They adopted a strikingly aggressive orientation, an assertiveness that represented a deviation from the developing world culture. They were the new barbarians preaching the advantage of violence. Had these regimes been victorious, they would have set back by many generations the evolution against the use of force in international life. As it happened, the barbarians lost, a remarkable case of more-militaristic regimes being defeated by less-militaristic ones.

Were the dictatorships of Germany, Japan, and Russia the last aggressors the world will see? Almost certainly not, for, as I discuss later, the more violence-prone cultures of the economically undeveloped regions may be expected to supply bellicose regimes for some time. But the German, Japanese, and Soviet dictatorships may well have been the last *major* militaristic regimes. Their demise has left relationships between the great powers remarkably calm. Historian Paul Johnson commented in 1995 that "the 50 years of peace between the Great Powers [1945–95] is a significant landmark in human history. Never before, and indeed never since there have been Great Powers to fight each other, has a general peace lasted so long." Johnson contrasted the current era with other times of peace: "What is notable about our half-century of general peace is that the likelihood of general war has been steadily declining throughout these five decades, and that the risk of war now is smaller than at any time in the last 50 years."[17] (While the great powers have ceased to fight each other, they have not yet left all thought of war behind, of course—as their numerous "police actions" demonstrate.)

Political scientist John Mueller makes the same point about great power war. By his reckoning, in 1984 "the major countries of the developed world had managed to remain at peace with each other for the longest continuous stretch of time since the days of the Roman Empire." This turning away from war, he says, is not attributable to luck or to the advent of weapons of mass destruction. Instead, it is "the culmination of a substantial historical process."[18]

Statistics on War

Although there has been a general decline in the emphasis on warfare, a decline especially noticeable in the past half-century, popular attitudes and perceptions have not caught up with this reality. Most people believe that war and military preparations for war are a growing problem for humanity. This prejudice encourages the media to publish biased claims and even outright fabrications that exaggerate the extent of modern violence compared with the past.[19] These spurious claims, in turn, reinforce the popular prejudice. Public figures, think tanks, and lobbying groups also attempt to attract media attention by exaggerating present evils: claiming that violence is a growing and alarming problem is a useful way to get their names in the paper. Another ingredient in the distortion is changing attitudes. As we develop a growing distaste for violence, we become more sensitive to those episodes of violence that do occur, and we therefore tend to exaggerate them.

Leaving aside subjective feelings and distortions in the media, the data on the incidence of war provide little support for the belief that warfare has been increasing. Although there are difficulties in working with the incomplete information about warfare in the past, the facts suggest, on balance, a declining intensity of warfare over the centuries. In order to discern this conclusion in the evidence, however, one needs to be aware of and compensate for a serious methodological problem that has affected all attempts to study the changing incidence of war: the missing-data bias. The basic cause of this bias is the fact that as one moves closer to the present, one encounters increasingly complete information about events. This bias will make it appear that many different kinds of events—from droughts and hurricanes to the writing of poems—are becoming more frequent.

A good way to illustrate the missing-data problem is to examine the trend in knowledge about the starting and ending dates of wars. In 1942, historian Quincy Wright published a comprehensive history of fighting, *A Study of War,* in which he made a tabulation of the major wars from 1480 to 1940 and included the date when each began and ended. For the first part of this period, 1480 to 1650, in only 13 percent of the cases was Wright able to establish the beginning and ending day or month. For the rest of the wars in this period, the dates were known only to the nearest year. Knowledge about war chronology increases as we move forward in time so that Wright was able to establish precise beginning and ending dates in 99 percent of the wars in the period 1875 to 1940.[20]

This same pattern of increasingly comprehensive coverage characterizes information about all aspects of wars, *including the number of wars themselves and their casualties.* The closer to the present we get, the higher the numbers become—not because the real frequency is increasing but because we have an increasing level of information. Most of the scholars who have studied the incidence of war over time have been unmindful of this bias. For example, Wright, relying on the tabulations made by several military historians, reported that the number of battles had increased from 106 in the sixteenth century to 882 for just the first part of the twentieth century. He took these numbers at face value and concluded that "the intensity of war measured by the frequency and duration of battles has certainly increased."[21] The conclusion is unwarranted. All we really know is that the Associated Press is a more comprehensive source of information about battles around the world than were sixteenth-century monks.

Two more recent studies of the changing intensity of war have to some extent overcome the missing-data problem by restricting attention to the recent past. These works are *Statistics of Deadly Quarrels* (1960) by Lewis F. Richardson and *The Wages of War 1816–1965: A Statistical Handbook* (1972) by J. David Singer and Melvin Small. Neither of these studies found, on balance, any overall trend, up or down, in the incidence of war over the past century and a half.[22] However, both studies have serious biases that tend to exaggerate the incidence of modern war. First, the missing-data bias is controlled only somewhat by confining attention to the past 150 years. Information about wars in the nineteenth century is often quite sketchy, and it is reasonable to suppose that many episodes went unreported. In many cases, the casualties were unknown, a circumstance that led the analysts to ignore the event altogether. For example, Richardson reports having to exclude some 80 revolutions in nineteenth-century Latin America and 477 wars and revolts in nineteenth-century China owing to the lack of data about them.[23]

A second problem with both studies is that they take a biased, nonarbitrary starting point: their data collection period begins after the conclusion of the Napoleonic Wars. Those years of fighting (1803–15) constituted a major world war, one that left many millions dead. To exclude this episode from the count of nineteenth-century wars—and to begin data collection in the period of war exhaustion immediately following—makes the nineteenth century look much more peaceful than it was. In both studies, then, two serious biases—the missing-data problem and the biased starting point—lead to an underestimate of warfare in the earlier period. The fact that *even with* these serious biases in their methodology the authors found no upward trend in the incidence of war strongly suggests that the real trend is a declining one.

Recent Trends in Military Forces

The three major studies of the incidence of war just discussed—Wright's, Richardson's, and Singer and Small's—conclude around the middle of the twentieth century. They thus fail to reflect the truly remarkable decline in fighting since midcentury. Western Europe, as noted, has set an historic record, with the European countries not fighting each other for more than fifty years. Latin America is another area that has seen a remarkable decline in military conflict. In the nineteenth century, Central and South America saw more than two dozen international wars, many of them quite costly.[24] For example, in the War of the Triple Alliance (1864–70), Paraguay lost 220,000 men, the majority of its military-age male population.[25] In the past half-century, these regions have seen only four *international* armed conflicts, all of them quite small: the "soccer war" between El Salvador and Honduras in 1969, the Falklands War between Britain and Argentina in 1983, and the U.S. interventions in Grenada (1983) and Panama (1989).

The decline in tension among the established countries is seen in the declining size of their military forces. For years, the popular press has decried an "arms race" supposedly taking place among the major powers. It is widely believed that countries have been furiously expanding their military establishments in a contest to dominate each other. As it happens, this view is rather far from the reality. There has been, of course, a development in military technology. Planes are faster, submarines are bigger, radios are smaller. And the stockpile of certain weapons, especially nuclear weapons, has increased. Overall measures of national military effort show a substantial decline, however, both for the United States and for other long-established countries.

One way to document this point is to examine the trend in the "force ratios." The force ratio is the size of a country's military forces relative to its population (expressed as the number of men under arms per 1,000 population). A number of tests and analyses show that this ratio is a good indicator of a country's overall commitment to military forces, one that well reflects other measures of military effort.[26] Beginning in 1961, the U.S. Arms Control and Disarmament Agency began publishing the force ratios of the countries of the world, using the data collected by the U.S. military intelligence community. These figures enable us to assess recent trends in the emphasis given to military forces.

Overall, the average force ratio for all countries in the world has declined from 6.6 in 1961 to 3.6 in 1999.[27] This overall figure is rather crude, however, for it is dominated by a handful of large countries and does not show what is happening in the typical country. The better figure to use is the unweighted average, which gives each country equal weight in the computation. A second problem with the overall figure is that it is based on a shifting number of countries. In the 1961 tabulation, there were 91 countries; in 1999, there were 167. To keep the series consistent, it is necessary to leave newly created countries out of the tabulation. Newly created countries create a third problem. When a new country comes into existence, after being a protectorate or colony of a great power, it is likely to have quite small military forces. Then, as neighbors become independent and rivalries start up, it builds up its military forces. Hence, the process of decolonization involves a pattern of increasing military forces.[28] We would not want to confuse this temporary upsurge with the long-run trend. For this reason, it is best to confine attention to countries that have been independent for a full generation (twenty-five years prior to 1961).

Figure 6.1 shows the trend in force ratios of 63 long-established countries, that is, countries independent since before 1936. The list includes nations of eastern and western Europe, North and South America, as well as 14 countries in other areas, such as Turkey, Saudi Arabia, Japan, Thailand, and China. (The list excludes most of the countries of Asia, Africa, and the Middle East because they were under outside control until recently.) The figure shows that the emphasis on military forces in these 63 countries has declined significantly in recent decades. It is important to note that this decline has been going on throughout the whole period. The demise of communism and the breakup of the Soviet Union in 1989 only accelerated an already apparent trend.

Figure 6.1

Relative Size of Military Forces, 1961–1999
(63 long-established nations)

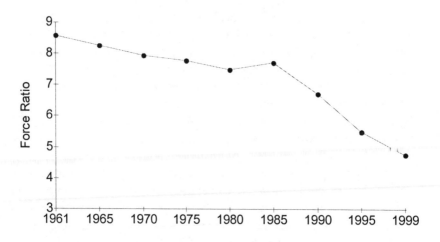

Note: The force ratio is the number of people under arms per 1,000 population. The figure shows unweighted averages—that is, averages that give equal weight to each country in the tabulation.
Source: U.S. Arms Control and Disarmament Agency, U.S. Department of State, *World Military Expenditures and Arms Transfers*, various editions (Washington, D.C.: Government Printing Office).

Another change that marks the declining emphasis on military forces is the decline in the practice of conscription—that is, using force to compel citizens to serve in a nation's military forces. Conscription practices have varied widely over the ages, depending on the military systems in use. In medieval Europe and Japan, warfare was seen as a noble activity, not suitable for peasants. Furthermore, rulers were reluctant to give peasants weapons and military skills, fearing—quite rightly—that these weapons and skills would be used in uprisings against them. In this period, therefore, conscription was not used. Military forces were generally paid mercenaries led by nobles, and the peasants were forced by severe tax levies to supply the funds to support the military forces.

As the disadvantages of the mercenary system grew more apparent, nations turned to conscription. In France, conscription began under Louis XIV in 1688, and the practice was copied by the German state of Hesse in 1701.[29] By the time of the Napoleonic Wars, all the major European powers were employing some system of conscription. England employed informal—and brutal—"press gangs" that arbitrarily seized available men for service in the army and navy. In the United States during the Revolutionary War, the Continental Navy was raised almost entirely through the use of press gangs.[30]

In earlier times, conscription requirements were absolute: everyone had to serve. Anyone who claimed religious or moral scruples against serving in the military was treated harshly. Nations gradually began to recognize a right of "conscientious objection" to military service. England, Holland, and the United States were leaders in this trend. Perhaps the first legal recognition of conscientious objector status came in 1864, when the U.S. Congress amended the Civil War draft act to allow noncombatant duties for those sincerely opposed to bearing arms. Some of the European countries were extremely slow to recognize conscientious objectors. Belgium did not allow them until 1964. France had 150 conscientious objectors in prison as late as 1962 (the measure allowing for conscientious objection was passed in 1963).[31]

The modern period of declining international tension appears to have reduced the emphasis on conscription. Countries are lowering the length of the period of conscripted service or abolishing conscription altogether. This point can be seen by looking at the International Institute for Strategic Studies surveys of the conscription practices of long-established countries.[32] As shown in figure 6.2, in the period 1970–2000 the average length of the conscription period fell from 17.4 months to 8.6 months.

Figure 6.2

Average Length of Military Conscription Period, 1970–2000
(48 major, long-established nations)

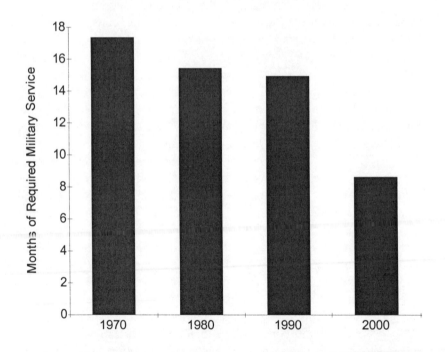

Source: The International Institute for Strategic Studies, *The Military Balance*, various editions (London: IISS).

Primitive and Prehistoric Warfare

The data from recent times indicate, then, a decline in war: fewer countries are engaging in war, for shorter periods, and with lower overall casualty rates. How does this decline fit into the larger picture of war through the ages, going back to before civilization?

Prior to the 1960s, social scientists supposed that preliterate peoples, both modern and ancient, were relatively peaceful. More recent research—especially Lawrence Keeley's comprehensive survey of primitive warfare, *War Before Civilization*—reveals that the belief in a peaceful distant past is a myth.[33] The problem was that archeologists and anthropologists had little actual data on the subject, and what they had was disregarded because they had succumbed to preconceptions about primitive life. One of these errors might be called the "bucolic fallacy," the idea that rural life is more peaceful than urban life. This impression is fostered by the low absolute incidence of violence in a sparse rural population. A village that has one murder in ten years looks peaceful compared to New York City which has hundreds every year. But if you calculate the per capita murder rate for both places, the village's might be much higher. This is the kind of error anthropologists made when noting that skirmishes between tribal peoples entailed only a few deaths. Compared to the carnage at the Battle of the Somme, these tiny losses made primitive war seem a "relatively harmless sport."[34] Only when you look at the war casualty *rate* does it emerge that war losses of primitive peoples are many times those sustained in World War I.

Another fallacy at work is the assumption, dating back to the French philosopher Jean-Jacques Rousseau (1712–78), that civilization corrupts the character of human beings, which is assumed to be gentle and harmonious in a state of nature. Perhaps this idea traces to a false analogy: just as civilization can pollute natural beauty with its garbage and sewage, one could suppose that it also pollutes the pure, natural character of humankind.

Another misconception is the idea that because primitive peoples are relatively inefficient at the ordinary tasks of life—building homes, raising food—they must also be inefficient at the killing presumed to constitute the essence of war. At first glance, this argument seems persuasive: guns, tanks, and atomic weapons can kill more people, and with less effort, than clubs and spears. What the observer overlooks, however, is that efficiency of offense is matched by a corresponding efficiency of defense. Modern soldiers don't stand up in defenseless rows for tanks to mow down. They get into reinforced concrete bunkers, or they keep tanks at bay with antitank rockets. Furthermore, the objective of war, especially in modern times, is not to kill people. War aims to change the will of the enemy, to cause retreats, concessions, and surrenders. When these political goals are achieved, the weapons are silenced.

Influenced by misconceptions about war and primitive society, the social scientists at first refused to perceive the violence of primitive warfare that was apparent in their own data. Archeologists would excavate structures with ditches and palisades that common sense would suggest were forts, and interpret them as merely expressing a "symbolism of exclusion." Masses of human bone fragments found on these palisades were assumed to reflect some kind of peaceful burial ritual. The swords and shields buried with males did not make them "warriors;" these implements were merely harmless "status symbols."[35]

Eventually, more data began to overturn these innocent interpretations. Masses of arrow points were found around the entrances of the presumed "symbols of exclusion," rather clearly indicating that someone was shooting at somebody. Graves were unearthed that revealed a high proportion of violent deaths, with arrowheads imbedded in skulls, for example.[36] The anthropologists, too, eventually went beyond the communities of easy-to-study "natives" already pacified by European administrators and missionaries. They began to find that primitive peoples with virtually no contact with civilization were, for the most part, remarkably warlike. One of the first studies that shook the belief in the "gentle savage" idea was the 1968 research of Napoleon Chagnon on the Yanomamo, a tribe inhabiting the jungles of Venezuela and Brazil. Chagnon found that 24 percent of the adult males of this tribe die in the incessant warfare that takes place between villages.[37] Other recent studies of both modern primitive tribes and prehistoric peoples studied through archeology have also found elevated war death rates. Keeley collected the findings of twenty-three such studies, and these show, in the median case, that 15 percent of the deaths in primitive and prehistoric societies were owing to warfare. By comparison, less than 1 percent of deaths in Europe and the United States in the twentieth century were attributable to war.[38] Keeley concludes, "primitive warfare was much deadlier than its modern counterpart."[39]

The decline in the intensity of war in the past few centuries, then, is not an anomaly. It is part of a much broader decline that has been taking place since the beginning of civilization.

War in the New Nations

If war and conquest are in decline, what accounts for the fighting that still prevails in the world today? To answer this question, we need to appreciate that the great majority of these modern conflicts are taking place in the areas of Asia, the Middle East, and Africa where new nations are being formed. Seen in historical perspective, this fighting does not represent an increase in a tendency toward violence in these areas. Instead, it is probably the reemergence of bellicose tendencies long present, but suppressed by the colonial empires.

By the seventeenth century, the development of political organization, military technology, and methods of transportation in the more economically advanced countries—such as England, Holland, France, Spain, and Portugal—gave these nations a great advantage over less developed areas. At relatively low cost, these European countries were able to seize and control remote regions that were centuries behind them in technology and economic organization.

Prior to this period of conquest, a vast number of independent tribes, clans, kings, and warlords governed these regions. In West and Central Africa, for example, the British encountered some three hundred native states and tribes; they signed treaties with each of these tribes to form the colony of Nigeria.[40] In Melanesia, the collection of Pacific islands including Fiji and the Solomons, there were more than twelve hundred tribal groups with different languages.[41] In the area that was to become the lower forty-eight American states, there were more than three hundred Indian tribes; California alone had sixty.[42]

From what we just observed about warfare among primitive peoples, we know that these many primitive empires, warlords, and tribes saw considerable fighting in the times before contact with Europe. Smaller groups engaged in raids, pillage, and slave taking, while larger units saw wars of conquest and wars of revenge. Even the most primitive societies engage in warfare. One survey of thirty-one hunter-gather societies with virtually no contact with the modern world found that 64 percent were involved in war at least once every two years.[43] Centuries ago, around the world, how many wars would all these primitive conflicts have amounted to in a given year? One can only guess, of course, but it helps to keep in mind the number of independent groupings capable of fighting with neighboring units. Because these units numbered in the thousands—or even tens of thousands—it seems probable that there were hundreds, even thousands, of wars per year in Asia, Africa, the Middle East, and the Americas before the arrival of Europeans. Many of these military actions would have been rather small, but given the tiny populations of the day, the per capita death rate owing to military conflict was most likely quite high.

Western colonialism played a pacifying role in these primitive areas. With their superior technology and organization, the European countries were able to subdue and unite these independent units, thus essentially ending war between them. Violence by no means disappeared, for there were revolts against the colonial powers, but it appears to have diminished considerably.

This state of affairs did not last, however, because the evolution against force eventually undermined colonialism itself. European nations became less willing to make the necessary military sacrifice to put down rebellions, and they increasingly questioned the morality of maintaining an empire through violence. In a relatively short period— from around 1940 to 1980, most of the protectorates, dependencies, and colonies in the Middle East, Asia, and Africa became independent states. With no outside power to suppress conflict, the impulse to violence reasserted itself in a number of wars, both between the new nations as well as within them.

The same evolution has led to the breakup of other types of empires. The Russian empire was built by the military conquest of divergent ethnic communities. After 1917, the communist Soviet Union took over this empire, holding it together by ruthless force. When the communist regime collapsed in 1989, more than a dozen regions were given—or took—independence and began violently to assert themselves. In a similar fashion, the ethnic minorities that made up Yugoslavia had been held together by the communist dictatorship that suppressed their agitation for independence. When that dictatorship ended in 1989, ethnic groups gained enough freedom to mount bloody protests and revolts.

We thus encounter a strange paradox: a decline in the use of force at one level has led to an increase at another. The declining willingness of the more economically developed countries to use military force to subjugate less-developed areas has led to a proliferation of independent political units among less-developed, violence-prone groups. The result has been an *increase* in bloodshed in these areas.

It is important to keep this violence in perspective, however. In 1998, some twenty-seven wars took place in the world, twenty-four of which were in the recently independent areas of Africa, Asia, and the Middle East.[44] This tabulation, made by the Stockholm International Peace Research Institute (SIPRI), includes both civil wars as well as international conflicts. This figure may well represent more fighting than Asia, Africa, and the Middle East saw seventy-five ago, at the height of colonial control, but it probably represents a substantial *decline* compared to the many hundreds of conflicts that characterized these areas many centuries ago, before the pacifying effect of European empires.

How Quickly Will Newly Independent Countries Catch Up?

What will be the course of conflict in newly independent countries? If the lesson of the established countries is any guide, these new regions will move, in the long run, toward domestic and international peace. But predicting the speed of their evolution is not easy. The violence in many of these areas resembles the mayhem seen in places such as France and England four or five centuries ago, suggesting that peace in these regions is perhaps hundreds of years away.

It is possible, however, that the evolution against force has been accelerating, perhaps owing to the effect of modern communications. Fears and superstitions are breaking down more rapidly than before, and the lessons learned from both good and bad examples are transmitted more rapidly and more widely than in ages past. For this reason, peace may come to these troubled regions much more rapidly than the historical record of the established countries indicates. Indeed, this evolution may be already visible. A comprehensive tabulation of armed conflicts in the post–World War II era recently published in the *Journal of Peace Research* supports the points I have been making about trends in warfare. First, for countries existing at the start of the period (1946), the authors found a decline in the tendency to be involved in war. Second, they found that as the creation of new countries from colonial empires proceeded, the total number of armed conflicts in the world rose, from 17 in 1946 to 55 in 1992 (in this tabulation, rather small fights are included as armed conflicts). Since 1992 there has been a dramatic decline in the number of conflicts, to 34 in 2001.[45] In assessing an evolutionary process that can take centuries, one is reluctant to put much emphasis on a trend only a decade long. It may well be that the new nations of Asia and Africa have not yet experienced the full effect of their underlying potential for violence and that extremely bloody episodes still lie ahead. But the recent figures suggest that the level of warfare in these areas is no longer growing, but is in fact declining with surprising rapidity.

7

Beyond Political Murder

To modern American eyes, the Roman Empire seems a familiar, earlier version of our own society. The Romans had hot running water, well-built roads, and, with the games of the coliseum, public spectacles that match NFL football in both popular appeal and inanity. Rome had an impressive code of laws, an extensive tax system, and a senate that clashed with the executive branch. Rome also had thinkers who expressed modern ideas about liberty and the proper role of government, and philosophers such as Cicero, the noted orator and statesman of the first century B.C. To us, he seems a familiar figure of Western culture, like Jefferson, Madison, or Adams.

Similarities there may be between Rome and modern democracies, but they obscure one really enormous difference, a difference that commentators and historians almost always overlook or fail to weigh sufficiently: the normal operation of the Roman system of government involved a level of political violence that is unthinkable by today's standards.

We get a glimpse of this chilling pattern by noting what became of Cicero. Cicero may have been a distinguished statesman like Jefferson, Adams, or Madison, but he did not end his days like them, in peaceful, respected retirement. He was one of the thousands of leading politicians slated for execution by the victors of the civil war that erupted after the murder of Julius Caesar in 43 B.C. He was caught and beheaded on the Appian Way. His head was brought back and nailed up in the Forum, where the wife of one of the victorious generals (Flavia, wife of Antony) pierced his tongue with a stiletto to mock his oratorical powers. A shocking, gruesome end to a noble life, but a typical episode in the political life of Rome.[1]

In the subtle, complicated history of the effort to reduce the use of force in human affairs, perhaps no aspect is more paradoxical than the development of government itself. Government is an agency for wielding force over a given territory. In its most primitive form, it is simply an army holding sway over a particular place, often an army of invaders who choose to remain in the conquered territory and exploit the people in it. At first glance, then, government seems to promise humankind nothing but grief. Violence is bad enough: How could a system of permanent, organized violence extended over an entire territory represent any kind of improvement?

In ancient times, however, it generally was an improvement. When government first emerged, human beings were not living peacefully with each other. Violence loomed everywhere. Tribes attacked tribes, clans attacked clans, and thieves, pirates, and marauders menaced from all sides. Many primitive groups, such as the Bedouin of Arabia, the Apache of North America, the Goths of Gaul, and the clans of the Scottish Highlands, thrived on pillage. It was their way of life. Unless protected by an accident of geography or by exceptional fortifications, few people could plant a field or build a house in safety. Trade languished, and the development of the civilized arts was nearly impossible. In this condition of nearly perpetual war, life was, as the English philosopher Thomas Hobbes put it, "solitary, poor, nasty, brutish, and short."

The introduction of a permanent, overarching military force—government—made it possible to end, or at least to curtail, the primitive pattern of invasion, feuding, and pillage. By exercising a monopoly of force in a given territory, government could ward off invaders and suppress brigands, thus ensuring a degree of peace under which commerce, communication, and the arts could thrive.

Although the emergence of government represented a step in the reduction of violence, it opened up a grave problem: Who was to control government? With its awesome powers of coercion, government stood as a great prize, a pinnacle of power that attracted the ambitious, the vengeful, and the greedy. Because violence was so rooted in primitive cultures, it was natural that the struggle to control government would take a violent form. Those who aspired to rule would resort to killing to gain place, and those in power would kill to destroy their opposition. The result was a cycle of massacre and civil war almost as bad as that caused by the invaders and brigands in the days without government.

Eventually history laid its hand on this process. Systems of uniformly bloody leadership change gave way to peaceful arrangements. The end result of this long and difficult evolution is the modern system we call democracy, the system where, as we take for granted, no one is slain when political offices change hands. To appreciate this system fully, we need to understand the tremendous evolution it represents, how far the human race has traveled from political processes deeply permeated with violence.

The Killing Fields of Rome

One hallmark of virtually all ancient political regimes was the practice of political murder: the killing of political leaders by other political leaders. It is important to distinguish what I call *political murder* from the murders of political figures that sometimes occur in modern democracies today. In the case of these modern assassinations, the killer is a stranger, someone not personally known to the victim, not a leader or high official, and not a representative of any faction or party. The assassin has no hope of gaining office by killing; he is committing an act universally recognized to be a crime, and he is punished if he is apprehended.

In political murders, the killers come from *within* the elite. They are high officials, generally acquaintances or even family members of the person they are slaying. Furthermore, they expect to profit politically if they are successful. They anticipate that their deed will be approved or at least excused. Similarly, when incumbent office holders kill opposition leaders, these executions are approved—or at least accepted as normal. It is the *acceptability* of killing that makes political murder so different from a modern assassination. The failure to make this distinction between acceptable and unacceptable killing leaves one unable to detect the sweeping reduction in political violence that marks the modern political system.[2]

The Roman Empire affords an extensive panorama of the system of political murder. The basic rule of the political game in imperial Rome was, literally, kill or be killed. If a leader was displeased enough with the emperor to want him removed, he had to kill him. Of course, there were complexities and nuances to the system. Emperors could employ various tactics to enhance their popularity, so as to reduce the number of conspirators disposed to rise against them. They funded circuses for public amusement; they distributed free bread to demonstrate their compassion; they went among the nobles and "pressed the flesh," as we say today. They carefully managed the praetorian guard that was supposed to protect them, giving bribes to the officers and bonuses to the troops.

For most emperors, however, these tactics proved unavailing. In the 334 years from the rise of Julius Caesar to the division of the empire (49 B.C. to A.D. 285), Rome had forty-nine emperors. Thirty-four were murdered, and only eleven died a natural death (two others were killed in a foreign war, and in two cases the cause of death is unclear).[3] As we inspect the killings of these thirty-four Roman emperors, we discover that they all were political murders: all were carried out by high officials or family members. Indeed, half of them, seventeen, were carried out by members of the same praetorian guard that was supposed to protect the emperor. (So much for the theory that lavish fringe benefits buy employee loyalty!) We see the pattern of political murder in the first killing of this era, the famous slaying of Julius Caesar. Caesar wasn't killed by a stranger who had no role in Roman government. He was stabbed to death by a group of senators, including men he knew and trusted. He had made two of them, Cassius and Brutus, provincial governors.[4] For an American assassination to resemble a Roman one, we would have to imagine that some high official—say the chairman of the Joint Chiefs of Staff—kills a president and that, thereafter, majorities in Congress acclaim the chairman's deed and make him president!

Why can't this happen? The answer appears to lie in the modern rejection of violence. Neither congressional representatives nor the public will approve of a murderer, even someone who kills an unpopular president. For us, there is no such thing as a "good" murder; for Romans, there was. This difference reveals how far we have traveled in our evolution against the use of force.

As Roman emperors could be killed with public approval, so they also could kill with public approval. That was the other side of Rome's violent political coin. Emperors protected their position with all sorts of violent tactics, the most common being an accusation of treason. They could level this charge at anyone who seemed unfriendly, on the assumption that anyone who was critical of the emperor was plotting to murder him. We would find this assumption absurd today, but in those bloody days it was everyone's working hypothesis. In those days, treason was anything the emperor said it was: tax evasion, sorcery, even failure to praise the emperor's poems.

The decisive fact about all the murders and executions that regularly took place in Rome was that leaders and the public generally acquiesced in them. There was surprisingly little shock or revulsion—even when family members slew each other. When, in A.D. 59, Nero murdered his mother, Agrippina, he was well received when he returned to Rome. "From one province and another," reports the Roman historian Suetonius, "loyal addresses duly poured in."[5]

Of course, if emperors went overboard with their killing, they ran the risk of provoking a reaction. Caracalla massacred twenty thousand people in A.D. 212, provoking public protests—and eventually his own murder.[6] Moderation in killing generally proved to be the best policy. The typical emperor would execute only a few dozen senators and only a few hundred equestrians (nobles).

It wasn't just the emperors who employed murder. Senators would eliminate rival senators by bringing *maistres* (charges of treason) against them, holding snap trials dominated by their supporters and convicting and executing them within hours. This vicious tactic was encouraged by the practice of giving one-third of the executed person's property to the leader who had denounced him. Politicians also made use of violent street gangs, which murdered opponents and sacked their homes, and which intimidated public officials, including, on occasion, even the emperor, with their demonstrations and riots.

The Right of Brothers to Slay Brothers

How widespread was this pattern of political murder? Were some ancient communities able to shake it off or at least to make progress toward a nonviolent alternative? The sketchiness of historical accounts makes it difficult to answer this question with certainty. But based on the information that has come down to us, it appears that no ancient regime was able to put such violence truly to rest. Perhaps the earliest government we know about in some detail is that of the Hebrew kings, which was founded around 1025 B.C. It was a government steeped in blood, fulfilling the curse that the prophet Nathan laid on King David that "the sword shall never depart from your house." David's son Absalom formed a conspiracy against him, forcing David to flee from Jerusalem; David eventually gained the upper hand, and his general Joab slew Absalom, along with twenty thousand of Absalom's supporters (2 Samuel 15 and 18). The Bible undoubtedly skips over many rebellions and executions, but from what it does report, the violent pattern is clear. For example, in the year 845 B.C., a general named Jehu murdered King Joram by shooting him in the back with an arrow and then had Joram's wife thrown from a window and ran over her body with his chariot. Next he had all seventy of Joram's male relations slain. Their heads were delivered to him in baskets, which were dumped out in two piles at the city gates. Not to leave any loose ends, Jehu went on to slay everyone else connected with the prior regime—all officials, friends, and even the priests of the former ruler—"until he left him none remaining" (2 Kings 9–10).

In the Ottoman Empire, Mohammed II (A.D. 1429–81) enshrined the principle of royal fratricide in his *Book of Laws:* "Those of my illustrious children who shall ascend the throne shall have the right to execute their brothers, in order to ensure the peace of the world; they are to act accordingly."[7] As the edict indicates, this harsh practice was made necessary by the sinister tendencies of royal siblings. If they weren't killed, they could be expected to organize plots and revolts against the ruler.

Ancient laws and customs also sanctioned the killing of rulers. These laws generally were couched in the form of justifying the slaying of leaders who—as an ancient Greek law put it—"rise up against the people with a view to tyranny."[8] Because deciding who was or was about to become a tyrant was a highly subjective decision, the legitimization of tyrannicide was an open-ended invitation to kill rulers.

One regime does depart somewhat from the pattern of political murder in ancient times: the early Roman Republic. The republic was the government that existed in Rome between the fall of the Tarquin monarchy in 509 B.C. and the period of the emperors beginning in 49 B.C. It was a remarkable regime, characterized by a number of interesting and commendable features, but perhaps the most unusual was its record of having surprisingly few murders of incumbent rulers.

A closer look reveals, however, that the idea of killing was not really laid aside in the republic. Instead, a constitutional device tended to make killing unnecessary. The Roman Republic had a strong version of term limits. Those holding executive power—the consuls and other magistrates—were elected by popular assemblies for terms of one year and could not be reelected to a consecutive term. The effect of this practice was to produce leadership change automatically, without the necessity of a murder or revolution. Under the republic, if you didn't like your rulers, all you had to do was wait a few months and they would be gone.

Although this measure reduced the number of political killings, it did not end them. Despite the extremely short terms, impatient opposing factions still slew consuls and other officials. Spurius Cassius was killed in 486 B.C. by patricians who opposed his policies of land redistribution; Spurius Maelius was slain by an emissary of the Senate in 439 B.C.[9] In 133 B.C., the tribune Tiberius Gracchus was clubbed to death by a large group of senators and their followers, who also slew three hundred of Tiberius's supporters at the same time. Eleven years later, Tiberius's brother Gaius, also a tribune (the highest executive position), was murdered, and three thousand of his supporters were executed (in 122 B.C.).[10] One of the reasons these men were slain was that they had broken the prohibition against term limits, and their opponents feared they were about to become dictators. After that time, the term limits principle was not reestablished, and conspiracies, executions, and civil war became the normal pattern in Rome. It appears, therefore, that in the early Roman Republic, political violence was not outgrown, but only held at bay by a constitutional device.

Well into the Middle Ages, the pattern of political murders was common. In *The Age of the Despots,* nineteenth-century English historian John Addington Symonds describes the pattern in the Italian kingdoms—including Padua, Florence, Bologna, Milan, Genoa, and Pisa—in the fourteenth and fifteenth centuries. The history is a spine-chilling account of bloody deeds—a history, as Symonds concludes, "of crime revenged by crime, of force repelled by violence, of treason heaped on treachery." For example, in Bologna, Giovanni Bentivoglio began to rule in 1400 but was stabbed to death the following year (then "pounded in a wine-vat"). A few years later, his son was beheaded by a papal legate, along with other members of his family. In 1445, a group of nobles murdered another member of the Bentivoglio line, Annibale, along with all his kinsmen, while they were attending a christening feast. Then, Annibale's supporters hunted down the killers and, after slaying them, "nailed their smoking hearts to the doors of the Bentivoglio palace."

The excesses of violence led Symonds and other historians to a provocative query: Were rulers of those days in the grip of a mental disease called "haematomania," an insane desire for bloodshed? Symonds concludes that the violence was too general to fit this theory. "If we answer this question in the affirmative," he says, "we shall have to place how many Visconti, Sforzeschi, Malatests, Borgias, Farnesi, and princes of the houses of Anjou and Aragon in the list of these maniacs?"[11]

A Mysterious Evolution

How was the system of political murder overcome? From a modern perspective, the case for moving beyond it seems elementary.

The killings were in themselves tragic and horrible, and the resentment they caused led to feuds and civil wars as friends and relatives attempted to avenge them. Furthermore, they handicapped the rational conduct of governmental affairs. How could anyone make thoughtful policy or give sound advice knowing that the threat of death lurked behind every glance? Common sense should have led people to say, "There's got to be a better way." Yet this does not seem to be how political murders were overcome. The elimination of violence from the process of leadership change was not a conscious, rational step. No one came forth with the theory that violence works against human happiness and achievement. No assembly passed a law or constitutional clause to mark a switch from violent to nonviolent practices.

It's doubtful that we can call this transformation a learning process. Hebrews and Romans went along century after century with destructive political violence, yet came away still murdering, no wiser than before. Furthermore, the inhibition against this kind of slaying emerged surprisingly quickly when it did emerge. Nations went along for thousands of years in the violent mold, and then, in the space of a few generations, they put political murders behind them.

We get a sense of this mysterious evolution from the history of one of the first countries to make the transition to a nonviolent politics, England. Up until the sixteenth century, its politics resembled the violence of the Roman Empire. We all have heard how Henry VIII (who ruled from 1509 to 1547) executed inconvenient wives, yet these deaths were just a small part of his mayhem. Fearful that enemies might plot to overthrow him, Henry murdered dozens of relatives with some distant tie to the throne, including children. He also executed a number of his own appointees who had served him with energy and distinction, including Thomas More, Cardinal Thomas Wolsey, Bishop John Fisher, even his former chief minister Thomas Cromwell. The striking thing about this bloodshed was that it was socially approved. Henry wasn't repudiated as a monster—as he would be today. Records indicate that he was a popular king. In the climate of the times, palace murders were simply normal.

In the space of about a century, this view shifted. One indication of the change was Elizabeth I's reluctant execution of her niece, the rebellious Mary Stuart. Captured and imprisoned, Mary continued to plot with Catholic conspirators to overthrow Elizabeth. For this reason, Elizabeth's advisors repeatedly urged her to execute Mary for treason. In 1587, she did so, but only after nineteen years of hesitation.

The execution of Sir Walter Raleigh some thirty years later was another example of a reluctant slaying. Like Mary, Raleigh had involved himself in conspiracies against the sovereign—in this case, James I. He was convicted of treason in 1603, but James stayed the execution, and Raleigh became a "death row inmate" (even writing a history of the world while in prison). In 1616, James gave Raleigh provisional freedom to command a mission to Guiana to bring back gold supposed to exist there, with express orders not to attack any Spanish community. Raleigh violated the orders by attacking Spanish settlements (thus provoking an international dispute)—and found no gold. Returning to England in disgrace, he tried to escape but was captured, and the original sentence of execution was finally carried out—in 1618.[12]

The execution of Raleigh appears to be the last time an English monarch used the death penalty against opposition leaders. When, in 1629, Charles I arrested leaders of the parliamentary opposition on charges of sedition, their punishment was limited to fines and imprisonment. This more lenient treatment of opponents undoubtedly encouraged later parliamentarians to be bolder in contradicting the king.

But political murders were not quite over with. In 1641, the Puritan Parliament ordered the execution of Charles's minister, the earl of Strafford, on trumped-up charges of treason. Then came the Puritan Revolution (1642–49), which produced years of civil war and culminated in the execution of Charles I. This was another reluctant execution. Charles had been defeated by Oliver Cromwell's Puritans and was made prisoner in January 1647. Nevertheless, he was not killed immediately. In the ensuing two years, he was offered many reasonable compromises, ways of saving his life if he would agree to certain Puritan demands concerning church-state arrangements. The stiff-necked Charles spurned all of these offers. Worse still, he defied his captors by escaping to the Isle of Wight and organizing a revolt against them. The revolt was defeated, and he was recaptured and offered another deal, which he again refused. He was finally executed on January 30, 1649.[13] In spite of all the vexation that Charles had cost the Puritans, some in that faction opposed his execution, including Oliver Cromwell's own son, Richard, who pleaded on his knees for the sparing of Charles's life.[14]

The execution of Charles I may be taken as the last political murder in England—that is, the last killing of a leader by other leaders.[15] In 1660, just eleven years later, the Puritans were overthrown, and the royalists were back in charge. Instead of taking vengeance against members of the prior regime, the victors made the new monarch, Charles II, agree to limit reprisals to those who had specifically ordered the death of his father. When Parliament later tried to expand reprisals to others, Charles went to the House of Lords to urge it to "join me in extinguishing this fear [of being slain] which keeps the hearts of men awake. Mercy and indulgence," Charles said, "is the best way to bring men to a true repentance [and] make them good subjects to me, and good friends and neighbors to you."[16]

The events of 1688 confirmed that England had put political murder aside. The Dutch prince William III invaded England—with the approval of virtually the entire English political elite—to depose the unpopular James II. Because James's army declined to obey him and fight for him, it was a bloodless revolution with no significant clash of arms. James fled, and William was welcomed as the new monarch. English historians have called this event the "Glorious Revolution" because it reasserted the role of Parliament, but it also marks a glorious milestone in the reduction of political violence. William's forces captured the deposed James II, but they did not execute him—as would have happened in an earlier day. He was allowed to go into exile in France (where he caused no end of vexation for the English government that spared his life). Furthermore, there was no bloodbath against James's supporters—again a marked departure from the usual practice after a ruler was overthrown.

The English experience affords a useful insight into the relationship between democracy and the practice of political murder. There is a tendency to treat democracy as a political system that people simply choose to have and that, once adopted, guarantees political calm.

The causality seems to run in the other direction, however. A people must first set aside the practice of resorting to violence to get and retain power; then, and only then, can freedom of expression be respected and meaningful elections carried out. In England, it was the fading of the practice of political murder in the seventeenth century that made possible the system of electoral democracy—which came more than a century later.

When elections are held in a country whose people are still strongly disposed to political violence, the elections are not sufficient to establish democracy. Practices of political murder and violent revolt reassert themselves, and the country collapses into civil war or dictatorship. Russia held several elections in the early years of the twentieth century, and, of course, did not achieve democracy. Elections in the Weimar Republic in Germany (1919–33) did not guarantee the establishment of democracy in the face of the violence of the Nazi and communist leaders. Other illustrations of the same point come from modern Africa, where many former British colonies began independence under democratic arrangements, yet these arrangements could not withstand the lingering impulses toward murder and civil war. In the final analysis, the politically tolerant system we call democracy can exist only when violent practices such as political murder have been set aside.[17]

Backsliding in France

In France, the elimination of political murder followed the same general pattern as in England, though the timing was considerably later. All the way into the early seventeenth century, political murders were common in France. In 1588, King Henry III arranged for assassins to murder his own army commander, Henry of Guise, and also decreed the execution of that commander's brother, the cardinal of Guise. In 1617, Louis XIII secretly ordered the murder of Concino Concini, his chief minister and a favorite of his mother, and had Concini's wife beheaded and burned for sorcery.[18] After this time, however, we find no further episodes of monarchs' slaying individual political leaders.

The reign of the Louis XIV (1643–1715) confirmed that murder was passing from the repertoire of power techniques. Though Louis was a vain, imperious personality and exercised virtually unlimited powers in an absolute monarchy, he did not kill personal and political enemies. When he moved against his shockingly corrupt chief tax collector, Nicolas Fouquet—a man Louis envied because of his ostentatious wealth—he simply had him tried for peculation (the trial lasted three years). The upshot was that Fouquet was imprisoned, and Louis confiscated his property for himself.

Especially remarkable was the treatment Louis accorded François Fenelon, a churchman whose advanced opinions were a direct insult to Louis's policies and beliefs. Before Louis knew where Fenelon stood, he had appointed Fenelon as tutor to his grandson and rewarded him with the archbishopric of Cambrai. But Fenelon's opinions gradually came out, especially when he published a book in 1669 that condemned war as "a shame of the human race" and deplored absolute monarchy. Louis, who spent the best years of his life in wars of national expansion and who fully believed "I am the state"—even if he did not actually say it—was furious. The printer of the book was arrested, and the police confiscated all copies they could find, but Fenelon was untouched and even kept his archbishopric. The worst that happened was that Louis forbade his grandson to visit his former teacher for a period of 2 years.[19]

Although the era of palace murders had passed, there still would be, as in England, deliberate slaying of high officials in connection with revolutionary upheaval. The difference was that France's last revolution came 150 years later than England's last revolution, in 1789. As in England, the monarch, Louis XVI, was executed—along with his queen Marie Antoinette (in 1793). Thereupon ensued 6 years of political turbulence in which a great number of political murders and many massacres were committed. With fitting justice, some of the revolution's bloodiest leaders—including Hébert, Saint-Just, Danton, Robespierre, and Westermann—were themselves executed as political tides shifted. In Paris alone, twenty thousand people were slain on the guillotine.[20]

In retrospect, it seems clear that this period of revolutionary violence was a brief backsliding from a broader, stronger trend against political murder. By 1796, the Terror had ceased. The last murder of a major figure was the 1804 slaying of the duc d'Enghien, whom Napoleon suspected—falsely—of treason.[21] Thereafter, even those leaders who seemed to deserve death were let off lightly. When Talleyrand, Napoleon's foreign minister, was discovered plotting with the British in 1807, Napoleon did not have him shot but merely dismissed him with a tongue lashing. Napoleon himself was treated with remarkable leniency when he abdicated in 1814, after his military defeat by the coalition of European countries ranged against him. He had sacrificed a million men in an ill-judged campaign to conquer Europe, yet neither the victors nor the French felt it fitting to slay him. He was sent to a comfortable exile—from which he returned a year later to head another disastrous military campaign, and when he lost, he was sent to exile again.

Another instance of remarkable leniency was the treatment of his nephew, Louis Napoleon, who led an uprising in Strasbourg in 1836. It failed, and Louis Napoleon was captured, but instead of being shot, as he expected, he was shipped off to North America. Four years later, he attempted another uprising, in Boulogne, and failed again. This time he was sentenced to life imprisonment—a gentle confinement that allowed him a valet, a dog, a mistress, and an opportunity to escape—which he took.[22] Later, in 1848, he was elected president of France.

Russia and China Move away from Political Murder

In England and France, the sheer passage of time since the last political murder—350 years and 200 years, respectively—demonstrates that this form of political violence has been transcended permanently. In the case of Russia, we lack this kind of chronological confirmation, however, for the last political murders took place less than 50 years ago. Nevertheless, recent events suggest that the era of political murder may be past.

In turning away from various uses of force, Russia lagged behind England and France. Even late into the nineteenth century, savage corporal punishments were applied, both in the military and in civil law enforcement, and torture was routine. Military service was for a period of 25 years—virtually a death sentence for the conscript.[23] Serfdom, the forcible attachment of agricultural workers to the land, was not abolished until 1861.

In political violence, Russia exhibited the same delayed evolution. In 1718—a century after palace murders had ceased in England and France—we find Peter the Great brutally torturing his own son Alexis and condemning him to death for disloyalty (he died of the injuries before the execution could be carried out). Many of Alexis's friends were also tortured and executed.[24] The time of Catherine the Great (1762–96) represents perhaps the beginning of a turning point in the pattern of palace murders. It is a fact that both Peter III and Ivan VI were murdered in prison during her rule and that these deaths were convenient for Catherine. These men, though personally inoffensive, served as possible replacements for her as emperor, at a time when she was surrounded by conspiracies. However, their killings were done clandestinely, under quite confusing circumstances, and apparently not ordered or approved by Catherine—though public opinion blamed her for them.[25]

In 1801, the emperor Paul was murdered by a high-level conspiracy led by the military governor of St. Petersburg.[26] This event may mark the last of the palace murders—that is, killing within the royal and aristocratic circles, but it did not end the threat of political violence. Nineteenth-century Russia was marked by persistent terrorism and revolutionary violence. Although the terrorists were political outsiders, they were so numerous that government officials, including the czar, lived in constant fear of assassination. The slaying of Alexander II in 1881 illustrates how ubiquitous this threat was. Returning from a state function, Alexander took a route that was lined with not less than four assassins. The first—a student—threw a bomb that missed the royal sledge. Alexander was unhurt, but he stopped to help the wounded soldiers. Thereupon another student threw another bomb, which killed him. This was the seventh major attempt against his life.[27] Nineteenth-century Russian political leaders may have been relatively safe from being killed by each other, but they were not safe from being murdered by revolutionaries.

The Bolshevik Revolution in 1917 demonstrated that political murder was not over. As with the French Revolution 128 years earlier, the Russian Revolution unleashed a spasm of bloodshed, including civil war, massacres, and political murders. In 1918, Czar Nicholas II and his family were murdered—a deed that was for many years regarded as "the highest revolutionary service."[28] Vladimir Lenin and his comrades set up a secret police—the Cheka—that was directed at murdering anyone, high or low, who seemed to contradict the purposes of the revolution. In that same year, Lenin's revolutionary committee publicly executed former members of the provisional government.[29]

Joseph Stalin, the dictator of the Soviet Union until his death in 1953, institutionalized the revolution's violent impulses. He relied on terror, using the secret police to eliminate any possible rival, sometimes in quiet executions, sometimes in show trials for "treason." The victims included fellow revolutionaries such as Sergey Kirov, Grigory Zinoviev, and Lev Kamenev, and high military officials such as Marshall Tukhachevsky. Right before Stalin died in March 1953, he seemed about to begin another violent purge of top officials; some historians suspect that these officials may have killed him to protect themselves.[30]

After Stalin's death, top officials shared power in a period of collective leadership that attempted to put an end to the climate of terror. The head of Stalin's secret police, Lavrenti Beria, was tried and executed, as were a number of his subordinates. These executions, it appears, were the last political murders in Russia. In 1956, Nikita Khrushchev—who was gathering the reins of power in his hands—made a speech denouncing Stalin and the climate of fear his killings had created.

A test of the new climate came the following year, 1957, when some party leaders attempted to oust Khrushchev by voting against him in the central committee. Khrushchev brought enough members to his side to outvote them, and as a result they were disciplined. However, their punishments were simply political demotion. One of these insurgents was Vyacheslav Molotov (after whom the "Molotov cocktail" firebomb is named). He was removed from the Central Committee and given a minor post. He kept on criticizing Khrushchev, however, and in

1962 lost all his party and governmental positions and went into re- tirement. Another of the defeated insurgents was Georgy Malenkov. He was expelled from the Communist Party, but was given a job as a manager of a hydroelectric plant in the far-off Kazak Republic.[31]

Journalists called this leadership reshuffling a "purge," without noticing the dramatic shift in the treatment given to the losers. In the days of Stalin and for most of Russian history, leaders who openly sought to displace the ruler were punished by death or, rather, torture and death. It reflected a monumental stride in the conquest of violence when a leader who unsuccessfully challenged a Soviet dictator came away with a hydroelectric plant in his pocket.

In 1964, Khrushchev, who had seemingly made himself master of the Soviet Union, was ousted by the Central Committee. Again the transition was bloodless. Khrushchev was simply voted out of office and pushed into a peaceful retirement. He was allowed to write his memoirs. Although they were not permitted to be published in the Soviet Union, they were published abroad with no ill effect on the author.

In 1991, another difficult leadership transition took place, and again it did not result in any deliberate killings. A reformist president, Mikhail Gorbachev, was forced out of office in the double coup that ended communist rule and produced the breakup of the Soviet Union. The leaders of the coup put together a retirement package for Gorba- chev that included a small house in the country, a small pension, and office space for a foundation in Moscow.[32]

The most significant thing about this nonviolent transition was that it was completely unexpected. It is understandable that everyone was caught off guard. We expect the future to resemble the past. Be- cause Russia has had a history of appalling political violence, where practically every major change of regime involved slayings, if not civil war and massacre, the toppling of the communist regime—we would reason—should have been bloody and devastating. After all, this sev- enty-four-year regime had been born in bloodshed and was maintained by terror. How could the whole edifice collapse with scarcely more than an "excuse me"?

This transition becomes somewhat understandable if we factor in the idea that there is a historical trend against the use of force. It is incorrect to assume a constant potential for violence in Russia. That potential clearly declined during the course of the twentieth century— as the events of 1957 and 1964 suggest. There was reason to expect, therefore, that Russia was finally moving beyond political murder and that future transitions would be characterized by the absence of this kind of violence.

A similar movement away from political murder appears to have been accomplished in China in very recent times. Politics in China historically has been extremely violent, characterized by frequent revolutions, civil wars, and massacres, as well as by slayings within the circle of political elites. Sociologist Daniel Tretiak has examined the pattern of political killing in a study of the deaths of more than five hundred high Chinese officials in the period from 1600 to 1968. He observed three common types of political deaths: execution, suicide (almost always to forestall execution), and assassination. He notes that the assassinations were political murders by our definition because they were plotted by other high officials. "In contrast with what appears to be the case in the United States, for example, assassinations in China have generally not been the result of random acts committed by individuals acting alone. Rather . . . assassinations are part of the process of elite conflict."[33] His tabulations show that political murder (execution, forced suicide, and assassination) has been a significant cause of death among members of the political elite in China, accounting for between 13 and 28 percent of the deaths of high officials.[34]

After the unification of China under communist control in 1950, the pace of political murders seems to have declined considerably. In 1971, the commander of the armed forces, Lin Piao, and his wife were slain, apparently for plotting to kill Mao Tse-tung. In 1972, a daughter of Lin Pao was shot, on grounds of treason. After Mao's death in 1976, a power struggle ensued, and the four losers, including Mao's third wife, were jailed. Mao's wife was later tried and sentenced to death in 1981, but the sentence was suspended. That act of clemency may well mark the passing of the practice of political murder in China, for since that time there appear to have been no more high-level killings in China.

Overcoming political murder does not guarantee a peaceful, democratic politics, of course. It is only a first step. China and the former Soviet countries are still generations behind the established democracies in overcoming the emphasis on force. There is reason to hope they may cover ground more quickly than Western countries did, but, even so, they are likely to be the scene of many disruptive, violent episodes, including assassinations, riots, and terrorist acts. Their government officials may be expected to employ force arbitrarily in denying freedoms of speech and assembly. But it does seem likely that their leaders have largely stopped killing other leaders. This would seem to be an essential foundation for making progress against other kinds of political violence.

8

Whatever Happened to Revolution?

When the Constitution of the United States was drawn up in the late eighteenth century, the framers were preoccupied with the danger of revolution. They knew that throughout history countries had been ravaged by violent struggles between factions trying to gain control of government. In the Greek city-states, the conflicts often took place between the haves and the have-nots, as the poorer classes rose up to destroy rulers and seize the property of the wealthy. "The revolutions which aimed at such a redistribution of property were utterly disastrous for Greece," says historian Michael Rostovtzeff. "Revolution and reaction followed each other with brief delays, and were marked by the wholesale slaughter or expulsion of the best citizens."[1] Even in Athens under Pericles—supposedly a golden age of democracy—violence was never far away. Leaders of the faction opposing Pericles conspired with Athens's enemy, Sparta, to carry out an invasion of Athenian territory, which was to be coordinated with an uprising against Pericles. The invasion (of Tanagra in 457 B.C.) succeeded, but the uprising failed to materialize.[2]

The Roman Empire was the scene of an almost continuous series of revolutions and civil wars (along with political murders, of course), as were the later medieval Italian city-states, with the striking exception of Venice. And, of course, both France and England were ravaged by uprisings and civil wars throughout the Middle Ages. To the eighteenth-century observer, such as James Madison, it seemed that the "violence of faction" was the great enemy of humankind. "The friend of popular governments never finds himself so much alarmed for their character and fate," he wrote in *Federalist No. 10,* "as when he contemplates their propensity to this dangerous vice."

This preoccupation with the violence of faction led the Founding Fathers to invent the complicated system of "checks and balances" for the U.S. Constitution. As tradition has it, this precious document—now carefully preserved in helium at the National Archives—is responsible for the political stability and freedom the United States has been able to enjoy.

A thoughtful analysis reveals rather considerable difficulties with this interpretation. For one thing, the Constitution did not produce political stability for the first seventy-five years. Even if one doesn't count the small Whisky Rebellion of 1794 as a significant uprising, the Civil War of 1861–65 certainly was, a rebellion that drowned the nation in rivers of blood. The domestic peace that we credit to the Constitution dates from after that time: since the Civil War, the United States hasn't seen any *more* violent uprisings.

A study of English history casts further doubt on the theory that legal and constitutional arrangements are responsible for the political peace of modern times. Before the seventeenth century, politics in England was as bloody as anywhere in the world. The country was dominated by local warlords who fought among themselves and in alliances with kings and would-be kings. In addition to wars involving the nobles, there were numerous uprisings of workers and peasants. In 1450, for example, peasants and workers led by a Jack Cade marched on London demanding a reduction of oppressive taxation. They defeated the forces of Henry VI and entered London, where they beheaded the officials responsible for the tax system.[3] Following the conclusion of the Wars of the Roses in 1485, the central government began to gain a predominant position, but it was still beset by military challenges. For example, in 1536 the regime of Henry VIII faced two major rebellions, one in Lincoln and another at York. The year 1541 saw another rebellion in the north of England. In 1549, Henry's successor, Edward VI, faced an uprising of peasants and small landowners (Ket's Rebellion).[4]

Over the next hundred years after 1550, the pace of revolutionary activity slackened. Then domestic peace was broken quite dramatically by the Puritan Revolution of 1643, which involved two quite bloody civil wars, one right after the other. A generation later, in 1685, there was a Puritan rebellion in Dorset. This was the last domestic military conflict in England.[5] There were uprisings later in English possessions, including the United States, India, Scotland, and Ireland. England also subsequently saw many riots, instances of terrorism, and, as I discuss below, the bloodless revolution of 1688. But it saw no more civil war.

Thus, more than a century before the American Founding Fathers drew up their constitutional system to control the danger of factional violence, the English had already overcome the problem! And they overcame it without the aid of any formal system of checks and balances, indeed without any legal document at all. The government of England does not have a written constitution. It has a highly centralized political system without any of the separation of powers that the Founding Fathers thought essential for stable government. Those who have a majority in the House of Commons control both the legislative and executive branches and, in effect, can oppress any group they wish with whatever outlandish or repugnant legislation might strike their fancy.

How, then, do we account for England's overcoming the violence of faction? It is difficult to resist the conclusion that this transformation was part of the broad historical trend I have been exploring in this book. *Owing to the evolution against force, the tendency toward revolution has been decreasing.* This trend is most evident in the countries furthest along the evolutionary path against violence, especially in Europe and the Western Hemisphere. In these areas, human beings are not so inclined to take up arms against each other as they used to be. When in opposition, they are not so ready to kill—and to be killed—to overthrow the government. And when in power, they are not so likely to provoke a bloody reaction by the excessive use of force against their opposition.

This broad cultural change would seem to be the main explanation for domestic peace in the United States. The American Founding Fathers had the good fortune to draw up their constitution at a time in history when political violence—in the Anglo-American subculture—was in striking decline. They got credit for a broad historical trend that had little to do with the document they drafted.

The Decline of "Customary" Violence

At first, it may seem implausible to say that civil violence is decreasing, for our television sets positively scream with episodes of civil strife in the world. We need to remember, however, that modern communication has shrunk the world and brings us detailed reports from the new countries in Africa, the Middle East, and Asia. As just noted, in these newly independent regions the evolution against violence is centuries behind the West. Their politics resembles the bloody struggles of sixteenth-century Europe, complete with political murders, armed uprisings, and civil wars. If we focus on the Western countries, we see a clear decline in the frequency of revolution. Indeed, in most of these countries, violent revolution appears to be a purely historical phenomenon, a type of event that has passed away forever.

Consider the case of France. Although somewhat behind England in moving beyond violent politics, France seems to have followed the same evolutionary path. Over the course of approximately 200 years, from the 1660s to the 1870s, one sees a gradually decreasing frequency of revolt. From a distance, it may seem that civil life under the old monarchy was one of stability and order, but in truth the country in those early times was seething with rebellion. Historian Norman Davies gives a glimpse of this political violence during the heyday of France's greatest king, Louis XIV: "The long procession of provinces in open and bloody revolt continued—Béarn (1664), the Vivarais (1670), Bordeaux (1674), Brittany (1675), Languedoc (1703–9), Cahors (1709). Rural riots and outbreaks of château-burning were mercilessly punished with military repressions and mass hangings."[6] One tabulation of political violence in the period 1630–1715 shows twelve peasant revolts and thirty-one urban riots where rebels seized control of a town or city.[7]

The eighteenth century culminated in the revolution of 1789, or perhaps one should say *revolutions* because the period 1789–99 involved a series of bloody clashes and campaigns. In the nineteenth century, the pace of rebellions slackened, there being only three, in 1830, 1848, and 1871. Although these rebellions were not on the scale of the revolution of 1789, they were major episodes of strife. In the 1848 uprising, for example, more than 10,000 people died as General Jean-Baptiste Cavaignac's troops crushed the rebels in Paris.[8] Since the time of the last of these uprisings—the Paris Commune of 1871—France has not seen any major rebellions—a period of 130 years.

The pattern of declining civil strife is not confined to the West, however, as the case of Japan demonstrates. Japan was unusual because as an island, like England, it was relatively protected from invasion, and—again like England—it had developed early on a common culture that included a written language and institutions of higher learning. Whether these advantages explain its progress, the fact is that Japan overcame the problem of civil war just as France and England did. In the Middle Ages in Japan, fighting was a more or less continuous activity. The country was ruled by hundreds of independent warlords who fought against each other, singly and in alliances. In addition, the country was plagued with pirates, bands of robbers and marauders, as well as frequent and violent agrarian uprisings. In the fifteenth century, in the central province of Yamashiro, there were agrarian rebellions every two or three years.[9] An eleven-year civil war that raged from 1464 to 1477 (the Onin War), devastated the country and led to a century of civil war, which Japanese historians call Sengoku, "the Warring States."[10] Toward the end of the sixteenth century, the more ruthless and skillful warlords began to achieve hegemony. One of the first steps in this process of centralization was the destruction of Buddhism as a center of power. In 1571, the leading warlord, Nobunaga, razed three thousand monastic buildings in the city of Hieizan and slaughtered thousands of monks.[11]

Though founded in blood and conquest, the Tokugawa regime that finally emerged in 1615 was able to bring a substantial degree of pacification to the country. The revolts that did occur were put down rather easily, thus teaching the lesson that rebellion did not pay. Two centuries later, in the mid–nineteenth century, the Tokugawa regime fell into disrepute, and opponents gathered to overthrow it. However, a major civil war was not necessary to accomplish this purpose. A show of force was sufficient to enable the opposition to take control of the government with relatively little fighting in 1868. The transition was followed by a number of revolts, as the samurai (displaced warriors and officials of the old regime) protested their exclusion. The greatest of these conflicts took place in 1877 in Satsuma; it took troops of the Tokyo government six months to suppress this rebellion of some thirty thousand former samurai.[12] The Satsuma rebellion was the last civil war in Japan's history.

The twenty countries of Latin America provide a useful laboratory to gauge trends in political violence. After the wars of liberation from Spain in the period 1810–25, most of these countries fell into a pattern of almost continuous uprisings and civil wars. During the course of the nineteenth century, the frequency of these violent episodes gradually diminished, so that after around 1920 revolution became the exception, not the norm. Since World War II, there have been only three cases in which a regime has been overthrown by military action against the government: the revolutions in Bolivia in 1952, in Cuba in 1958, and in Nicaragua in 1979. At the current time, there are only two rebellions in progress in Latin America, a major one in Colombia and a largely contained conflict in Peru.[13]

Uruguay provides a good illustration of this political evolution in South America. "Uruguay," said a historian writing in 1904, "has experienced to a marked extent the unrest customary in South America, where armed revolution is the climax of discontent with the authorities, or the outcome of ambitious politicians seeking office."[14] At the time, his observation seemed entirely justified, for the country had seen some fourteen rebellions in the period between 1832 and 1904. Uruguayan politics of this era bore an uncanny resemblance to the strife of England in the fifteenth century during the Wars of the Roses. Just as England had its Lancaster (red rose) and York (white rose) factions, Uruguay had two contending parties known by the same colors, Colorados (the Reds) and Blancos (the Whites). And, like the English factions, these two parties were divided by no ideological or policy point. Their life-and-death struggle was simply over who should hold office.

Yet the strife that seemed so "customary" to the historian writing in 1904 was in fact undergoing a remarkable diminution even as he was writing. The bloody revolution of that year—an uprising of Blancos who controlled six of the country's *departamentos,* or states—was the last major civil war. To some extent, the pacification was promoted by a policy of conciliation by the Colorado president, José Batlle y Ordóñez, and by the adoption of a political arrangement for permanently sharing power between Blancos and Colorados. This legal arrangement itself should not be given too much credit for the relative calm, however. The idea of political conciliation and sharing offices was not obscure. Politicians of the region had known about it for a century. They just didn't put it into effect earlier because too many of them preferred fighting to the idea of sharing power.

The threat of revolution in Uruguay did not entirely subside after 1904. One uprising in 1910 and one in 1935 were on a smaller scale than the civil wars of the nineteenth century. Since 1935, there have been no significant armed rebellions. This is not to say that politics in Uruguay for the past sixty-five years have been calm or that the country is a well-governed utopia. There have been violent strikes and demonstrations, terrorism, irregular transfers of power, and at least one attempted military coup. But civil war is a thing of the past.

Political Protest in Modern Times

It is difficult to pin down the underlying causes of the general trend away from revolution and civil war that we have noted in so many cases. One ingredient is probably a growing reluctance to cause bloodshed, a reluctance that traces to an increasing value being placed on human life—one's own as well as that of others. In the nineteenth and twentieth centuries, this change showed itself in an increasing number of "comic opera" uprisings. These events resemble the plots and conspiracies of earlier times in almost all respects except that when the time came to sacrifice human life, the participants held back. For example, Louis Napoleon—nephew of Napoleon Bonaparte—was a driven young man who believed it was his destiny to rule France. In pursuit of this aim, he organized two uprisings to put himself in power, one in Strasbourg in 1836, another in Boulogne in 1840. His aim in each insurrection was to overpower the local military garrison and convert it to his side. Yet in each case, when it came time to shoot and kill someone, Louis and his comrades held back—as did the military forces lined up against them. In both cases, Louis was captured without bloodshed.

In modern times, many actions against constituted authority have involved little or no bloodshed. One recent example took place in Fort Davis, Texas, in 1997, where a small group of protesters proclaimed themselves to be an independent country, the Republic of Texas. The leader, Richard McLaren, was the object of state and federal warrants (for minor offenses), which could not be served peacefully because of McLaren's and his bodyguards' threats to use force to defend their "country." The state police decided to wait the problem out. "We're not going to go risking people's lives over this particular silly notion," said one official.[15] After six months, the standoff ended when McLaren signed an agreement to surrender in return for an opportunity to appeal to the United Nations.

It is not always the case that government officials react with sophistication and sensitivity when their authority is challenged. There are occasions when the old impulses of brutality and revenge dominate, and the result is considerable violence. The raid by the Federal Bureau of Alcohol, Tobacco, and Firearms and the Federal Bureau of Investigation on the Waco compound of the Branch Davidians in April 1993 is an example. In pursuit of the almost trivial alleged crime of not paying taxes on certain firearms, the government forces under the direction of Attorney General Janet Reno bumbled their way into a massacre that killed seventy-six people, including twenty children.[16]

However, when modern government officials overreact with excessive force to those who resist authority, there is not an escalation of violence, as there often would have been in an earlier age. The public is shocked, and government officials apologize (and those with integrity resign). Few citizens are tempted to take up arms to avenge the violence with more violence. In the case of the Waco massacre, one person did take up arms in retaliation, and his action produced a dramatic violent result. Timothy McVeigh bombed the Oklahoma City federal building on the anniversary of the Waco massacre in retaliation for the government's deed. To understand why revolution was endemic centuries ago, imagine that instead of just one individual prompted to use violence in retaliation for the massacre at Waco, there had been thousands!

Another factor in the decline in revolution is the reduction of mob violence. In pre-twentieth-century Western societies, street violence was quite common, easily provoked, and difficult to calm down. The result was that crowds and demonstrations easily degenerated into armed bands that constituted the beginning of a military uprising against the government. In France, for example, virtually all of the military uprisings of the eighteenth and nineteenth century began as protests and riots. In modern times in Western societies, participants in strikes and demonstrations generally make an effort to restrict violence and avoid bloodshed.

The demonstrations in France in May and June 1968 that affected Paris and much of the rest of the country offer a good example of the modern pattern of restraint. Though primarily provoked by the university students with grievances against the educational system and their opposition to the war in Vietnam, these disturbances also included unionized workers who occupied factories and who organized a nationwide general strike. Altogether, there were thousands of sit-ins, blockades, and demonstrations, yet in each clash officials and demonstrators showed remarkable patience by the standards of earlier times. Most of the sit-ins and occupations were resolved peacefully through negotiations. The police were taunted—and pelted—in numerous street clashes, yet they generally acted with restraint in clearing demonstrators and street blockades. It is estimated that only 12 people were killed in connection with the disturbances.

Historian Charles Tilly contrasts this figure with the costs of political violence in France in earlier days. In the 1830 Paris uprising, for example, 650 people died, and in the same year 350 more people died in other riots and demonstrations. In the 1871 Paris uprising, some 20,000 were killed. "Over time," concludes Tilly, "French people have moved toward forms of collective action having less likelihood of generating violence."[17]

The Bloodless Revolution

A revolution is a form of protest against an unpopular govern-ment. Perhaps rulers have been vicious or oppressive; perhaps they have pursued unsound policies; perhaps they are blamed for problems beyond their control. Whatever the cause, rulers become so unpopular that opposition leaders are willing to use force to displace them. The result, then, is a civil war.

There is a way of getting beyond a revolutionary situation without bloodshed, however: the unpopular rulers can be asked to step aside—or be made to step aside—thus allowing the opposition to take over the government without any fighting. The result is a bloodless revolution. In effect, the opposition uses the threat of starting a civil war to achieve its goal with little or no actual destruction of life and property.

Although there were occasional bloodless revolutions in me-dieval times, this type of event became common only in relatively modern times. In earlier days, participants on both sides were too eager for violence to be able to emerge from a revolutionary situation peace-fully. The soldiers who represented the incumbent rulers were too eager to engage opposition forces in battle and too ready to risk their own lives, on which they placed a low value, even in a losing cause. In later times, soldiers began to have qualms about violence. They became hesitant about slaughtering their countrymen and grew reluctant to plunge their country into the maelstrom of civil war. They also became more "cowardly," more reluctant to risk their own lives in civil war.

The same change in attitudes affected opposition forces. They, too, grew less bloodthirsty toward opponents and more concerned with their own survival. Therefore, they became more patient, more willing to temporize, looking for ways to get rulers to step down quietly, with-out a bloody battle. Of special importance, opposition forces grew will-ing to respect the lives of the officials and soldiers of the defeated re-gime, which naturally made it easier for the defenders of incumbent rulers to lay down their arms.

An example of this kind of relatively peaceful leadership

change took place in England in the late seventeenth century. In 1659, the London Puritan army led by Major General John Lambert closed Parliament and took control of the government. The Lambert regime was extremely unpopular, however, and faced opposition from virtually all sectors of the country. In 1660, the army division stationed in Scotland, under the leadership of General George Monck, undertook to represent this opposition and made a march on London. Though Lambert sent troops to oppose Monck, his soldiers deserted, allowing Monck's forces to proceed freely to London—and compelling Lambert and his associates to resign. In this way, a change of rulers was effected without civil war.

A quarter-century later, the pattern was repeated. The highly unpopular James II had come to the throne. Among other things, James was attempting to force Catholicism on a country that had been Protestant for more than a century. In 1688, opposition forces invited William III of Holland to invade the country and to become, with his wife Mary (the English pretender to the throne), rulers of England. William landed with his troops at Torbay on November 5, 1688. Everyone expected a civil war, but it didn't happen. When James tried to gather his troops in Salisbury to oppose William, they deserted, leaving him defenseless. He was forced to flee, and William entered London unopposed. This episode is known as the Glorious Revolution, but it was not a revolution that involved a military struggle between government and opposition forces. It was a bloodless revolution, accomplished by the threat of military action.

The decline in vindictiveness played a critical role in this episode. As discussed in the preceding chapter, during the seventeenth century the practice of political murder was left behind in England, with the reluctant execution of Charles I in 1649 being the last clear example. By the time of the Glorious Revolution of 1688, participants on the losing side of political disputes could expect to have their lives spared. Even the deposed king, James II, was allowed to escape to France unharmed. This more tolerant context made soldiers employed by an unpopular government more inclined to desert it when revolution loomed.

The bloodless revolution stands as an important transition

phase in the development of the modern democratic regime. It is a sign that leaders are moving beyond the practice of kill or be killed. When that stage is achieved, it becomes possible to use elections to decide questions of leadership succession.

The Rise and Decline of Military Coups

The experience in Latin America parallels the transition to democratic rule that occurred in England two centuries earlier. As noted, most Latin American countries had gone beyond the pattern of revolution and civil war by the beginning of the twentieth century. But the decline of revolution did not mean that these countries immediately went to democratic systems of leadership change. There was a transitional period characterized by bloodless revolutions. In the Latin American setting, these bloodless revolutions have been known as military coups.

A military coup—the removal of the chief executive by the country's armed forces—is an action that involves the threat of force, but not the actual use of force in a battle. The president is told to step down—and does so. In most cases, a coup represents an attempt to defuse a revolutionary situation peacefully. Most coups take place in times of great political turbulence, when the government is carrying out—or is accused of carrying out—wrong or oppressive policies, and when opposition forces are clamoring for a change in rulers. The military then steps in and removes the chief executive, thus producing a peaceful change in government.

Arturo Bray, a retired Paraguayan colonel who made a comprehensive study of military coups in Spain, Portugal, and the Latin American countries describes the perspective of the military officers in the crisis leading up to a coup. "If the constituted government, because of its incapacity or immorality, is proceeding to lead the country on the path to a disaster which could end even in national dissolution, or if it deprives the people of their rights, drowning all legitimate opposition in blood and arbitrary acts," Bray points out, "it is difficult to understand on what basis the military—who are, after all, armed citizens—must resign themselves to contemplating, impassive and Olympian, the impending catastrophe."[18]

Since 1945, the twenty countries of Latin America have experienced a total of seventy-two military coups. Whether one approves or disapproves of these episodes, they represent instances of peaceful, or nearly peaceful, changes of rulers. In many cases, they defused a severe conflict between opposition forces and incumbents that otherwise might have developed into a bloody civil war.

Although the military coup represents an improvement over the violence of revolution, it still involves the threat of force. In order to prompt the military to act, opposition groups threaten to escalate their violence against the government. And the military, once it decides to depose the incumbent chief executive, threatens to do battle against him and his supporters if they will not leave office quietly. Thus, the military coup represents a quasi-violent system for changing leadership. We therefore should expect that over time this pattern would fade away.

This appears to be the case. The seventy-two military coups Latin America has seen since World War II have not been distributed evenly over this period. As figure 8.1 shows, the frequency of coups in the region has declined from approximately two per year in the early part of the period to about one-tenth that rate in recent times. Indeed, the evidence of recent years suggests that the military coup, which used to be the hallmark of politics in Latin America, has almost disappeared. The coup that occurred in January 2000 in Ecuador was the first one since a 1993 coup in Guatemala.

Figure 8.1

Frequency of Military Coups in Latin America, 1945–2000
(10-year moving average)

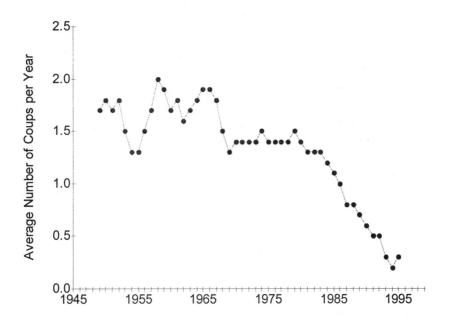

Freedom of Expression and the Decline of Revolution

The possibility of civil war is not a constant in the life of a nation. Revolutions are not equally likely to happen anywhere, anytime. The overall historical trend against the use of force brings about, over time, a turning away from force as a way of settling political disputes.

This observation is not, at first, easy to accept. Americans like to think of the revolution of 1776 as just around the corner, and it figures, even today, in political discourse. One reason why the right to bear arms needs to be preserved, say some, is to give citizens a chance to rise up militarily against an oppressive government, just as our forefathers did. My analysis suggests, however, that in a country such as the United States the probability of a violent uprising is extremely remote. Our politics has moved beyond it—not necessarily, as the reader might suppose at first, to the advantage of rulers. As discussed in chapter 16, governments in the advanced democracies are being undermined by many moral and psychological challenges. Their officials can still be confronted and even overthrown, but with verbal and emotional weapons. Guns have become unnecessary as well as unseemly.

The feeling that revolutions are always possible is kept alive by the experience of the new countries of Asia, Africa, and the Middle East. These countries have indeed seen revolutions and civil wars in recent times. But as noted previously, these lands are centuries behind the West in their evolution against force. Each country and region is following its own evolutionary path. We should not suppose that recent revolutions in places like the Congo or Sudan show what is likely to happen in the United States or France. The interpretation needs to be reversed. The absence of revolutions in the United States and France indicates the likely future trend in places such as the Congo and Sudan.

The decline of revolution has many effects on the shape of modern government and politics. For one thing, it has figured significantly in the general increase in freedoms of expression. Down through the years, the threat of revolution has been one of the principle reasons why governments restricted civil liberties. National rulers felt—not without reason—that freedom was, in Madison's metaphor, the air that fed the fire of violent faction. In mid-seventeenth-century England, for example, censorship was seen as a necessary tool to block the growth of a violent opposition. If opponents of the government were left free to communicate and organize, the logic went, they would begin a bloody uprising. Once the revolutionary times were past, by the 1690s, freedom of the press and other civil liberties began to be more widely respected.

This pattern is being repeated in modern times. As more countries move past the danger of civil war, civil liberties are observed more widely. Freedom House—an independent organization that rates the countries of the world according to the degree to which they respect civil and political freedoms, including religious freedom, freedom of association, and freedom of the press—has documented this trend. When Freedom House made its first tabulation in 1972, it rated 42 countries "free." This was 30 percent of the 139 countries surveyed. Since that first measurement, the proportion of countries rated "free" has grown. In the 2001 survey, 57 of these same 139 countries—41 percent—were rated free.[19]

It may seem difficult to believe—and sometimes it seems we almost don't want to believe it—but the nations of the world are making progress in turning toward a less-violent politics. This process is slow and halting, with backward steps as well as advances, but the overall trend is clear.

9

From Hell to Hot Meals:
The Evolution of Criminal Punishment

Every society faces the problem of dealing with wrongdoers, with those who have violated its laws and customs. And from time immemorial, every society has relied on the use of physical force to punish these wrongdoers. Yet despite the continuity, an enormous change has occurred in this practice. The past four centuries have seen a dramatic reduction in the severity of criminal punishment. In a relatively short space of time, the civilized world moved from extremely bloody penalties, applied hastily and almost indiscriminately, to milder punishments, given with reluctance after considerable deliberation.

As with so many of the changes involving the use of force, this contrast is often taken for granted, as if today's practices were simply the right way, and our ancestors were too unintelligent to see it. A closer look suggests that the changes in criminal punishments were not only, or even mainly, the product of reason and argument. They were propelled by cultural changes. Our ancestors did things differently not because they didn't know particular facts, but because they had a different attitude toward the use of force.

Before Prison

It comes as something of a surprise to learn that until relatively modern times prison was not recognized as a punishment for wrongdoers. There were prisons and dungeons all over the world, of course, but their function was to hold captives until their punishment was decided upon or carried out. The idea of sentencing someone to a period in jail would have seemed rather ridiculous to the ancients, an action almost meaninglessly light. When a crime could not be redressed by restitution or a fine, the punishments employed in ancient societies always involved the infliction of physical harm.

One of the milder corporal punishments was whipping, a penalty widely employed from ancient times. In Deuteronomy (25:1), whipping is recognized as a punishment for an offender, the number of lashes given "in proportion to his offense," but not to exceed forty. In colonial Massachusetts in the seventeenth century, whipping apparently was the main punishment for minor transgressions, including petty theft, cursing, lying, drunkenness, absence from church service, criticism of the governor, even courting without the permission of the girl's parents.[1] In Massachusetts, the biblical limit of forty stripes was observed, but not in other places. In the British navy in the eighteenth century, an offender could be given as many as one thousand lashes, and sentences of five hundred to eight hundred were common, a punishment that bordered on execution.[2]

Other types of "mild" punishment involved restraining the offender in public so as to combine the discomfort of a fixed position with public humiliation. These "engines of punishment," used especially in England and New England, included the stocks and the bilboes, a device that pinned the offender's legs with an iron bar. The pillory held a prisoner's head in a vise and presented it to a public that was permitted—and expected—to throw things at it. These missiles included rotten eggs and dung, but also stones that could cause the loss of an eye or even, in a rare case, death. The punishment was thus a form of legal mob violence. The action of the mob could be prevented, on occasion, if the victim had supporters to defend him. In one famous case that took place in London in 1814, a highly regarded English navy officer, Lord Thomas Cochrane, was condemned to the pillory for spreading false financial news. His supporters, led by a Sir Francis Burdett, who stood by his side, inhibited bystanders from harming the prisoner.[3] (Naval fiction writer Patrick O'Brian adapted this episode in his novel *The Reverse of the Medal,* putting his hero Jack Aubrey in Lord Cochrane's predicament.)

In addition to whatever the spectators did to the victim, the pillory usually involved an additional punishment of mutilation. Sometimes the victim's ears were nailed to the restraining block that held his head, and, after the period of punishment, he was freed by cutting the ears away from the nails. Thus, having "both ears cropped" was often an official part of the punishment by pillory.[4]

More severe punishments included using a hot iron to burn a letter onto the victim, the idea being to combine public shame with pain. Thieves were branded with the letter T, and "rogues" with the letter R. Crimes involving the exercise of religion and the expression of political views were also often punished by branding. In England in 1628, a Scottish preacher charged with writing a book critical of king, peers, and prelates had one ear cut off and his face branded with SS, for "sower of sedition."[5] In New Haven, Connecticut, a Quaker being persecuted by the Puritans in the 1660s was whipped, put in stocks, and branded with a red-hot iron with an H for "heresy."[6] In Brussels, criminals were—rather incongruously—branded with an angel.[7]

Mutilation was another way of punishing lesser crimes. Cutting off ears was commonly used to penalize minor forms of sedition, such as speaking against the king or government. Religious deviancy was often punished by piercing the tongue—or removing it. In France in 1766, a seventeen-year-old follower of Voltaire had his tongue cut out after a period of torture.[8] In ancient times, some victims had an eye or both eyes put out. This practice was not so common in medieval times, though not unheard of: it was employed in both Amsterdam and Venice, among other places.[9]

The death penalty was widely used in ancient and medieval times. In many cases, it was not merely an execution—which could be accomplished by beheading or hanging—but a killing that involved considerable torture. In Palestine and Greece, stoning was common. The Romans used crucifixion. In medieval times, burning became a popular form of execution, especially for religious heresy. In Germany and France, officials employed a slaying known as "breaking on the wheel," wherein the prisoner was strapped to a large wheel, his limbs were beaten and broken, then he was slain by a killing blow. England was known for executing by "drawing and quartering." With each limb tied to a different horse, the victim was pulled apart when the horses were driven in opposite directions (if necessary, the executioner aided the process by hacking the limbs). In Hanover, sophisticated executioners contrived to have a mass of wasps sting the prisoner to death.[10]

The death penalty applied to numerous crimes beyond murder, including theft, forgery, counterfeiting, homosexual acts, religious and political dissent. In early Athens, stealing cabbage was punished by death.[11] In eighteenth-century England, lawmakers went on a capital punishment binge, adding more than a hundred new crimes to the list of those punishable by death, including robbing a rabbit warren and cutting down a tree. In 1820, forty-six persons were hanged for forging Bank of England notes (some of the allegedly false notes proved, when analyzed by modern techniques, to be real, unforged currency). In 1820, England had some 222 capital offenses in its legal code. Many were not being applied, but others were. One observer noted that in 1829 twenty-four persons were hanged in London, not one of whom had committed murder.[12] By 1861, however, the number of capital offenses in England had been reduced to four.[13] In France in 1789, 115 crimes received the death penalty; this number was reduced to 30 by 1871.[14]

Punishment generally recognized a distinction between men and women, but the practices in no way favored the fairer sex. The ducking stool, which added immersion in cold water to the humiliation of public exposure, was used in both England and America typically to punish women for offenses of speech, such as "scolding." Public whipping—the woman being stripped naked—was another common punishment for offenses such as prostitution and adultery. (A seventeenth-century English critic of the practice observed it was "designed rather to feast the eyes of the spectators than to correct vice.") It wasn't until 1820 that England abolished whipping as a corporal punishment for women. When convicted of a crime deserving the death penalty, women generally were burned alive—in well-attended public spectacles. In England, public sentiment shifted against this form of torture-execution, and it was abolished in 1790.[15]

In earlier times, punishments not only were severe, but also applied carelessly, with the result that many innocent people were made to suffer them. In effect, the judicial process operated with such reckless partisanship that arrest often automatically meant punishment. It has been calculated, for example, that the average length of a criminal trial in London's Old Bailey in 1833 was only 8.5 minutes.[16] Over the centuries, a broad movement of legal reform has taken place, giving accused persons the ability to combat charges and thus to escape the state's use of force. These reforms include the right to a trial by a jury, the right to a defense attorney, the right to face accusers, the right not to be forced to testify against oneself, and so on. Even after being convicted, defendants still are given opportunities to overturn their conviction. A recent Supreme Court decision (*Bounds v Smith,* 1977) gives prisoners the right to a law library, legal assistance, paper, pencil, envelopes, and stamps.

The Movement away from Cruelty

The rationale of harsh punishments in olden times was deterrence. Punishment, as one writer puts it, "was offered as an example and a lesson. The spectacle of human suffering was intended to put the crowd in mind of the vastly greater terrors of hell, the only fear that most magistrates believed could overawe a fallen humanity."[17] As a theory, the deterrence idea is difficult to refute: it is true that the more terrible the punishment, the more people are dissuaded from committing the deed that leads to it. By this logic, the best punishment is the most hellish.

To modern thinking, this formulation is repugnant because it so obviously ignores the pain and suffering of the victims, including innocent victims swept into the criminal justice system by accident. But in earlier times, people ignored this aspect because they saw life as having less value, and also because people were less sensitive to the suffering of individuals. This seems to be the simplest way to explain why ancient and medieval societies adopted the extreme version of deterrence: they didn't object to the suffering caused by the harsh criminal penalties.

By this theory, then, punishments started to become less harsh as people began to feel a degree of sympathy for victims of the criminal justice system. What might have caused this growth in empathy? One plausible explanation points to the growth of wealth and comfort made possible by economic development. General poverty meant that people were poorly protected against starvation, illness, and the ravages of nature. Historian Barbara Tuchman raises this point in accounting for the violence of the fourteenth century. "Accustomed in their own lives to physical hardship and injury, medieval men and women were not necessarily repelled by the spectacle of pain, but rather enjoyed it."[18]

The theory that wealthier and healthier people empathize with the pain of others helps explain why the trend against force seems to have accelerated in recent times. In the case of most violent practices, including criminal punishments, the world went for thousands of years without much apparent change. Most of the progress seems to have come in the past two or three centuries—that is, since the Agricultural and Industrial Revolutions. This theory also helps explain why certain countries—specifically the wealthy countries, such as England and Holland—led others in the evolution against force. Even today, the pattern still holds: it is in the poorest regions where violence, both official and unofficial, are most widespread.

In Europe, a turning point in criminal punishment seems to have arrived toward the end of the sixteenth century. Officials began looking for an alternative to the harshest methods of punishment. The obvious one was the prison or "workhouse": a place where offenders would be confined, yet maintained alive with food and shelter, and made to observe a strict regimen of work and discipline. Holland was one of the first countries to develop the prison as a punishment. The first house of correction was established in that country in 1588, following a jury's refusal to vote the death sentence for a sixteen-year-old boy accused of theft.[19] By the end of the seventeenth century, prison was a well-recognized alternative to whipping or execution as a punishment.[20] In England, the first house of correction was established at Bridewell, in the City of London in 1556. In 1609, legislation provided that each English county was to have a "bridewell."[21]

The early prisons may have been an improvement over execution and mutilation, but only a slight one, for they were extremely harsh institutions. Jailers charged prisoners for everything, including food, straw, and clothing. Those who couldn't pay went without. In some places, prisoners were also charged for "easement of irons"—that is, they had to pay a fee to be let out of spiked collars around their necks or released from iron bars that pinned their legs to the floor. With all these charges—paid by family members and friends of the wealthier prisoners—prisons became profitable investments and were bought and sold for thousands of pounds.[22] In addition to punishments and depriva tions, prisons were extremely unsanitary, so death from infection and disease was common.

Most prisons included a regime of strenuous forced labor. In Holland, prisoners were often given the job of rasping wood powder from logs of dye trees, the first step in making dye. The prisoners in the "rasphouse" were expected to produce fifty pounds of powder a day and had to work ten to twelve hours a day to do it.[23] When meaningful work wasn't available, prisoners were forced to do exhausting exercise activities. In the early nineteenth century in England, a huge circular stair machine called the treadwheel was employed in many prisons. The sickly, underfed prisoners were driven for six-hour periods in these exercise machines that ran at a speed selected by the taskmaster.

The Dilemma of Prisons

As the cruelty of prison treatment became known, reformers took up the task of humanizing prisons. One early group of reformers in England established the Society for the Promotion of Christian Knowledge, which produced a report on the deplorable conditions of London prisons in 1702.[24] A committee appointed in 1729 condemned the "cruelty, barbarity and extortion" that they found in prisons.[25] Perhaps the best-known eighteenth-century reformer was John Howard, whose 1777 book *The State of Prisons in England and Wales* led to legislative measures to improve conditions.[26]

The nineteenth century saw a number of experiments in operating penal institutions along more humane lines. One notable success was achieved at the penal colony on Norfolk Island. This South Sea island had been a place of incarceration for the most hardened and violent criminals in the British penal system, and it had been operated along extremely harsh lines, complete with floggings, chains, and starvation. In 1840, Alexander Maconochie, a retired Scottish naval captain, took over as superintendent and implemented a new approach. Maconochie believed that the object of prison was "to prepare men for discharge." He saw that brutal treatment worked against this end because it demoralized the convicts and left them less able to function in normal society. He abolished all arbitrary punishments and deprivations and set up a clear system of rewards for constructive behavior. Sentences were varied according to the work accomplished by the prisoner. Prisoners earned credits that allowed them to buy choice foods and other amenities. They could wear ordinary clothing and were allowed to smoke. They worked their way up a ladder of privileges, the highest rung of which was a conditional freedom before release. Within a few years, Norfolk was a model prison. Inmates were relatively cheerful and well behaved, and they showed low recidivism when released.

Unfortunately, a happy prison was more than the English public and politicians could stand. When London learned that the convicts had celebrated the queen's birthday by playing games, acting in a play, and drinking a toast to Her Majesty, Maconochie was recalled, and Norfolk was turned back into the "turbulent, brutal hell" it had been previously.[27]

The episode at Norfolk Island points up a major dilemma that confronts modern prison practice. On the one hand, we are increasingly concerned about humane standards, and modern policy is opposed to deliberately injuring prisoners. Furthermore, we know that the healthiest regime of rehabilitation is one where prisoners are constructively occupied and, indeed, "happy." Yet we have not consciously abandoned the idea of using prisons to punish—that is, to make a wrongdoer suffer. We want inmates to be *unhappy;* we want prison to be a place people hate to be—on the theory that fear of more suffering will deter them from doing the things that put them in prison.

The prison system is caught in the conflict between these opposite impulses. In physical terms, the modern prison system is, in most cases, an extremely mild form of punishment. Prison life is covered by extensive regulations designed to ensure the health and comfort of prisoners. For example, the standards of the American Correctional Association require that prisoners be served three meals a day and that at least two must be hot meals. Meals must meet basic nutritional requirements, and prison kitchens are expected to accommodate special diets prescribed by dentists and doctors, as well as the dietary restrictions of different religious groups.[28] A 1982 lawsuit by prisoners in a Massachusetts prison established the point that every cell must have flush toilets and sinks with running water; a plastic bucket was ruled unacceptable. (This court decision cost the state's taxpayers $1.2 million in cash awards to prisoners.)[29]

Most prisons provide many cultural services for prisoners, including libraries, classes, church services, support groups, sports and recreation, television, mail, and visiting privileges. It costs a great deal to provide all these services and to follow all the regulations governing prisoner rights and treatment. In the U.S. prison system, each inmate costs taxpayers more than $22,000 per year, almost exactly the tuition at Harvard.[30] In effect, prisons now seem to punish taxpayers more severely than criminals!

Yet in spite of their enormous costs, prisons are unhealthy places. The forced boredom, the forced association with undesirable individuals, and the breaking of normal ties to family, community, friends, and coworkers put great psychological strains on prisoners. In many cases, modern prisons unwittingly inflict or exacerbate mental illness, leaving inmates less able to function normally when released— and therefore more likely to commit further offenses. Prisons could be an excellent setting to apply firm systems of uplift and rehabilitation— along the lines of the Norfolk Island experiment. But modern prisons unfortunately have become so bureaucratic and so paralyzed by the micromanagement of far-off judges and legislators that uplifting systems of "tough love" are almost impossible to implement. Prisons thus serve mainly as holding tanks that accentuate the vices and weaknesses of the alienated individuals they confine.

Prison is thus an increasingly futile, yet expensive, approach to the punishment of wrongdoers. Correctional authorities in most of the advanced nations widely recognize this point. As a commissioner of the Canadian Correctional Service put it, "increased reliance on incarceration is not only unsustainable financially, but also largely ineffective in preventing future crime compared to other forms of intervention."[31] The United States is somewhat out of step with this trend. The current "tough on crime" mood combined with the "war on drugs" has led to a sextupling of the prison population over the past three decades, leaving this country with an incarceration rate six times that of other economically developed countries including France, Spain, Italy, Greece, Germany, England, and Canada.[32]

In the future lie perhaps even milder punishments, *even punishments that involve no use of force.* To a degree, we have already arrived at this point. A suspended sentence is an example. It amounts to a declaration that the defendant has done wrong, but he will not be made to pay a physical penalty. It is a psychological penalty, a social condemnation. Private groups, such as universities and trade associations, also formally criticize individuals for wrongdoing. Other modern punishments that involve little use of force include probation, parole, and community service. In the United States, these methods are the mainstays of the modern criminal justice system. In 1996, fully 70 percent of the 5.5 million offenders under supervision of correctional authorities were not in prison; they were on probation or parole. The popularity of these alternatives to incarceration indicates that, almost in spite of ourselves, we are drifting away from the use of force to address the problem of criminal punishment.

The Decline of Sadism

In reviewing the attitudes that have led to milder treatments of criminals, we need to note the declining role of sadism—that is, the human tendency to take pleasure in the pain of others. Most of us today would claim that we do not feel any such impulse. To the extent this claim is true, however, it is because our culture and reason have worked to overcome what appears to be an instinctive orientation. The popularity of killings on television—including torture killings—and the appeal of violent sports such as boxing and videos of "ultimate fighting" show that this fascination still lies in the human makeup.

As I have observed previously, sadism is not a socially constructive impulse, for it impedes the trust necessary for human cooperation. It's difficult to feel benevolent toward people who enjoy seeing blood and gore because that blood and gore could include our own! Therefore, the human race has gradually moved away from sadism. As noted in the discussion of human sacrifice, the first step in this evolution was the perception that sadism is not among the highest values—and therefore not a plausible trait to impute to a superior, virtuous god. When it was assumed that gods do not enjoy human suffering, human sacrifice passed from the scene.

This is not to say that with this perception sadism was thereupon condemned. A long period ensued during which sadism was considered an innocent, if frivolous, pleasure—perhaps akin to the way we view television programs today. A really superior being, such as God, probably would not find *The Flintstones* entertaining, but we consider this show an acceptable diversion for lesser beings. This, it appears, was the view of sadism through the Middle Ages: an innocent pleasure. We note, for example, that in sixteenth-century Paris, cat burning was a popular entertainment. A special stage was built where cats were lowered into a fire. Historian Norman Davies reports that "the spectators, including kings and queens, shrieked with laughter as the animals, howling with pain, were singed, roasted, and finally carbonized."[33]

This desire to watch suffering most likely contributed to the popularity of vicious criminal punishments. Not surprisingly, these punishments were made public spectacles and probably were the best-attended public events in medieval times. All over Europe, huge crowds gathered to watch the torture-executions of criminals, as well as the lesser tortures of branding, maiming, and whipping.

With the passage of time, however, the evolution against sadism continued. It passed from the category of innocent pleasure to vice. By the eighteenth century, attending executions was an activity for the lowest classes, not a spectacle appropriate for the well-to-do. Changes in practice followed the change in attitude. In London, the tradition was to hold a grand procession of the condemned prisoners from Newgate prison to Tyburn Hill, where they were executed. This vulgar parade was stopped in 1783; after 1868, public executions themselves were stopped. In the United States, the last public hanging took place in 1936 in Owensboro, Kentucky, where a crowd of twenty thousand came to watch in a light-hearted mood. The news services' pictures of holidaymakers enjoying an execution stirred up a storm of protest, however, leading the Kentucky legislature to ban public executions.[34]

The Decline in Torture

The decline in the acceptability of sadism seems also to have played a role in the decline of torture. In ancient and medieval times, torture was an approved practice, not only for convicted criminals, but also against criminal suspects and witnesses—that is, against those who were innocent of any crime. In Greece and Rome, slaves would be tortured to reveal the wrongdoing of their masters. Flogging, the rack, and burning with red-hot irons were the common ways of eliciting "evidence." In medieval times, torture was regularly used on suspects in ordinary criminal cases as well as in cases of witchcraft and heresy. The Inquisition, the Catholic Church's system for rooting out critics and nonbelievers, became infamous with tortures so appallingly sadistic that it makes us uncomfortable today even to describe them.

A famous early critic of torture was Cesare Beccaria, whose essay *On Crimes and Punishments* was published in Milan in 1764. Beccaria made the obvious logical points that confessions wrung out through torture were of dubious value and that the torturing of suspects meant the state was punishing suspects before it knew if they were guilty. Though Beccaria is often credited with inspiring the shift away from torture, this seems an oversimplification. Torture had already been abandoned in many places before his book was published. Judicially sanctioned torture ended in England in 1640 and was abolished in

Scotland in 1708. In Prussia, Frederick the Great abolished torture in 1740.[35] The enthusiastic reception of Beccaria's book further suggests that he was confirming views already held, not trying to persuade a hostile audience. By the eighteenth century, the educated elites of Europe were already of the opinion that it was wrong to indulge sadism through the use of torture. This is not to say, of course, that torture in law enforcement agencies ceased. Even today it still occurs at the hands of sadists who make their way onto the police and prison staffs. But when it occurs, it is recognized as an abuse and a crime; it is not officially sanctioned as it was before the eighteenth century.

The Death Penalty: The United States Bucks a Trend

The history of the death penalty provides an interesting lesson in the twists and turns in the evolution against the use of force in punishment. Like other uses of force against criminals, the death penalty has undergone a general decline. The arguments against it, which have steadily gained ground, are, first, that it is a cruel and extreme use of force; second, that it is an irreversible punishment in the event that it is applied in error; and, third, that it demeans those of us who punish by revealing the low value we place on human life. The point applies even if capital punishment is reserved for the crime of murder. To take human life deliberately as a punishment blurs the social lesson that taking human life is wrong.

The movement to abolish the death penalty began in Europe and Latin America in the nineteenth century. Some countries became "de facto" abolitionist: although the death penalty remained on their statute books, they ceased applying it. For example, Iceland has had no executions since 1830, although the death penalty was not legally abolished until 1928. Portugal hasn't applied the death penalty since 1849. Costa Rica was the first country officially to abolish the death penalty for all crimes, in 1877. Other early leaders in abolishing capital punishment—for ordinary crimes—include Holland (1870), Norway (1905), and Sweden (1921). After World War II, and especially since 1970, many countries have moved to lay aside the death penalty. By

1999, sixty-eight countries had abolished the death penalty for all crimes; another fourteen had abolished it for ordinary crimes including murder; and another twenty-three countries had abolished it in practice, by not applying it for more than ten years.[36]

Until the 1970s, the United States seemed to be on this same evolutionary path. Public support for the death penalty was declining, going from 60 percent in 1937 to 45 percent in 1965.[37] The number of executions was declining, from approximately 150 a year in the 1930s to approximately 50 per year in the 1950s. In the 1960s, legal appeals in death penalty cases were so numerous and so successful that executions ceased altogether in 1968. Then, in 1972, the Supreme Court found existing death penalty statutes of the states unconstitutional.

After that point, however, the United States underwent an abrupt right turn. Support for the death penalty climbed to record-breaking levels—80 percent in a 1994 poll. States passed new capital punishment laws that met the Supreme Court objections, and in 1976 executions began again (there were 66 in 2001).

What is the outlook for capital punishment in the United States? It seems most unlikely that the move away from it has simply stopped. As my review of the world picture has shown, the movement toward more humane punishments is a massive, long-term trend. The power of this trend is seen even in the data on capital punishment in the United States. Although the current level of executions may seem high, it is extremely low by historical standards. Figure 9.1 shows the trend in the execution rate in the United States—that is, the number of executions relative to the size of the population of the country. It shows that the execution rate has been falling for more than three hundred years, with the recent increase in executions producing a barely discernible uptick on the graph. This long-term change has been dramatic: if the United States were applying the death penalty at the same rate it was applied in the 1640s, there would have been more than 88,000 executions in the decade 1990–99, instead of the 478 there actually were. Even to match the execution rate at the beginning of the twentieth century (1900–1909), there would have to have been 4,000 executions in the 1990s. The data on executions show, then, that the United States has in effect come very close to abolishing capital punishment.

Figure 9.1

Execution Rate in the United States, 1640–1999

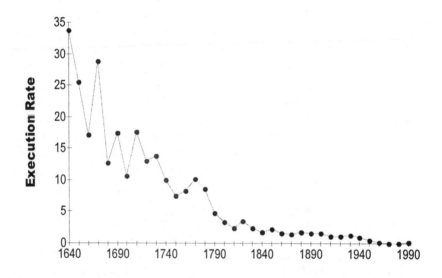

Note: The execution rate is the number of executions per 1,000,000 population per year. Each data point in the figure shows the average execution rate for the entire decade.
Source: Calculated from the data file compiled by Watt Espy and John Ortiz Smykla, *Executions in the United States, 1608–1987*, updated (Ann Arbor: Inter-University Consortium for Political and Social Research, University of Michigan, 1987). I am indebted to Professor Keith Harries of the University of Maryland for assistance in processing this data.

The decline in capital punishment in the United States is seen not only in the dramatic decline in numbers, but also in changes in the nature of the punishment itself. In bygone days, executions were brutal deeds, made deliberately painful for the condemned. This brutality served the purpose of retribution—making the criminal suffer for his action—and also fitted in with the theory of deterrence: the more painful the death, the better it served to frighten others away from committing the same crime. Hence, the use of torture-deaths such as crucifixion, burning, breaking on the wheel, and drawing and quartering. Today, sentiments of compassion have overpowered these arguments. Modern lawmakers have chosen to substitute swifter, less-painful killings. For a time, hanging and the electric chair were used, but even these forms now offend modern sensibilities, so lawmakers have turned to lethal injection. The result is a death that a number of prisoners have actually requested—hardly the scary deterrent of yesteryear. Nor does lethal injection provide a satisfying retribution for heinous crimes. It can hardly be said that society "balances the books" against a mass murderer by putting him to sleep.

Executions formerly were public events, open to a maximum audience, including children. Making executions a public spectacle served both deterrence and retribution. The theory was that if people—especially children—could see the horrible death, they would be given a lasting, vivid memory that supposedly would deter them from crime. And enabling the public to see the malefactor die a painful death enhanced the satisfaction of those seeking revenge. In modern times, lawmakers have shrunk from these theories and have closed executions to the public. Human life is too sacred, they say, to let killing become any kind of public spectacle; the act of deliberately slaying a human being is too unsettling to allow children to watch.

One defense of the death penalty used to be that it was cheaper to execute a criminal than to maintain him alive for scores of years in prison. Now, because of our modern sensibilities, even this argument has been reversed. Because we are so hesitant about taking life, especially an innocent life, we have surrounded the death penalty with elaborate legal safeguards—automatic appeals and so on—that end up costing taxpayers far more than life imprisonment. In addition, because waiting times on death row now average twelve years, a death sentence in fact often becomes a sentence of life imprisonment: the prisoner dies of natural causes before society gets around to killing him. In effect, no one is sentenced to death in the United States. The guilty are sentenced to prison and an extremely long period of appeals, one possible outcome of which is an execution. This vagueness and uncertainty allows prosecutors, judges, juries, and the public to suppose they are not "really" ordering anyone to his or her death by selecting the option of capital punishment.

We see, then, that in reform after reform lawmakers have moderated the death penalty so that it is now but a vestige of its former self. It is not terrifying, it is not swift, and, in its present restricted use, it is not certain (only about one murder in two hundred leads to an execution). What does it mean, then, to say that the United States "has" the death penalty? If the United States had a death penalty in robust, traditional form, we would be executing approximately 10,000 prisoners a year, including scores of perfectly innocent people. The victims would be killed in torture-deaths, and these events would be shown on nationwide television to be viewed by all citizens, including children (at 27 executions a day, this would leave little time for any other television fare).

That defenders of capital punishment would be appalled by this prospect shows that even they have felt the leavening effect of the increasing respect for human life. Given this profound, long-run trend in attitudes, the recent shift in the United States back to supporting capital punishment is almost certainly only a temporary deviation from the underlying trend against it.

What caused this deviation? It seems to have been a popular backlash against legal elites who attempted to reform the criminal justice system too rapidly. The 1972 Supreme Court decision to suspend capital punishment was only one of a string of court decisions that aimed at softening the criminal justice system. Among these decisions was the famous *Miranda* case decided by the Supreme Court in 1966. In this decision, the court ordered the release of a convicted rapist because his confession, though apparently voluntary and genuine, had been obtained without advising him of his right to remain silent. In the abstract, this and related decisions were laudable efforts to enhance the rights of defendants against police and prosecutors. But the judicial leniency coincided with—and probably contributed to—a dramatic nationwide rise in crime. Between 1960 and 1980, the homicide rate nearly doubled, and other crimes of violence—rape, robbery, and assault—grew at an even faster pace. As a result, the public viewed the judicial liberalization with alarm. The overuse of suspended sentences, parole, and probation added fuel to this fire. From a distance, it appeared that judges and prosecutors were irresponsibly turning loose thousands of dangerous and violent criminals.

Public opinion turned toward a "tough-on-crime" stance, and the politicians responded by striving to make their toughness visible, especially by coming out in favor of capital punishment. The power of the popular mood was shown in the 1988 presidential campaign, when the Republicans issued campaign literature citing the case of Willie Horton, a convicted murderer in Massachusetts who had been allowed on a furlough program with rather lax supervision. He escaped and subsequently raped a woman and stabbed a man in Maryland. The governor in charge of the furlough system that gave Horton his freedom was Michael Dukakis, the Democratic presidential candidate. The advertisement and the campaign issue it raised were widely regarded as one of the main reasons for Dukakis's decisive defeat in the election.

Perhaps the lesson of the modern turnaround on capital punishment in the United States is that the evolution against the use of force must play out at its own pace. The judges of the 1960s and 1970s who attempted to liberalize criminal prosecution and punishment ignored both social realities and public opinion. In attempting to implement their view before the rest of the country understood it and was ready for it, they provoked a backlash that set the movement to abolish capital punishment back by several generations.

10

Violence for Show:
Terrorism in the Modern World

No book about uses of force would be complete without a discussion of terrorism. Indeed, since the September 11, 2001, attacks on the World Trade Center and the Pentagon, terrorism has become the most-discussed use of force, looming larger in our thinking than genocide, war, or even nuclear war.

We don't get very far into this subject, however, before realizing that it is a strangely slippery one. Everyone who writes about it begins with the observation that there is no generally accepted definition of *terrorism*. One researcher went to the trouble of combing through scores of works on terrorism and came up with 109 definitions. Beyond the fact that they allude to the use of force, these 109 definitions have very little in common. Nothing daunted, this researcher offered a 110th definition, a 211-word disquisition that—as other scholars soon informed him—merely compounded the ambiguity that surrounds this term.[1]

The main reason for this confusion is that writers are attempting to develop their definitions using the root word *terror* as their starting point. Dictionaries follow this approach, defining *terrorism* as "the systematic use of terror." This way of arriving at a definition is understandable, but it leads to an impossibly broad conception because any use of force can be said to cause some degree of fear or terror. War certainly terrifies, as do genocide and crime. Even taxation can involve terror on occasion (people have committed suicide in response to threatened collection actions by the U.S. Internal Revenue Service).

A second problem is that *terrorism* is a highly value-laden term. It doesn't just mean a use of force that inspires fear. It connotes a use of force that the speaker deplores. "Our use of force is good," we say to our enemies, "your use of force is terrorism." With people on all sides accusing each other of being "terrorists," it's no wonder the term lacks clarity.

Given this semantic tangle, it is necessary to proceed cautiously. In advancing a definition in this discussion, my tactic here will be to bypass the many semantic overtones of the term and limit the definition to those episodes that most people have in mind today when they employ the word. The definition that I believe serves this purpose runs as follows: *terrorism is political violence by nongovernmental entities that is premeditated, clandestine, and focused on publicity.* To introduce the subject, it is helpful to explore the implications of this definition.

"Terrorism" and Government

The term *terrorism* was first coined in connection with the French Revolution of 1789 when the new government turned to widespread repression in order to silence critics. It organized networks of spies and informers, and relied on arbitrary arrests, snap trials, and waves of executions on the guillotine. The revolutionary leaders were openly proud of this deliberate use of state violence to instill "terror" in their opponents. English commentators such as Edmund Burke picked up on the word, calling this policy of repression *terrorism.* But for them—and for the rest of the world ever since—*terrorism* came to have a strong negative connotation, referring to a deplorable use of force.

Thus, for about a century, *terrorism* referred to government violence or, rather, to government violence highly disapproved of by the speaker. And the term is still occasionally used in this way—as when we speak of Stalin's "reign of terror," for example. However, in the latter part of the nineteenth century, *terrorism* began to be applied to a rather new type of political violence: violence directed *against* governments by out-of-power groups as a way of attracting support to their cause, in actions that were called "propaganda of the deed." One of the first groups to practice this form of opposition was the Narodnaya Volya (People's Will) revolutionary group in Russia, active in 1878–81. This group began an extensive campaign of assassinating high government officials in the expectation that these highly publicized murders would arouse the masses to revolt. (They succeeded in slaying Czar Alexander II in 1881.) This type of violence came to be called *terrorism,* and this is the principal meaning it has today.

Limiting the use of the term *terrorism* to violence by nongovernmental actors should not be taken to imply anything about the moral status of government violence compared to that of opposition groups. Governments do many deplorable things, from dropping bombs on innocent civilians to exterminating whole peoples. But it is confusing to lump all of this kind of violence in with terrorism.

Violence by nongovernmental actors takes many forms, and the term *terrorism* is reserved for a subcategory with special features. To begin with, the violence has to have a political aim—that is, a focus on a collective interest beyond the personal interests of the participants. The political goal may be quite broad—such as trying to take over a government, remake a society, or advance a religion—or it may be limited—such as an effort to repeal a particular law or to protect an ethnic group. But, in all cases, the aims go beyond the personal interests of the participants. As one terrorism specialist has put it, "The terrorist is fundamentally an altruist: he believes that he is serving a 'good' cause designed to achieve a greater good for a wider constituency."[2]

Thus, this definition of *terrorism* excludes ordinary criminal acts of murder, arson, extortion, and so on, which are prompted by personal motives. Perhaps rather ironically, we seem to be less shocked by these crimes than by terrorism. When an arsonist or extortionist blows up a building for money, we take it in stride, apparently because we find it fitting that selfish people would do harmful things. When people blow up a building out of supposedly idealistic motives, we are shocked because deliberately doing harm in order to produce good seems perverse.

This definition of *terrorism* also excludes the violence of mentally deranged individuals. Sometimes individuals go on killing sprees that are quite shocking, and, as in the case of a serial murderer (the Boston Strangler, for example), they can create as much fear or terror as a terrorist organization. But this kind of violence does not have a political purpose.

Terrorism is further distinguished from other types of political protest in that it is premeditated. The perpetrators arrange, usually many months in advance, the time and place of their action as well as its results. This level of organization makes it different from other forms of protest such as sit-ins, street blockages, and riots. Although these mass protests usually reflect some degree of planning, any resulting violence is unpredictable, depending on many variables, especially on how the authorities respond to the crowds. Thus, after a riot that may have left many dead, it is difficult to say that anyone deliberately intended these deaths. In the case of an action by terrorists, we can point to individuals who did indeed intend the harm. This premeditation makes their violence all the more reprehensible, of course.

Another distinguishing feature of terrorism is that it is clandestine: the perpetrators act in secret and with the element of surprise. In this respect, terrorism differs from the more open, public acts of political opposition such as sit-ins, riots, and military rebellions. The clandestine feature of terrorism further adds to its repugnance. One is inclined to give some credit to perpetrators who fight openly, who announce where and when they will take their stand. Terrorists are often called "cowardly" for striking without warning, though, in truth, terrorists have no lack of courage, for they risk and sometimes deliberately sacrifice their lives (in suicide missions) for their cause.

Is Terrorism New?

Were terrorism defined only by the features already mentioned—political motivation, premeditation, and secrecy—we would have to say that it was an ancient type of violence. Ever since the advent of governments, there have been violent oppositions to these governments, and this opposition has often taken clandestine form. For example, two thousand years ago in Palestine, the *sicarii,* a Jewish opposition to the occupying Roman forces, would make surprise attacks on Roman officials (and on Jews who collaborated with the Romans), stabbing them in the marketplace and then melting into the crowd. Guerrilla warfare, a close relative of terrorism, is also very old. The idea of harassing a vastly superior force by attacking and then fleeing—refusing to "stand and fight"—surely dates to the beginning of warfare itself.

However, modern terrorism incorporates a new ingredient to these old forms of violence: an emphasis on publicity. The clandestine violent deeds of yesteryear were performed with the main objective of harming enemy agents and disrupting enemy aims. Some bystanders naturally would come to know about them, but this publicity was a by-product, an incidental feature. The assassination or the guerrilla attack would still have been considered a successful action even if the world in general didn't learn about it.

With the terrorism of modern times, publicity is the focus of the violent deed. Perpetrators are aiming for mass media coverage. They pick targets that will be prominent for the media, including politicians, diplomats, and leading businessmen. They are active in large cities where the media is present and ignore the countryside. Targets are chosen for their symbolic value: government buildings, monuments, and centers of commerce are preferred targets. Furthermore, the groups often supply the media with press releases and manifestos to make sure their deeds are publicized. In some cases, they even distribute photographs of their killings.

Many commentators seem to overlook the importance of publicity seeking in identifying terrorist groups, especially when it comes to distinguishing a terrorist group from a criminal secret society. The criminal society resembles a terrorist group in many respects: it is clandestine; it uses violence in a premeditated way; and it usually has some kind of collective orientation or political aim. What it lacks is the emphasis on publicity. A group such as the Molly Maguires illustrates the distinction. The Molly Maguires was a secret society of Irish miners active in Pennsylvania coal country in 1860–77. The Mollies relied on death threats and murder in order to punish hated foremen and to intimidate mine owners in order to set favorable working conditions. A typical note sent to a mine foreman showed a picture of a coffin and the words, "We will give you one week to go, but if you are alive on next Saturday, you will die." Scores of murders were attributed to the Molly Maguires. The organization was suppressed in 1877 with a far-ranging prosecution that led to nineteen executions.[3]

Although clandestine and political, the Molly Maguires should not be considered a terrorist organization because their violence was not directed toward achieving publicity. Their killings and death threats were used for the purposes of intimidation and extortion, and to recruit members. Although the Mollies did have a policy purpose—advancing the interests of miners against employers—they did not use publicity to advance this agenda. They did not stage violent events for purposes of getting press coverage or attracting nationwide attention. The same point would apply to a number of other secret criminal societies of yesteryear that are sometimes called "terrorist" groups.

The publicity-seeking feature of terrorism makes it a relatively new type of violence. An emphasis on publicity did not exist in earlier times simply because it could not, owing to the lack of organs of mass communication. The beginning of the mass media can probably be set in the 1830s with the advent of the rotary press that dramatically dropped the price of daily newspapers and put them in reach of the average consumer. Later, nineteenth-century developments—especially the telegraph, wire service news reporting, and the transatlantic cable—were important in expanding the speed and scope of news reporting.

In addition to the emergence of the mass media, another trend has further encouraged the growth of publicity-oriented violence—namely, the growing respect for human life in the societies where terrorism is practiced. In earlier times, life was cheap and death was commonplace; as a result, acts of violence did not have much power to shock. When brutal official violence was a routine occurrence—public hangings, mutilations, massacres—the deliberate shedding of blood did not attract unusual attention. Today—especially in developed countries with a heightened sensitivity about violence—bloodshed now has great shock value. Hence, it can be used as an advertising technique for a political cause.

To illustrate how the publicized violence of terrorism works, consider the Jewish terrorist organization known as Irgun, active in Palestine in the period 1937–48. At the time, Palestine was a territory of mixed Arab and Jewish population administered by the British. The aim of the Jewish leaders was to force a British withdrawal from the area so they could establish a Jewish state. The Irgun (whose leaders included later Israeli prime minister Menachem Begin) followed a policy of carrying out highly publicized acts of violence to reach public opinion in Britain. Their theory was that Britons would turn against the Palestine occupation when they saw the bloody resistance to it.

To this end, Irgun activists murdered policemen, soldiers, and British officials and bombed government offices, including the immigration agency and the tax office. The biggest blow was the July 1946 bombing of the King David Hotel in Jerusalem, where many British officers were staying. The attack killed 91 people, including many other hotel guests, Jews as well as non-Jews. Another slaying that especially shocked the British public was the hanging of two British sergeants whom Irgun had captured. To assure maximum coverage of the atrocity in Britain, Irgun sent the British media photographs of the men in the act of being slain.

Deplorable as these deliberate, sadistic killings were, the Irgun terrorism succeeded. The British were indeed shocked and demoralized by the violence so visibly used against them, so they eventually withdrew their forces, allowing the Jewish state of Israel to be established in 1948. The victory of the Jewish leaders was not unalloyed, however. With sad symmetry, the state founded by terrorism has become engulfed in terrorism.

The Two Terrorisms

What is the trend in terrorism? Is this use of force, like the others I have reviewed in this book, on the decline? Or, as the events of September 11 seem at first to indicate, is it growing? To answer this question, we need to make a distinction between the terrorism emerging within the economically developed countries and that generated in more strongly force-oriented cultures. Modern transportation makes it possible today for people from any culture to travel anywhere. Hence, terrorists from violence-prone areas can carry out an action in a country far away from the culture that spawned them. One can suddenly have terrorism in the Netherlands, let us say, not because the Dutch have become more inclined toward terrorism, but because natives of other areas where violence is more acceptable have traveled there.

For rough purposes of making an overall analysis, we may divide the countries of the world into two broad groups, developed and undeveloped. The developed areas comprise the countries of Europe, North and South America, and the more prosperous countries of Asia, including Japan, Australia, and New Zealand. In these areas, processes of economic growth and communication have been at work for some time in reducing the acceptability of violence. In the underdeveloped countries—most of Asia, Africa, and the Middle East—the evolution against the use of force is far behind that of the developed regions, as is evident from the prevalence of many violent practices, including political repression, political murder, violent criminal punishments, massacres, and civil war. The disparity in the orientation toward force in these two segments of the world leads to two different patterns in terrorism. In the rest of this chapter, I look at terrorism in the less-force-oriented developed countries. In chapter 11, I discuss terrorism originating in the more strongly force-oriented countries, especially in the culture of Islam.

Terrorism in the West

In the developed world, terrorism has followed a remarkable pattern of rise and fall. Prior to the 1960s, there was relatively little terrorism. There was a great deal of violence, of course, including two world wars, plenty of riots with many fatalities, lynchings, killings by political gangs, organized crime, and labor "wars." But there was relatively little terrorism as such—that is, the deliberate use of violence for publicity purposes. In the United States, a lone anarchist assassinated President McKinley in 1901, and in 1919–20 anarchists were apparently behind several bombings, including one on Wall Street that killed 38 people. On the West Coast, a small group of left-wing labor leaders were responsible for the bombing of the *Los Angeles Times* building in 1910, which killed 20 employees. But there was no sizable terrorist group, by which I mean a politically oriented group with more than a dozen members using violence primarily for publicity.

This changed in the 1960s. As table 10.1 indicates, some sixteen sizable terrorist groups emerged in the United States between 1966 and 1987. Most of these groups committed only a handful of crimes, but several were very active. The Weathermen were responsible for some 800 bombings in the period 1969–72, including explosions at the University of Wisconsin Math Center, the U.S. Senate office building, and the Pentagon. Omega-7, the anti-Castro group, was responsible for some 50 bombings in the United States. Puerto Rican separatists—especially the FALN and the Macheteros—carried out some 100 bombings. As a result of the activities of these groups, the United States experienced a wave of terrorism in the 1970s and early 1980s.

Then the picture began to change. Many of the terrorist groups were eliminated by the arrest and prosecution of their major figures. In others, leaders and participants fled the country or retired from active involvement, and organizations failed or were unable to recruit new leadership and new members. As a result, by the year 2000, most of these groups had either disappeared or had greatly declined. This decline has not been counterbalanced by the emergence of an equal number of new terrorist groups. There appear to be only two significant active terrorist groups coming into existence in the United States in the 1990s, both concerned with the environment and animal rights. The decline in organized terrorism produced a corresponding decline in major terrorist incidents. The number of such incidents, as reported by the Federal Bureau of Investigation, went from approximately 50 a year in the 1970s and early 1980s to less than ten a year in the late 1980s and less than five a year in the 1990s.[4]

This is not to say that all forms of terrorism in the United

Table 10.1
Terrorist Groups in the United States, 1966–Present

Group	Orientation	Start	Demise
Black Panthers	Black power	1966	1971
Jewish Defense League	Anti-Arab	1968	1987
Weathermen/Weather Underground	Left-wing	1969	1977
Symbionese Liberation Army	Left-wing	1972	1974
Posse Comitatus	Right-wing	1973	1986
Omega-7	Anti-Castro	1974	1985
FALN	Puerto Rican	1974	1983
Macheteros	Puerto Rican	1978	1985
United Freedom Front	Left-wing	1975	1985
May 19th Communist Coalition	Left-wing	1979	1986
The Covenant	Right-wing	1978	1985
Aryan Nations	Right wing	1979	2000
The Order	Right-wing	1984	1987
The Order II	Right-wing	1987	1987
Earth First	Environmental	1981	1989
Earth Liberation Front	Environmental	1992	active
Animal Liberation Front	Environmental	1997	active

States have declined. Terrorism carried out by individuals or tiny groups still occurs. The 1990s saw several high-profile episodes carried out by individuals, including shootings of abortion providers by anti-abortion activists in 1993 and 1994, the letter-bomb campaign by Ted Kaczynski on behalf of radical environmentalism that killed 3 and injured 29, and the 1995 Oklahoma City bombing by Timothy McVeigh that killed 168 people. These episodes of "lone" terrorism generated great public attention, but they should not obscure the larger point that terrorism as a *collective, organized* form of violence by U.S. citizens has virtually disappeared.

Other Western countries have seen the same pattern. During the time that the United States was grappling with home-grown terrorist organizations, most of the other developed countries faced similar challenges from sizable domestic terrorist organizations. Table 10.2 identifies fourteen of the more important groups in Europe, Japan, and Canada. A number of these conspiracies were especially large and violent. The Red Brigades in Italy engaged in many kidnappings and murders, including the murder of former prime minister Aldo Moro. In 1979, the year of peak activity, there were 2,500 terrorist incidents in Italy. The Baader-Meinhoff gang in Germany killed 31 in its campaign of murders and bombings before it was brought under control in the late 1970s.

The two most costly terrorist campaigns in Europe have been those in Northern Ireland and Spain. In Ireland, terrorist violence peaked in 1972 with 474 killed in that year. From 1970 to the early 1990s, a total of almost 10,000 explosions killed more than 3,000 people. Since the truce of 1996, there have been only occasional incidents. In Spain, the violence of the Basque separatist movement continues, though at a considerably reduced pace compared to earlier times. The high point of this terrorist campaign was in 1979 and 1980, when more than 100 people were killed each year. Since 1995, an average of 10 people a year have been killed in ETA actions.

In Latin America, a large number of terrorist organizations emerged after 1960. Table 10.3 identifies nineteen of the more prominent groups. By the year 2000, almost all of these groups had disappeared or at least had declined to a greatly reduced level of activity. Only in Colombia has terrorism (along with banditry and guerrilla war) continued with full intensity.

In summary, the developed world saw the emergence of some forty-nine significant indigenous terrorist organizations in the post-1960 period. Of these organizations, only two continue at the previous level of intensity (in Colombia). The other forty-seven have either

Table 10.2
Terrorism in Developed Countries, 1969–Present

Country	Group	Focus	Inception	Demise
Britain/ N. Ireland	Provisional Irish Republican Army	anti-British	1969	1996
	Irish National Liberation Army	anti-British	1975	1987
	Ulster Volunteer Force	anti-IRA	1968	1976
	Ulster Freedom Fighters	anti-IRA	1972	1996
Canada	Quebec Liberation Front	Quebec separatism	1963	1971
France	FLNC	Corsican separatism	1975	1990
	Action Direct	left-wing	1979	1987
Italy	Red Brigades	left-wing	1970	1988
Germany	Baader-Meinhoff group	left-wing	1970	1989
Greece	November 17	left-wing	1975	2002
Japan	Red Army Faction	left-wing	1969	1988
	United Red Army	left-wing	1972	1972
	Aum Shinrikyo	religious cult	1988	1995
Spain	ETA	Basque separatism	1968	1996

Table 10.3
Terrorism in Latin America, 1961–Present

Country	Group	Focus	Inception	Demise
Argentina	ERP	left-wing	1970	1989
	Montoneros	left-wing	1970	1989
Brazil	YPR	left-wing	1968	1971
	ALN	left-wing	1968	1971
Chile	MIR	left-wing	1967	1988
	FPMR	left-wing	1067	1988
Colombia	FARC	left-wing	1964	active
	ELN	left-wing	1964	active
	M-19	left-wing	1973	1990
El Salvador	FPL	left-wing	1970	1992
Guatemala	FAR	left-wing	1962	1970
	MR-13	left-wing	1964	1970
	EGP	left-wing	1972	1996
Nicaragua	Sandinistas	left-wing	1961	1979
	Contras			
	(ARDE,	right-		
	FDN)	wing	1981	1994
Peru	Shining			
	Path	left-wing	1980	1992
	MRTA	left-wing	1984	1996
Uruguay	Tupamaros	left-wing	1963	1988
Venezuela	FALN	left-wing	1963	1967

greatly diminished their level of activity or have disappeared alto-gether. These groups have not been replaced by a significant number of new terrorist organizations. It is a pattern that begs for an explanation.

Explaining Modern Terrorism: New Grievances or New Media?

The first temptation in attempting to explain the rise and fall of terrorist movements is to look at motives. Terrorism requires a grievance—that is, a strong feeling about some injustice. So it might seem that terrorism arises when some objective "wrong" is particularly severe. For example, one might say that terrorism by the Irish Republic Army (IRA) in Northern Ireland was provoked by the disadvantages Irish Catholics suffered in Northern Ireland.

The problem with this approach is that it overlooks the subjective character of political grievances. Any society will have—or can be said to have—deficiencies. Whether these deficiencies give rise to anger and political action depends not so much on how serious they are, but on how they are perceived.

For example, one source of anger and agitation is resentment against the wealthy. This hostility has been one of the main grievances of terrorists for well over a century—and a focal point for riots and revolutions since the beginnings of recorded history. Yet outbreaks of hostility in recent times seem rather unrelated to poverty and poor working conditions—the evils supposedly attributable to wealth and capitalism. Who would have predicted, for example, that revolutionary terrorists such as the Weathermen, the Symbionese Liberation Army, and the May 19th Communist Coalition would emerge in the United States in the 1970s, an era that saw relative prosperity and pampered workers and students? The same question can be asked about the Marxist terrorists who emerged at the same time in Italy, Germany, and France. And why was there no comparable Marxist terrorist movement in England, where—one could easily argue—the lowest classes are shockingly dispossessed?

With a little reflection, we discover that an infinite number of possible grievances can form the basis of a terrorist movement. This is especially true in a rapidly changing modern society. Migration and immigration bring different cultural and religious groups into contact, providing an opportunity for new fears. Rapidly changing customs and moral standards produce shock and dismay. The transformation of urban and rural landscapes, genetic engineering, nuclear power, the growth of government, new religions and cults, the use and abuse of drugs, trends in art and music: all provide abundant sources for the hysteria about "what the world is coming to" that forms the psychological foundation of terrorism.

Adding to the hysteria is the mass media, which has made it easier than ever for people to learn frightening partial truths about distant dangers and faraway wrongs. As anyone can easily confirm by exploring the Internet, many people today do indeed hold rather extreme opinions about modern dangers and wrongs, and readily voice apocalyptic solutions to these problems. If terrorism were caused simply by shallow and extreme social, economic, and religious ideas, bombs would be exploding daily on every street in the country.

It is implausible to argue, then, that the rise of terrorism in the 1960s and 1970s in developed countries was the result of a sudden increase in social wrongs. In searching for a cause, it makes more sense to look for a change in the environment that made this kind of political protest—publicity-oriented violence—more attractive in that era. As soon as we pose the problem in this way, the answer immediately emerges: the appearance of television. Television represented a quantum leap in the publicity available for terrorist actions. Prior to the advent of television, media coverage of events was fragmented. Newspapers covered events with considerable delay and involved hundreds of separate markets. Radio could be instantaneous, but lacked the visual component. Television created a national—and soon, global— live audience. It gave reality to the slogan "the whole world is watching." It offered the publicity hungry of all kinds—from deranged adolescents to status-seeking politicians—an intoxicating draught of publicity. It is no surprise to find, then, that the advent of this medium fueled the rise of terrorism.

The Terrorism Life Cycle

Television may account for the rise of domestic terrorism in the developed world, but it certainly will not account for its demise, for this medium has continued to expand the opportunities for publicity-oriented violence.

In order to understand the decline of terrorism in the developed world, we must realize that most terrorist organizations go through a rather short life cycle. Terrorists begin their campaigns under the assumption that their violence will galvanize large numbers of sympathizers to rise up in support of their cause. A growth in support may occur initially, when the violence is relatively low key. But when terrorists escalate and commit one or more truly shocking acts of violence, a turning point occurs in the fortunes of the terrorist organization.

For one thing, the extreme violence alienates sympathizers and makes it more difficult to recruit additional activists. It also encourages former sympathizers to side with the police and become informers. Furthermore, the extreme violence gets the attention of security forces. Terrorists assume that their shocking deeds will demoralize security forces and provoke some kind of governmental collapse, but they are almost always wrong. Their violent excesses prompt government officials to make an energetic effort to suppress terrorism—an effort that often includes brutal methods and the violation of civil rights. The public and the political elites, appalled by the violence of the terrorists, accede to the high-handed methods being used to suppress them. With most of its leaders imprisoned or killed, and with little or no recruitment of new activists, the terrorist organization rapidly declines.

Most terrorist groups in the developed countries have gone through this life cycle. For example, the Red Brigades in Italy began pursuing their Marxist agenda in 1969 with restrained, almost playful acts of violence, kidnapping and then releasing political figures. In this early period, they recruited many hundreds of supporters and were viewed indulgently by the public and the police. But in 1974, their violence began to turn ugly. A government prosecutor was kidnapped with a demand for the release of imprisoned Red Brigade members. A deal was struck, but the government reneged, and the prosecutor was later murdered. Many more serious kidnappings and murders followed. The turning point came in 1978 with the kidnapping and murder of former prime minister Aldo Moro—an atrocity that the terrorists deliberately drew out for fifty-five days and milked for its publicity value. Another murder that shifted opinion against them was the killing of the communist labor leader Guido Rossa.

With the support of the public, the Italian Parliament approved special antiterrorism powers for the police, who carried out an energetic campaign of rounding up terrorists and sending them to prison. By 1982, the back of the movement was broken—though occasional episodes of violence continued to occur for many years thereafter.

The first explanation for the decline in domestic terrorism in the developed world, then, is that the existing terrorist organizations ran through their life cycles, committing violent excesses that stripped them of support and provoked an effective repression. However, this explanation leaves a critical question unanswered: Why has there been so little development of new terrorist organizations? The same possible grievances still exist. The Marxist illusion—that poverty is caused by evil capitalists and can be alleviated by government programs for sharing wealth—still captures naive minds, the supply of which has in no way diminished. Racial tensions still exist; regional and cultural differences still cause resentment; policy issues from abortion to environmentalism still arouse extreme views. If the tendency toward terrorism within the developed countries were constant or increasing, we should have seen the formation of scores of new domestic terrorist organizations in recent decades. What has happened?

One possible answer is that the process just needs more time. The recent wave of government repression—this theory runs—has chastened activists for the time being. But in a decade or two, a new generation of activists will again reach for guns and bombs to make their political points.

There is, however, an alternative explanation for the failure of organized terrorism to reappear to any significant degree in the West: violence is increasingly losing its appeal—or, to put it another way, people in developed countries are viewing violence in an increasingly negative light. Some opinion poll data supports this idea. A Times-Mirror poll of a national sample of respondents found that the proportion who said they were "personally bothered" by violence in entertainment shows jumped from 44 percent in 1983 to 59 percent in 1993.[5]

The growing disapproval of violence very likely has undermined the motivation for using it in a collective, "moral" way. For a terrorist organization to come into being, a number of people must agree that it is right to slay innocent human beings in cold blood to attract attention to a political cause. Of course, there are always likely to be isolated individuals who will accept this premise, and they may be expected to carry out acts of lone terrorism. But when violence is widely deplored, it becomes increasingly difficult to find a significant number of people who as a group will agree on the rightness of premeditated political violence.

This analysis suggests, then, that the countries of western Europe and North America have probably seen the end of domestic group terrorism. Only time will tell whether this prediction is correct, of course, but many clues suggest that collective political violence in these countries is rapidly fading away. Consider, for example, the tactics of protest by blacks in the United States. In the 1960s, resentment in black communities led to widespread and bloody rioting and to the formation of terrorist groups such as the Black Panthers. In the past quarter-century, there has been only one major riot (in Los Angeles in 1992 in reaction to the acquittal of the police officers involved in the beating of Rodney King, a black man), and no significant terrorist organizations. This relative calm is remarkable because agitation on the theme of "black oppression," if anything, has intensified, and episodes triggering outrage have continued to occur. For example, in 1999 a team of four New York police officers shot and killed an unarmed black man, Amadou Diallo, under suspicious circumstances. After the police officers were acquitted in a closely watched trial the following year, black activists were outraged, but protest did not take a violent form. "Let not one brick be thrown," said black leader Al Sharpton. "We are fighting violence."

We see a similar turning away from violent methods on the abortion issue. This has been an extremely emotional issue, with some opponents of abortion feeling that the practice is tantamount to murder and that therefore extreme measures are justified to oppose it. A number of individuals have accepted this logic and have committed acts of individual terrorism against abortion clinics. From 1977 to 2001, there were 41 bombings, 165 acts of arson, and 7 killings. However, no anti-abortion terrorist organization has been formed. The disapproval of violence (especially among the devoutly religious who form the core of the anti-abortion movement) has apparently been too strong to allow for the formation of such an organization.

We also see a shift in the tactics of the neo-Marxist activists in the most recent wave of agitation, this time directed against free trade, multinational corporations, and international financial institutions. Unlike the Marxist activists of yesteryear, these youthful idealists have not turned to terrorism, limiting their tactics to unruly street demonstrations.

The modern distaste for violence seems also reflected in the tactics of the newest terrorist organizations, the Animal Liberation Front (ALF) and the Earth Liberation Front (ELF). Although committing hundreds of acts against property in recent years, these groups have thus far rather carefully avoided harming people. "No one has ever been injured by the group's many actions," claims an ALF/ELF spokesman.[6]

It is likely that the terrorist action of September 11, 2001, has further increased the hesitation among domestic activists about using violence. In the West, this event galvanized a universal reaction of shock and disapproval. Most potential terrorists now realize that if their acts seem to copy this act of despicable violence, they will lose, not gain, support for their cause. Since 9/11, even the remnants of domestic Western terrorist organizations have been cautious about using violence. For example, in Spain, some members of the Basque separatist group ETA set off five bombs during a European summit in June 2002. Yet none of the bombs caused loss of life because the terrorists warned authorities to evacuate the areas.

The evidence suggests, then, that *organized* terrorism originating from within the developed countries is on the decline. This trend further reinforces the general pattern of a declining use of force that we have encountered in so many other areas. This is not to say that all terrorism in developed areas is at an end. First, one must keep in mind that terrorist acts can be carried out by individuals. The frequency of individual acts of terrorism presumably will decline as the culture grows more opposed to violence. But for the immediate future, acts of individual terrorism are certainly possible, and on occasion they may be quite spectacular and disruptive.

Second, there is the danger of terrorism from abroad, originating in cultures more strongly force oriented than the West. In these settings, violence is widespread and more likely to be socially acceptable. As a result, these areas are a breeding ground for terrorism directed both against local regimes and at far-off Western countries that may represent a source of grievance. The main source of this kind of "imported" terrorism is the religious culture of Islam. In chapter 11, I explore the background of this deadly pattern.

11

The Warlord's Religion:
Islam and Global Terrorism

In the preceding chapters, I have alluded to cultural and regional variations in the tendency to use force, suggesting that peoples with certain histories and traditions are more prone to violence than others. While we cannot explore all of these possibilities, it is useful to examine one of the most salient of these cultural variations: the impact of Islamic religion and culture. This topic is of particular importance today in the wake of the September 11, 2001, attacks on the World Trade Center and the Pentagon. As Americans reacted to and attempted to understand this event, it soon emerged that this sweeping act of mayhem had been carried out by devout Muslims. Many wondered whether the conjunction of the Muslim religion and extreme violence was just happenstance or part of a pattern. Does the religion and culture of Islam have a bias toward violence that would make it a natural breeding ground for terrorism?

The usual way of trying to decide what a religion stands for is to look at the written texts. This approach generally yields inconclusive results because—as is so often the case with doctrinal sources—one can find quotations on both sides of the issue. Some passages in the Koran are very militant: "Make war on unbelievers until idolatry is no more and Allah's religion reigns supreme," and "Slay the idolaters wherever you find them. Arrest them, besiege them, and lie in ambush everywhere for them." Yet other verses suggest peace and tolerance. "Let there be no compulsion in religion," says one oft-quoted declaration.

To settle the question about the connection between religion and the use of force, then, we need to look beyond the ambiguous realm of doctrine and interpretations of doctrine to the actual practice of the religion. In scores of countries, Islam is the dominant religion. By comparing these countries with the rest of the world, we can determine empirically whether Islam tends to be associated with a greater use of force.

We may start our exploration by looking at one of the most important indicators of a nation's emphasis on force, the relative size of its military. Countries that are peaceful tend to have smaller forces, whereas nations with a warlike orientation tend to have larger ones. We find, using data for 1999 (the most recent year for which data are available), that the countries with a majority Muslim population had an average of 7.95 military personnel per 1,000 population, whereas all the other countries had an average of 5.15.[1] In other words, the relative size of military forces in Muslim nations is 50 percent higher.

Another indication of a tendency toward violence is involvement in war. In the year 2000, according to the Stockholm International Peace Research Institute (SIPRI) there were twenty-three ongoing civil and international conflicts in the world. Twenty-three percent of Muslim countries were involved in these conflicts, and only 11 percent of non-Muslim countries.[2] The SIPRI tabulation focuses on major, relatively long-standing struggles. Other tabulations of violence that include smaller and more transitory conflicts show the same pattern. One such compilation, made by the National Defense Council Foundation for the year 2001, identifies fifty-six countries with some significant political violence, including ethnic clashes, labor unrest, and terrorism.[3] Using this tabulation, we find that 49 percent of the Muslim countries experienced significant violence, whereas only 27 percent of the non-Muslim countries were similarly affected.

The propensity toward the use of force also shows up in the denial of civil rights. A civil right is, in effect, the ability to do something unhampered by the government's use of force. The right of association, for example, means people can meet to form a labor union or stamp club without being forcibly disbanded by police officers wielding clubs. The right of free speech means one can criticize a government policy without being dragged to prison. Hence, a country that denies civil rights is using the threat of force to control culture and expression. The comprehensive survey of the presence of civil rights made by Freedom House for the years 2001 and 2002 shows a clear contrast between Muslim and non-Muslim countries. On a scale ranging from 1 (full respect for civil rights) to 7 (no respect for civil rights), Muslim countries drew an average score of 5.24, and non-Muslim countries a score of 2.96.[4]

Social practices involving the use of force tell the same story. Slavery is one example. As explained earlier, it is really state-sanctioned kidnapping. The practice of slavery was maintained in the Muslim world long after it passed from other parts of the globe. The last country to abolish slavery officially was Saudi Arabia in 1962. The bulk of the clandestine slavery that continues to this day is found in Muslim countries. In 2002, the U.S. Department of State identified nineteen "Tier Three" countries—nations with the most serious unaddressed problems of trafficking in persons. Thirteen of these nations are Muslim.[5]

The approach to criminal punishment is another indication of a country's emphasis on force. Muslim countries are unusual in applying brutal punishments, including maiming and branding. In many Muslim countries, for example, the cutting off of a hand is a common punishment for theft. The statistics on capital punishment provide a general indicator of the emphasis on extreme physical punishments. Data compiled by Amnesty International reveal that 73 percent of Muslim countries utilize capital punishment, whereas only 33 percent of non-Muslim countries employ it.[6]

The emphasis on the use of force also shows up in political practices. The custom of political murder illustrates the pattern. As defined in chapter 8, political murders are slayings of prominent leaders by other prominent leaders: opposition leaders murder rulers in the hopes of taking power, and rulers slay opponents who threaten their tenure—usually in executions for "treason." Political murder differs from an ordinary assassination, which is a killing carried out by an outsider. Political murder died out in the West centuries ago, but it still prevails in many Muslim countries. For example, in Saudi Arabia in

1975 King Faisal was murdered by his nephew Prince Faisal. In Pakistan, President Ali Bhutto was executed in 1979 by the military rulers who deposed him (Bhutto himself was accused of arranging a political murder in 1974). In Iran, several waves of executions followed the takeover by Muslim fundamentalists in 1979. One of the more prominent figures killed was foreign affairs minister Sadeq Ghotbzadeh, accused of plotting to kill the Ayatollah Ruhollah Khomeini, head of the new government.

Afghanistan has seen numerous political murders in modern times. In 1978, ruler Mohammed Daud was deposed in a military coup and executed. The following year his successor, Taraki, was in turn deposed and executed in another coup—an event that led to the Soviet invasion and decades of civil war. Iraq has been notorious for bloodshed within the ruling class. In the period 1968–82 alone, some eleven cabinet members and top officials of the ruling Baathist Party were executed.[7] High-level murders since that time include the 1995 execution of former air force general Mahmud al-Dulaimi (for plotting a coup) and the killings of two disaffected sons-in-law of Saddam Hussain in 1996.

Not all Muslim countries exhibit the pattern of political murder. Turkey, for example, seems to have transcended it. And it is also true that political murders occur in some non-Muslim countries, especially in Africa. But the salience of this pattern in the Islamic world is noteworthy.

After observing all the ways in which the Muslim community stands out in the use of force, it comes as no surprise to us to find that this culture is also a prominent source of terrorist movements. One measure of this point comes from a list of "designated terrorist organizations"—the largest and most troublesome terrorist groups around the world—compiled by the U.S. Department of State in 2002. Of this list of thirty-three groups, twenty-two or two-thirds are Muslim.[8] Since Muslims constitute only one-fifth of the world's population, this figure means that they participate in terrorist organizations at a rate eight times that of non-Muslims. Thus, it was not happenstance that the terrorists of 9/11 were Muslim: most of the terrorism in the world today originates in the culture of Islam.

Setting the Example of Violence

Many indicators, then, point to the same general conclusion: Muslim countries tend to be more strongly force oriented than the rest of the world. This conclusion might not be surprising if one could say that the Islamic world has lacked the advantages of civilization, that it has been a culture relatively untouched by the benefits of prosperity, communication, and the gentler arts. But the reverse is true. Years ago, Islam had a highly developed civilization.

In the tenth and eleventh centuries, when Europe was sunk in poverty and backwardness, the Muslim empire achieved extraordinary heights in art, science, learning, and literature. It had scores of thriving, prosperous cities, from Merv in northeast Persia to Cordoba in Spain. Working with the common language of Arabic, Muslim scholars made remarkable advances in medicine, mathematics, and astronomy. The great Arab cities were repositories of knowledge, centers of debate, and founts of creativity in art, literature, and philosophy. Baghdad—at the time the largest city in the world—had thirty-six public libraries and more than one hundred booksellers.[9]

One would suppose that this enlightenment would have had an effect in lowering the emphasis on force. Prosperity, ease of living, and better medical care should have made life more pleasant, thus increasing the value of human life. Communication and debate should have led scholars to see the folly of far-off wars and massacres, thus promoting skepticism about violence as a way of solving problems. The fact that no such transformation to pacific values occurred deepens the mystery. Apparently, something in Islamic culture caused it to resist and reject the civilizing lessons about the inappropriateness of force. What was it?

As noted earlier, most explanations of the traditions of a religious community tend to give too much emphasis to formal doctrine, to what written texts say about how believers ought to behave. Such passages have their impact, of course, but they are often less important than the effect of example. As parents know, it is difficult to teach children to "do as I say." All too often, they observe adult behavior and end up doing what we *do*. Religious communities follow this pattern, often adopting customs that are not necessarily emphasized in doctrine but that follow the example set by the founders of the faith.

In Islam, the founding prophet set a highly unusual example on the subject of force. In other religions, founders have been out-of-power teachers: they did not hold political office, and they do not command armed forces. Examples include the founders of Christianity, Jesus and Paul, as well as the founders of the great eastern faiths, Buddha and Confucius.

Mohammed (572–632) was different. He was a warlord—the head of an informal government and the leader of military forces. Mohammed began his career as a preacher who announced having visions that gave him the words of Allah. He began to preach this new monotheistic faith in his hometown of Mecca, attracting some believers, but alienating factions holding to polytheism. To escape persecution in Mecca, Mohammed and his followers fled to Medina in 622. One could perhaps say that he was thrust into the role of warlord by the absence of any formal government structure in his day. In the Arabia of the seventh century, people were organized into clans that enforced social norms and carried out military raids and reprisals. With no formal government in Medina, Mohammed became the de facto ruler. He decided disputes, punished those who did wrong in his eyes, and protected henchmen who carried out murders on his behalf.[10] He led the persecution of Jews in Medina and with his armed band drove them out of the city. Later, when the dispossessed Jews joined his enemies, Mohammed decreed the slaughter of six hundred who had been captured in battle.[11]

Seeking food and booty, Mohammed led his men in raids on caravans heading to Mecca. The result was a state of war with Mecca, with Mohammed directing the military campaigns against the Meccans in 624, 625, and 626. In 630, he conquered Mecca at the head of an army of ten thousand men and continued there in the role of warlord, dispensing personal "justice" and countering rebellions of neighboring tribes and clans until his death in 632. In sum, Mohammed was a religious prophet, but he also had a very full career as a specialist in violence. During his ten years in Medina building his political base, the

Prophet planned sixty-five campaigns and raids and personally led troops in twenty-seven military actions.[12]

The pattern continued for the disciples who became his immediate successors. Each of them also played the role of warlord, organizing military campaigns, both in actions of defense and in efforts to expand the Muslim empire. These early figures were all men who lived by the sword—and many died by the sword. With violence legitimated by Mohammed's example, his followers readily opted for bloodshed when a dispute arose. Of the four "rightly guided" caliphs who ruled in succession from 632 to 661, three were murdered. One of these murders was an individual vendetta, but the other two were carried out by Muslim factions with grievances against the caliph.

Each of these murders ignited a protracted civil war and set a pattern of internecine violence that continues to the present day: down through the years, more Muslims have been killed by Muslims than by followers of all the other religions combined. And, of course, the excessive violence in Muslim lands has been a main cause of their retarded economic development. Yet despite the havoc violence has wreaked on the Muslim community, Muslims have been reluctant to conclude that force represents a problem. No leader has advocated pure nonviolence, for example, and no pacifist sect has ever emerged within this religion. The explanation for the failure to condemn violence is obvious: saying that "violence is wrong" would have the appearance of criticizing the founding fathers of the religion, who practiced violence so fully.

Following the example of Mohammed, Muslim religious extremists throughout history turned to violent tactics to implement their theories of reform. The Assassins, for example, were an eleventh-century band of Muslim fanatics who believed that the faith had been corrupted by the existing Muslim rulers. Thinking to rid the world of these betrayers, they set out to murder them in individual attacks. The killer would get close to his victim by using a ruse or disguise and then quickly stab him to death with a dagger. These killings were suicide attacks because the assassin was certain to be apprehended and slain. In this respect, the tactic was typical. Since murder of the third caliph, Ali, by a suicide attacker in 661, the suicide attack has been a culturally reinforced form of religious or idealistic death in the Muslim world.

Another violent movement of Muslim religious extremists involved the Wahhabi sect that began in Saudi Arabia in the eighteenth century. A movement of military conquest as well as of religious renewal, the Wahhabi fought both the Ottoman Empire as well as local warlords in many bloody battles and vicious attacks. The movement finally succeeded in uniting Saudi Arabia under King Ibn Saud in 1926. The wheel of violent religious fanaticism came full circle in 1979 when Muslim extremists seized the Grand Mosque in Mecca—another suicide attack—declaring that the Saud dynasty had betrayed and corrupted Islam. In the battle to retake the mosque, 255 people died; sixty-three captured fundamentalists were later executed.[13]

The Christian Parallel—and Divergence

To understand fully the distinctiveness of the Muslim orientation toward the use of force, we need to compare it to the legacy of Christianity. In earlier times, Christianity was a violent religion, a tool of violent rulers who committed countless atrocities in its name. The parallel between Constantine, a Roman leader of the fourth century, and Mohammed is especially close. Like Mohammed, Constantine was a warlord, one among many in the turbulent, bloody days that marked the disintegration of the Roman Empire in the fourth century. The story goes that Constantine dreamed he heard a voice commanding him to have his soldiers mark their shields with the Christian cross; he did so and won the subsequent battle with a rival warlord (in 312). Constantine adopted Christianity and, using its organizing and motivating impact, was able to consolidate his rule—just as Mohammed later used Islam for the same purpose.

At that point, Christianity became a state religion, upheld—just like Islam—by violent conquest and bloody persecution. And, just as with Islam, different sects and heresies emerged, and their adherents fell to slaughtering each other with appalling zeal. But around the twelfth or thirteenth century, Christianity began to move in a new direction, gradually distancing itself from the use of force. Although the causes of this evolution are quite complex, central to the shift was a process of religious reform. Just as in the Islamic world, religious reformers came forth claiming that the true religion had been corrupted by existing rulers and church bureaucrats. And just as in the Islamic world, these reformers went back to the founders of the faith for inspiration.

That made all the difference. Christian reformers would never have thought of looking to the warlord Constantine for inspiration or example. They went back to the roots of their faith, to Jesus, Peter, and Paul—itinerant teachers who never used violence and who were objects of violent state persecution. Their example of nonviolence reinforced and made credible their preaching about loving neighbors, loving enemies, practicing meekness, and eschewing the sword.

One of the first sects of reformers that came out against war (and, incidentally, against capital punishment) was the Cathari, active in southern France around the year 1200. They took the Sermon on the Mount as their inspiration and preached the doctrine of loving enemies and never using force, even against infidels. This was, at the time, a minority and heretical view, and the Cathari and their allies were suppressed in the Albigensian Crusade.

In the early 1500s, another sect with similar ideas arose in Germany. The Anabaptists rejected all force-based government *and* the use of force in resisting government. They also opposed participating in military service on the grounds that it is sinful to take human life. The Anabaptists were persecuted but were not entirely eliminated. One branch, followers of Menno Simons, became known as the Mennonite communities that spread to Holland, Switzerland, Germany, and the United States. The following century saw the formation of the Society of Friends, or Quakers, an English Christian sect opposed to war, violence, and military service.

The individual Christians who took a stand against war and violence are too numerous to mention. The list might begin with Maximilianus, a Christian martyr executed in 295 for refusing to do military service. St. Francis of Assisi (1182–1226) preached love for all living things and urged his followers not to use force even to defend themselves against robbers. The renowned Dutch churchman Desiderius Erasmus wrote an antiwar tract, *Complaint of Peace,* in 1517. Basing his arguments on the New Testament, he argued that war was a shame of Christianity: "The wicked soldier, and hired for money to tear and murder men, doth bear before him the sign of the cross. . . . Oh thou wicked soldier!"[14] One cannot imagine a committed Muslim ever penning such a condemnation of the military career.

The opposition to violence in Christian culture came not only from pacifist sects and reformist clergy. Multitudes of ordinary believers, familiar with the example of nonviolence set by Jesus, came to the conclusion that war was not a Christian institution. For example, the first peace organization in the world, the New York Peace Society founded in 1815, was established by a devout Connecticut layman, David Low Dodge. He expressed his pacifist view in a book entitled *War Inconsistent with the Religion of Jesus Christ.*

This continuing tide of persuasion against the use of force obviously did not render Christian countries nonviolent. Most have participated readily in wars, and some—one thinks especially of the case of Nazi Germany—have committed appalling atrocities. Over the years, however, the Christian stand against killing percolated throughout society, bringing about a culture that viewed violence with a degree of hesitation. It is no accident that the evolution against force began sooner and has proceeded further in Christian countries such as Holland, England, and Switzerland than anywhere else. In broad terms, one can attribute the success of the West to the turning away from violence inspired by the Christian perspective. Its economic prosperity was made possible by a decline in banditry, civil strife, and massacre. Its institutions of democracy emerged when leaders stopped murdering each other to gain power, and when political factions became willing to refrain from civil war and accept the decision of the ballot box.

By similar logic, it is no accident that the Muslim world, which honors a warlord as its highest religious figure, finds itself far behind the West in containing the tragic and destructive effects of force.

The Ideology of Muslim Terrorism

Of the different uses of force in the Muslim community, the one of greatest interest today is terrorism. The American public became especially aware of Muslim terrorism after 9/11, but in truth the problem is long-standing. And it is not the United States or western Europe that bears the brunt of the destruction. Muslim countries themselves are impacted by terrorism far more seriously.

When the dawn of the television age gave rise to the modern period of terrorism, the first Middle Eastern terrorist groups to capture world attention were Marxist in orientation. These included the Palestine Liberation Organization, founded in 1964, and other groups related to the Palestinian cause, including the PFLP, PDFLF, Fatah, Abu Nidal, and Black September. These groups looked to the Soviet Union and socialist-oriented Arab states such as Syria and Libya for ideological inspiration as well as material and political support.

Less visible was another tradition of terrorism founded in the ideas of Islam. Developed by influential twentieth-century Muslim figures such as Mawlana Mawdudi in Pakistan, Ayatollah Khomeini in Iran, and Sayyid Qutb in Egypt, radical Islam looks back to the days of the Prophet Mohammed as a golden age that should be imitated today. Modern rulers of Muslim countries are seen as betrayers who have departed from this traditional Muslim ideal and who therefore must be destroyed and replaced. The United States and European countries are seen as enemies because they reflect and foster the spread of modern values and modern technology, and because they support many of the "impure" rulers in Muslim lands. The United States is a particular target because, in its role of world policeman, it has stationed troops in many Muslim countries and has opposed Muslims in many different settings.

The radical Islamic idea of returning to the lifestyle, values, and practices of seventh-century Arabia has many gaps, but it carries a strong appeal for those Muslims confused and frustrated by modern events. For the radical Muslim, the explanation for economic backwardness and for the decline of the Muslim empire is that Muslims stopped practicing the true religion. In his way of thinking, a country that made a complete return to the old religion would be both economically sound and militarily powerful.

Radical Islam, like Islam itself, is decentralized. Believers may hope for a single source of doctrinal and political authority as in the days of Mohammed and the early caliphs, but as a practical matter, Islam has no central intellectual or political authority. It is therefore possible for anyone to develop his own faction and to accuse all other Muslims—including those claiming to be radical themselves—of betraying the faith. For example, Saudi Arabia, founded on the extreme fundamentalism of the Wahhabi sect, has gone about as far as humanly possible in enforcing old-fashioned Muslim customs and religious dictates. Yet a number of radical Islamic groups view the Saudi regime as a betrayer of Islam. These opponents have included Khomeini's Iran (which has tried to foster a rebellion among the Shia minority in Saudi Arabia), the sect of Juhaiman Saif al Otaiba (which engineered the 1979 takeover of the Grand Mosque mentioned earlier), and the Al Qaeda group of Osama bin Laden.

Returning to the ways of the Prophet Mohammed may be an unrealistic goal in many respects, but there is one feature of the old-time religion that Islamic radicals apparently find simple and straight-forward: violence. They know well that Mohammed was a master at warfare and that they are on firm ground by imitating him in this respect. This makes radical Islam a natural terrorist ideology, for it directly legitimates the impulse to kill. The prospective terrorist may be uncertain about how to create an old-fashioned Islamic regime and confused about how it might operate, but he does not need to worry about any such issues. He can assume, following the example of Mohammed, that the first step must involve jihad—that is, a holy war against those he deems to be unbelievers, backsliders, or betrayers.

For Muslim terrorists, violence is not just a means to an end; it is attractive in and of itself. Therefore, they are more likely to engage in counterproductive violence and self-destructive violence. The suicide attack, which is so common among them, illustrates the point. Every terrorist who dies in a suicide attack is a soldier for the cause who will not be available to fight again. A rational commander, even one who puts no value on human life, would be reluctant to expend his forces in this manner. But if violence, not victory, is the *objective,* then a suicide attack is attractive, for it adds to the bloodshed and makes the catastrophe more complete.

The Muslim terrorists' eagerness for violence has resulted in many unproductive and self-defeating episodes. On numerous occasions, Islamic radicals have had their ostensible goal within their grasp only to throw victory away by resorting to extreme violence. For example, in Chechnya, Islamic terrorists have kept a war going that the Russians have been eager to stop. In 1996, the Russians tired of fighting, withdrew their troops from Chechnya, and signed a peace agreement that pointed to eventual independence for the "Islamic Republic." But Chechen terrorists wouldn't stop killing, and the new president, Aslan Maskhadov, could not control them. They made bloody raids into Russian territory, kidnapped Russian officials, including President Boris Yeltsin's personal envoy, and in late 1999 carried out the coordinated bombing of four apartments houses, two in Moscow and two in a provincial city, that killed three hundred people. Provoked by this violence, the Russians went back into Chechnya and laid waste to Grozny, the capital city, and much of the rest of the country, seeking to stamp out the terrorists.

Three years later, in the fall of 2002, history repeated itself. The Russians were again tiring of the war in Chechnya and looking for a way to negotiate a withdrawal. But a well-organized band of forty-one Chechen terrorists seized a Moscow theater, making hostages of the eight hundred members of the audience, and threatening to kill them all unless Russia withdrew from Chechnya. In the ensuing effort to recapture the theater, more than one hundred people were killed. The Russian public was shocked into favoring more severe military measures. "Last night," said one Russian legislator active in trying to work out a settlement with the Chechens, "I lost all my enthusiasm in trying to get through to these hard hearts."[15]

One could argue that the attack of 9/11 on the World Trade Center represents another example of irrational, counterproductive violence. In strategic terms, this event produced a severe reversal for Al Qaeda and its ostensible goal of spreading radical Islam. It led to the decimation of Al Qaeda forces and the loss of a secure base in Afghanistan; it triggered the destruction of the national regime that espoused the ideology of radical Islam to the fullest degree—Afghanistan's Taliban; and it galvanized countries all around the world, Muslim and non-Muslim, to make a concerted effort against Muslim terrorism.

A Life Cycle for Muslim Terrorism?

In discussing homegrown terrorism in Western countries in chapter 10, I pointed to a pattern of rise and fall. In its first phase, the terrorist campaign draws on the support of many sympathizers and is ignored or indulged by government officials and security forces. The terrorists then escalate their violence, provoking a popular backlash and triggering energetic measures of repression by security forces. As a result, the terrorist movement declines and eventually dies. In broad terms, this cycle also seems to apply to Muslim terrorism.

In Muslim countries, just as in the West, most people are spectators when it comes to terrorism. They have their lives to lead, families to take care of, and personal aspirations to pursue. Some may, to a degree, sympathize with the terrorists' aims. But, at the same time, inhabitants will be aware of the suffering and destruction caused by the terrorists' actions, so that when terrorists escalate their destruction, more people will be disposed to turn against them.

In many of Muslim countries where terrorists have been active, they have set in motion processes of resistance and backlash that have severely weakened them and impaired their cause. One example is Egypt, where terrorists associated with the Muslim Brotherhood and other radical Muslim sects have been active for at least half a century. The terrorists are no closer to victory today than they were fifty years ago, mainly because their shocking strokes of terrorism keep provoking government repression that decimates the movement. In 1954, terrorists tried to assassinate premier Gamal Nasser, and Nasser responded by executing six of the conspirators and arresting more than a thousand leaders and sympathizers, effectively crushing the radical Islamic movement—for a time.

In the 1970s, Egypt's new ruler, Anwar Sadat, encouraged the radicals by releasing many terrorists from prison and giving the fundamentalists freedom to preach and organize. The terrorist movement built itself up again and began collecting arms for an uprising. In 1981, one of the radical factions, Al-Jihad, assassinated President Sadat. The government responded with thousands of arrests and many executions. In the 1990s, another wave of terrorism by the fundamentalists produced many bloody clashes. Fundamentalists made violent attacks on Christians living in Upper Egypt, took over the Embaba District of Cairo, and made attacks on tourists and government officials. The result was, again, a sweeping campaign of repression that decimated the ranks of the terrorists. The terrorists also lost support among the public by their bloody deeds. In 1993, they tried to kill the prime minister with a car bomb. Although they missed their target, the blast injured twenty-one bystanders and killed a twelve-year-old schoolgirl. There had been more than two hundred terrorist slayings in the previous two years, and the public was fed up. At the girl's funeral procession, people cried, "Terrorism is the enemy of God!"[16]

The repression and public repudiation finally led the remaining leaders of the main terrorist group, Gamaa Islamiya, to call for a ceasefire in 1997. When a splinter terrorist group massacred tourists at Luxor in November 1997, many leaders of Gamaa condemned it. For the time being, the Egyptian government has won the war of terrorism that the radicals have declared on it.[17]

A similar shift against terrorists has occurred in Indonesia. One terrorist outburst, the Bali bombings that killed 183 people in October 2002, dramatically altered the political climate to the disadvantage of the terrorists and their radical sympathizers. Prior to the attack, the Indonesian government followed an indulgent policy toward the radical Islamic groups, refusing to arrest leaders that the United States, Singapore, and Malaysia identified as part of an international terrorist network. Foremost among these leaders was Abubakar Baasyir, a Muslim cleric who ran a religious school that endorsed Osama bin Laden and militant jihad. Some Indonesia officials not only ignored terrorism charges against Baasyir, but worked to gain his approval. In May 2002, Vice President Hamzah Haz invited Baasyir and other Islamic radicals to an official dinner. When asked about the dangers of Islamic terrorism, the vice president declared, "There is no such thing."[18]

Then came the bombings in the Bali nightclub district. Indonesians were shocked, both because of the bloodshed and also because of the economic impact: most of those slain were tourists, so the bombings threatened a mainstay of the economy. The government moved immediately to adopt strong measures against terrorism, making it easier to detain suspects. Local Muslims, including the leaders of the country's two largest Muslim organizations, approved the clampdown. Another action taken by the government—widely supported by the public—was the arrest of Baasyir. The extreme terrorist violence, then, undermined the radicals and their campaign to impose strict Islamic rules on the country. This broad pattern—violent excess by terrorists triggering repression and public repudiation—has been duplicated in many other Muslim countries in recent years, including Algeria, Syria, Malaysia, Pakistan, Saudi Arabia, and, of course, Afghanistan.[19]

Processes of repression are at work at the international level as well. Galvanized by 9/11, the United States spearheaded an international campaign to round up terrorists, deny them bases of operation, limit their movements, and deprive them of financial support. Many observers fear that some of the assertive U.S. moves—especially the invasions of Afghanistan and Iraq—may provoke still more terrorism by confirming the fundamentalist vision of a monster America intent on destroying Islam. There is undoubtedly some validity to this concern. However, the experience with Western homegrown terrorism (discussed in chapter 10) suggests that repression stifles more terrorists than it breeds, even when the repression is inept and excessive.

Of course, the Western experience is of limited value in predicting the course of terrorism in the Muslim world. Here, it seems, terrorism is likely to have an unusual resilience, given the ready acceptance of violence in that culture. By Western standards, the ease—indeed, the eagerness—with which many Muslim activists embrace violent death is really quite astonishing. One has to go back many centuries in the history of Western countries to find the same careless attitude toward death, and the same readiness to commit mayhem with such little regard for consequences. One hopes the Muslim community will not need centuries to transcend its emphasis on force. Modern means of communication, which enable third parties to note the horror of violence and observe its counterproductive effects, should speed the process of education along. Still in all, one suspects that Muslims are going to need many years to realize that, when it comes to violence, they must find some way to reinterpret or set aside the example of the Prophet Mohammed.

12

Violence in the Streets

In Paris on July 14, 1789, an angry mob invaded a government armory and seized thirty-two thousand muskets. With these weapons, the crowd mounted an attack on the Bastille, the government's fortress in the middle of Paris and the symbol of its oppressive rule. After four hours of fighting, ninety-eight of the attackers had died, still unable to penetrate the fortress. But because the defenders were without supplies and had no hope for reinforcement, the commandant surrendered, sending down the key to the main entrance. The mob surged in, killed six of the disarmed soldiers, and seized the commandant. He was dragged into the street and beaten to death. His head was cut off and raised on a pike for a victory march through the city. Thus began the French Revolution.

It is difficult for us today to imagine the extent of mob violence of earlier times. We know about incidents such as the storming of the Bastille, but we tend to assume they were isolated events, unusual episodes that stand out from an otherwise placid domestic history. A closer look reveals that this assumption of supposedly peaceful "good old days" is seriously mistaken. Bloody riots were a frequent occurrence in earlier times, a normal part of social life.

The storming of the Bastille was just an extension of a pattern of nearly continual rioting that had been going on for decades. Six cost-of-living riots occurred in Normandy between 1752 and 1768. In 1768, bread rioters seized control of the city of Rouen. In 1774, protesting silk workers seized the city of Lyon and had to be dislodged by army troops. Between 1770 and 1775, rioters seized granaries and broke into stores in Reims, Poitiers, Dijon, Versailles, Pontoise, Aix-en-Provence, and Paris.[1] In Paris in 1789 before the storming of the Bastille, rioting had been going on all year. Many of the disturbances focused on the shortage of bread. In the years before the revolution, mobs attacked shops, storehouses, and wagons and seized the grain. Another common grievance was the high cost of living and relatively low wages. In April of that year, a (false) rumor that wages were to be lowered at a wallpaper factory led mobs to sack the factory and the owner's house. In May, mobs forced their way into the meetings of the new parliament, the States-General. In June, mobs threatened and manhandled parliamentary members unsympathetic to their cause. Two days before the Bastille event, crowds clashed with soldiers in the Tuileries Gardens in the afternoon and forced their way into the Paris city hall in the evening. The next day, one mob broke into a monastery and seized grain, and another broke into the prison of La Force and freed the prisoners, mostly debtors.[2]

The closer we look, the more we find that the social and political life of earlier times was characterized by a pronounced degree of public violence. Rome, both in the republic and in the times of the emperors, was afflicted by violent mobs, as were the Italian city-states that followed the decline of Rome. For us today, the word *anarchy* refers to some vague, theoretical condition where no government exists. For the early Greeks who coined the term, however, there was nothing theoretical about it. Most of their city-states, including Athens, were frequently plunged into periods of mob rule and general pillage. In truth, rioting has been virtually universal around the world.

Popular violence has many causes, of course. These episodes generally grow out of real grievances and strongly held opinions. It is also true that they are seldom spontaneous. They generally have leaders, organization, and outside financing (certain nobles and wealthy businessmen financed the Paris mobs in the period leading up to the revolution).[3] In addition to these factors of causation, however, there is an additional variable, one that is often taken for granted: for riots to take place, the populace must have a ready disposition to violence. In an age of riots, risking life, taking life, and destroying property are normal tendencies. This disposition toward violence apparently has declined, for as we study the history of mob violence, we discover a general decline in this use of force.

England in the Age of Riots

This trend is perhaps best documented in the case of England. As historians are increasingly discovering, there never was a "Merrie old England." It was "violent old England," and one of most noticeable and recurrent forms of violence was rioting. It is difficult to say when the first riots occurred because the historical record of the earliest times is sketchy. As that record improves by around the seventeenth century, we begin to have considerable information about rioting, particularly in London. London mobs were active and influential in the political disturbances of 1641–42, and again in 1668, when the city saw five days of rioting by apprentices who tore down houses of prostitution. In 1688, the London mob's anti-Catholic rioting played an instrumental role in driving King James II from the throne in that year.[4]

The eighteenth century has been called the "Age of Riots," for it was an era that saw an enormous number of violent group challenges to life, property, and authority. One factor that contributed to the increase in protest was urbanization, which brought more people into proximity. The growth in printing and publishing, along with somewhat greater freedoms of expression, made it easier to organize and motivate crowds. Whatever the causes, violent rioting, especially in London, became the hallmark of the era. The century began with the so-called Sacheverell riots of 1709, wherein the followers of the High-Church preacher, Dr. Henry Sacheverell, rose up to protest what they considered to be his persecution by the Whig government of the day. Other major episodes of street violence occurred in 1715, 1732, and 1768.

In 1780, London saw the worst riots in its history, the so-called Gordon riots. Anti-Catholic mobs, organized by the London Protestant Association, practically took over London from June 2 to June 8, 1780, burning Catholic chapels, as well as attacking the homes of government officials and breaking into London's prisons and freeing the prisoners. In all, 800 to 1,000 people lost their lives, including 285 shot by army troops. Of the rioters arrested, 62 were given death sentences and 25 were hanged.[5]

Such great riots were just a wave in the enormous tide of group violence going on year after year, all around the country. Riots were taking place on almost every conceivable subject: against Catholics, Irish, Jews, and nonconformists; against exports and imports; against price increases and price decreases; against new machinery and new products; against employers; against taxes; against this political party and that one; and against governmental authority. The century saw hundreds, if not thousands, of food riots—that is, efforts by crowds to seize grain from farmers, transporters, and merchants. In the year 1766 alone, such riots occurred in sixty-eight places.[6] In the years 1830–32, there were more than a thousand rural disturbances where farm laborers attacked farms, destroyed threshing machines, and burned hayricks and barns.[7] A careful tabulation of civil disturbances in all of England between 1790 and 1810 found a total of 740 "full-scale" riots, 26 of which involved loss of life.[8] One count of group disturbances involving damage to persons or property, in just the city of London in the period 1790–1821, shows a total of 224 incidents, or an average of 7 a year.[9]

Although historians disagree about the causes of riots in England, they do agree on one point: the amount of rioting declined over time. This trend was in the making for many generations, but it showed up clearly after the mid–nineteenth century. One statistic that reveals the sea change is the number of persons tried for riot and sedition. In the decade from 1839 to 1848, 1,725 persons were committed for trial on these charges. In the twenty years after that, only 15 persons were tried on these charges.[10]

In addition to a dramatic decline in the number of riots, there was also a diminution in their violence. Labor groups, for example, had been quite destructive in the eighteenth and early nineteenth century, smashing machines and burning down factories. By around the 1840s, most unions had turned to more peaceful methods of bargaining.[11] Political protest also became more peaceful, and rallies were less likely to turn into riots. A good example of the shift came in 1848, when a large group of radicals held a huge demonstration in London to pressure Parliament to adopt universal manhood suffrage. Told by police that their planned parade to the Houses of Parliament would be blocked, leaders called off the demonstration, and the crowd disbanded peacefully.

Going along with the decline in group violence was a decline in government's use of force to control demonstrations and riots. In the earlier days, officials often considered group protests to be treasonable efforts to overthrow the regime, so participants were executed. The Riot Act, passed in 1715, provided for the death penalty for anyone failing to disperse after a magistrate had read the act publicly. This harsh measure led to scores of executions over the following century. By the 1840s, however, the death penalty for participation in a riot was no longer being applied. Contrary to what one might expect from the theory of deterrence, this milder treatment did not cause an upsurge in disturbances. As previously noted, it actually coincided with a marked decline in disturbances. The decline in mob violence apparently was not the result of particular laws or policies. It was a cultural evolution that affected everyone, protesters and government officials alike.

The data for other European countries indicate a similar pattern of declining street violence. In Germany, for example, rioting was extremely widespread in the first half of the nineteenth century. Using five German newspapers as his source, one researcher counted 142 food riots in just the eighteen months from January 1847 to June 1849 (a period of abnormally high mob violence).[12] These food riots, in turn, represented only approximately 10 percent of some 1,500 riots in this period. In the same general period, food riots were occurring elsewhere in Europe; for example, in France there were more than 400 riots in 1846–47.[13]

One should make a distinction between acts of public protest and the violence of riots. It is probably true that in most countries the number of demonstrations, parades, strikes, and sit-ins has increased—perhaps as a result of the growth in communication, increase in leisure time, and other such factors. However, these public expressions of opinion have been increasingly peaceful, so that the amount of deaths, injuries, and destruction of property has declined. Historian Charles Tilly makes this point in his comprehensive survey of four centuries of French civil strife: "Despite the rapidly increasing pace of strikes and demonstrations, the twentieth century brought a decisive decline in fatalities from civil conflicts."[14]

In Ireland, in addition to the usual kinds of riots, there was a type of communal violence called "faction fighting." In the eighteenth and nineteenth centuries, the country had numerous local and regional secret societies that were quite aggressive in their orientation. These Mafia-like gangs employed intimidation and violence against farmers, landowners, priests, and government officials—and against each other. They regularly attended fairs and other public gatherings for the purpose of recruiting members—and to do battle with each other, using sticks, clubs, swords, and sawed-off shotguns. At one fair in Golden in 1807, 20 people were killed in a faction fight. One historian estimates that hundreds of people died in faction fighting.[15] In a shift that historians have difficulty explaining, faction fighting virtually disappeared after around 1840.[16]

It's worth pausing to reflect on what all of this mob violence must have meant for commerce and trade. Not only were the entrepreneurs and merchants of earlier days assailed by government's overbearing taxation and crippling regulations, but their systems of production and distribution were constantly threatened by the violence of the streets. Consider the travails of Ireland's Grand Canal, which was opened in 1779. In an age when roads were little more than muddy tracks, the canal promised a quantum leap in the ease and efficiency of transportation. Unfortunately, its operations were constantly hampered by violence. On many occasions, unemployed workers would breach the canal—draining it dry, of course—in order to create work for themselves to fill in the gap. In one episode in 1820, a mob of some 300 pelted a repair crew with stones until the canal company agreed to hire additional local workers. During times of food shortage, mobs would attack the boats and carry away the flour and potatoes they were transporting. Mobs would also attempt to prevent foodstuffs from leaving the local area by breaching the canal or blocking it with large stones. Canal boats were also attacked for causing surpluses. Canal shipments lowered the prices of foodstuffs and peat, and local merchants striving to protect their high prices induced mobs to attack boats and to sink them or otherwise destroy their cargo. In addition to all the economic violence, the canal was caught up in political upheavals. The canal was closed for two months during the rebellion of 1798, and it supported a military guard for some twenty years thereafter. In the face of all this disruption, it is no wonder that the canal was not a profitable enterprise and often had to skip making payments to its investors.[17]

Strange as it seems, modern discussions of economic development almost entirely ignore the role of violence in crippling commerce. The textbooks on the subject write at length about other factors: natural resources, good harbors and the need for transportation, the importance of capital, the qualifications of the labor force, and the role of entrepreneurs. But surely all these factors are secondary to social peace. When mobs are burning down factories, how can there be economic development? What good are roads, bridges, and harbors when they are being shelled by artillery?

To some extent, the role of violence in economic development has been overlooked because we tend to view violence as a temporary phenomenon, a sort of brief intermission in the life of a nation. But this impression comes from the modern experience in the more economically developed countries. In earlier times, mob violence was more or less continuous—and in most of the less-developed areas of the world it still is. Many African countries, for example, experience commerce-destroying violence year after year. Mobs riot and loot, gangs extort, political factions engage in drawn-out civil war. Government officials, especially of the police and army, make war against trade, extorting cash and seizing lands, homes, and vehicles at gunpoint.

Perspectives on economic development need to be broadened. The main obstacle to prosperity is not so much a lack of creative, positive factors such as technology, capital, or entrepreneurship. It is the negative effect of violence. As a culture transcends this destructive impulse, economic development surges ahead.

Riots in the United States

The United States seems to have followed the British pattern of declining group violence, although the decline occurred somewhat later in time. In the mid–nineteenth century, when rioting in England was tapering off, the United States saw a great number of public disturbances. Just about all cities saw major riots. In the period 1830–60, Baltimore had 12 riots, Philadelphia 11, and New York 8. One historian suggests this period "may have been the era of the greatest urban violence that America has ever experienced."[18]

One of the main sources of group violence in the United States over the past 150 years has been labor disputes. Although such disputes occurred continuously since the earliest times, they gained a new ferocity in the latter part of the nineteenth century. The growth of industrial firms brought large numbers of workers together, and the emergence of ideologies of struggle and class hostility further embittered labor conflicts. The labor "wars" of this period typically began with a strike over some grievance, often a demand for recognition of a particular union as the bargaining agent for a firm. The owners would reject the demand and hire guards to protect facilities and, often, would bring in nonunion personnel to continue production. Union workers would then make armed attacks on the facilities and the strikebreakers.

One of the earliest major labor disputes, and apparently the bloodiest in U.S. history, was the nationwide railroad strike and riots of 1877. Rioters took over a railroad depot in Baltimore, set fire to it, and drove off firemen who attempted to battle the blaze. Troops were sent to Martinsburg, West Virginia, to combat strikers who had seized control of the yards there. In Reading, Pennsylvania, 13 people were killed in a clash between troops and strikers; in Chicago 19 were killed in a similar clash.[19] In 1894, there was another railroad strike that was almost as costly. In riots and battles around the country, an estimated 34 people were killed.[20]

Another industry that saw a large number of violent confrontations was mining, especially coal mining. In the Pennsylvania anthracite coalfields, a serious clash in 1897 left 18 dead. Seven years later, in the 1904 strike, a number of confrontations left 14 dead, as well as much destruction of property. Battles in the West Virginia coalfields in 1912–13 left a total of at least 29 killed.[21] In 1922, a strike at a Herrin, Illinois, coal mine cost 19 lives when union workers massacred a group of strikebreakers who had surrendered after a pitched battle.[22]

After the mid-1920s, the amount of labor violence—or at least the number of large, bloody clashes—declined. There still were many violent incidents, but almost always of a smaller scale, involving, at most, a few killed. Of course, this small-scale violence could add up. In Illinois, a running jurisdictional battle in 1932–37 between two unions—the United Mine Workers and the Progressive Mine Workers—cost an estimated 24 lives. The last major episodes of labor violence occurred in 1936–37. In the worst of the clashes, at Republic Steel in May 1937, 10 were killed and 30 wounded when a mob of picketing strikers charged a police line.

Since that time, labor historians agree, "violence has greatly diminished."[23] One sign of the change is the decline in the number of confrontations serious enough to require calling in the National Guard. In the earlier years, troops were frequently called out to quell violence that had gone beyond the capacity of local police to handle. In 1936 alone, they were called out eleven times for labor disputes. After the 1940s, this practice greatly declined. Troops were called out once in 1951 and once in 1959 for a strike in Kentucky, and very rarely since. This is not to say that the labor scene is entirely peaceful today. Scores of incidents occur in connection with labor disputes—scuffles, tire slashing, window breaking, and an occasional killing—but nothing like the large-scale battles and prolonged "wars" that took place in earlier times.

Another type of mass violence in America has been the race riot. Tension between whites and blacks goes back hundreds of years and has resulted in many violent confrontations. In New York City in 1741, fear of a slave revolt prompted a rampage by whites in which "scores of Negroes were burned, hanged, or expelled."[24] Probably the worst riot episode in the history of the United States was the so-called Draft Riot of 1863 in New York City. While triggered as a protest against the draft for the Civil War, these four days of rioting were

mainly an anti-Negro rampage. Some 50 blacks were lynched in disturbances that cost an estimated total of 1,300 lives (including the lives of
50 soldiers killed in the effort to put down the disturbances).[25]

In the South, the period after the Civil War saw a vast amount
of racial violence in the form of riots, battles, and massacres. In Texas,
a U.S. attorney estimated that 1,000 blacks were killed a year in the
period 1868–70. In Louisiana in the year 1868 alone, 1,884 people
were killed or wounded in racial strife (a riot in New Orleans in 1866
cost 38 lives). A riot and massacre in Wilmington, North Carolina, in
1898 resulted in an estimated 100 deaths.[26]

In the twentieth century, racial violence continued, but with
diminishing intensity. In one wave of disturbances between 1915 and
1921, there were major race riots in more than twenty-five cities,
including East Saint Louis (48 deaths), Chicago (38 deaths), Washington, D.C. (39 deaths), and Tulsa (85 deaths).[27] A less intense wave of
violence occurred between 1964 and 1967, with major riots in Detroit
(43 deaths), Newark (26 deaths), and the Watts District of Los Angeles
(34 deaths).[28] Since that time, there has been only one major race riot,
the 1992 Los Angeles disturbance in connection with the Rodney King
verdict, which resulted in 53 deaths. This episode reminds us that racial
strife has not disappeared, but an inspection of the overall historical
record does indicate that this kind violence has been declining. The
point is especially marked if one considers the growth of population.
On a per capita basis, the rate of deaths in race riots has been declining
dramatically over the past century and a half.

Racial clashes represent only one type of violence between
social groups in America. Down through the years, practically every
nationality group and every religion have been involved in serious
strife. Perhaps the first such instance of communal violence in America
occurred between Pilgrims and Puritans. Doctrinal and economic
differences led to a clash in 1634 that cost two lives.[29] From that time
until today, there has been serious mob violence against many religious
groups, including Quakers, Catholics, Mormons, and Jews, and against
many national and ethnic groups, including Indians, Germans, Poles,
Italians, Irish, and Chinese. Although this kind of strife still crops up in
modern times, it appears to have greatly diminished compared with

earlier times. All of the major episodes of religious and ethnic violence (excepting black-white clashes) occurred in the distant past.

One quantitative measure of the decline in group violence in the United States is provided by Sheldon Levy's study for the National Commission on the Causes and Prevention of Violence in 1969. Using certain newspapers as his source, Levy tabulated all reported instances of violent attacks on individuals or groups arising out of "economic, racial, religious, or political antagonisms." He found that there were fewer deaths per capita in the most recent period reviewed (1939–68) than in any other thirty-year period covered by the study, which began with the year 1819. When a correction was introduced to control for the fact that modern reporting of violence is more comprehensive, the lower level of group violence in the modern period was even more pronounced.[30]

Another index of the trend in group violence is revealed by the recorded statistics on lynchings since 1882. In the nineteenth century, lynchings occurred in many parts of the country in connection with riots and vigilante justice. In the 1880s, 1,203 people were lynched, 56 percent of whom were white. As time progressed, lynching became predominantly a form of mob violence against blacks in the South. In 1910–19, for example, 91 percent of the 621 people lynched were blacks. As figure 12.1 shows, lynchings of all kinds declined dramatically over the course of the twentieth century. By the 1960s, this form of violence had practically disappeared.

Another indication of the general decline in group violence in the United States comes from studying the activities of the National Guard. Down through the years, the Guard (or Militia as it was earlier called) has had two broad domestic functions: (1) to keep peace and restore order in the event of civil disturbance, and (2) to assist in providing public services in cases of natural disaster. Over the past century, the relative emphasis of these activities has shifted dramatically. In the late nineteenth century, the Guard was occupied almost entirely in controlling mob violence. A tabulation of the use of the Militia in the years 1877–92 counted 112 actions. Only 4 of these concerned a reaction to a natural disaster (one was the Johnstown, Pennsylvania, flood of 1889). The rest were responses to mob violence of one kind or another, including labor disputes, election riots, and lynchings.[31] In modern times, the emphasis has reversed. Of 9 domestic uses of National Guard units in the period 1987–93, 8 were responses to natural disasters, and only one—the race riots in Los Angeles in 1992— involved a civil disturbance.[32]

Figure 12.1

Lynchings in the United States
1882–1969

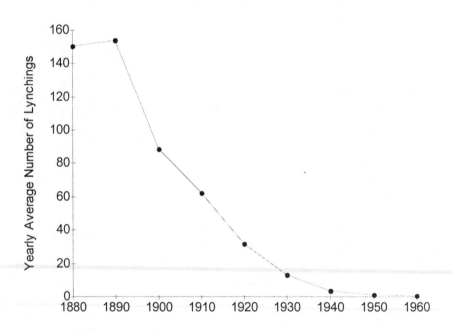

Source: Compiled from data given in U.S. Bureau of the Census, *Historical Statistics of the United States, Colonial Times to 1970*, part 1 (Washington, D.C.: Government Printing Office, 1975), p. 422.

Homicide

What application does the theory about the declining use of force have to the phenomenon of individual violence, especially in the form of murder? This is a difficult question because so many different factors affect the murder rate. Wars, especially civil wars, increase the homicide rate, whereas more intensive policing and higher incarceration rates can decrease it. In addition, one must consider the effects of social variables, such as urbanization and family breakdown, on the level of individual violence. Furthermore, there is the problem of migration and immigration. The homicide rate for people of a certain culture may be declining, but if people from another culture with a higher murder rate move into the area, then the overall rate will increase.

Although all these factors make an underlying change in the homicide rate difficult to spot, the decline-in-force hypothesis should apply to levels of individual violence. A decline in the general cultural orientation toward violence should affect the disposition of individuals to kill others, so that, everything else being equal, the result should be a lower homicide rate.

In order to test this prediction, we need good-quality data for a long period of time and for a country or region that has not changed to a significant degree its ethnic or cultural composition. These are demanding conditions, but they are adequately met in the case of England. Because of its insular condition, England was not as affected by the invasions and migrations that swept most countries of Europe, so that the cultural factor was kept rather constant over a long period of time. And although past records on homicides and population size (which we need in order to calculate a homicide rate) leave much to be desired, they are sufficient to identify the broad trend.

This trend is clearly one of a declining homicide rate. The most important evidence for this conclusion is James Given's path-breaking study on homicide in England in the thirteenth century. Given based his study on court records for seven different counties for various sessions in the years 1202 to 1276. The average homicide rate indicated by these records was 19 deaths per 100,000 population per year, more than ten times the current rate in England.[33] Because this thirteenth-century figure is based on court trials, not reported homicides, it almost certainly understates the homicide rate of the time.[34]

Other studies covering later periods in England confirm the picture of a generally declining murder rate.[35] This decline has not been smooth; some generations and even some centuries saw an increase in the homicide rate. Certain places at certain times exhibited unusual rates. For example, a careful study of murder in Oxford in the 1340s indicates it had a homicide rate of 110 per 100,000 population per year, or approximately one hundred times the modern rate in England.[36] When the trends for all the studies are combined, they show that the homicide rate declined from approximately 20 (or higher) in the 1200s to approximately 10 in the 1500s, and then to 1–2 in the modern period—that is, since 1860.[37] From the evidence, it is clear, as historian Michael MacDonald puts it, that "seventeenth-century villages bore no relation to the peaceable kingdoms anxious urbanites imagine made up 'the world we have lost'. . . ; hatred, fear and violence were endemic in rural England before the Industrial Revolution."[38]

It is difficult to find any other country where the data and existing research permit us to draw conclusions about long-term changes in homicide rates. Data for the United States are fragmentary for the early years and indicate a bewildering array of values for different jurisdictions.[39] Since 1933, when the Federal Bureau of Investigation uniform crime reporting program began, reliable nationwide statistics on homicide have been available. These figures show no overall trend in this period, a result that is not surprising, given that the United States has been a constantly changing country socially and culturally. It probably is true that the homicide rate for Anglo-Americans has declined, but the addition of other cultural groups with higher homicide rates—eastern Europeans, southern Europeans, Latinos, and African Americans—overlays this trend.[40]

Many observations of an impressionistic nature strongly indicate that levels of personal violence in other countries were very high in the distant past. French historians have observed that personal brutality and crimes of violence were strikingly common in medieval times.[41]

In accounting for the many homicides, private wars, and mob killings in medieval Europe, historian Barbara Tuchman points to an overall "habit of violence."[42] Historian Alex de Jonge notes that "Seventeenth-century Moscow was an extraordinarily violent city. Robbery and murder were commonplace, and every morning there would be a fresh batch of corpses to be found and laid out in the streets." He quotes a contemporary source who reported that "No night passes without a murder" and that the number of murders could reach as high as 15 in one night.[43]

Rome and other Italian cities were extremely violent places in earlier times. One source notes that in the middle of the eighteenth century, Rome averaged some 330 murders a year.[44] This figure indicates a homicide rate of approximately 180 murders per 100,000 population (the figure for modern Italy is 1.7). In medieval days in the Italian cities, it was apparently quite normal for enemies to settle scores through murder. The tenor of the times is illustrated in the autobiography of Benvenuto Cellini, the great Italian sculptor of the sixteenth century who lived in Rome and Florence. He reports that in those days "everyone" wore a sword, and he mentions more than twenty clashes and violent attacks in which he personally was involved. He also describes, with some pride, two ruthless murders he committed to satisfy grudges. In both cases, he surprised his victims and stabbed them to death. The authorities winked at both killings, even though in one case the victim was a blameless off-duty policeman.[45]

The Rise and Fall of Dueling

The staggering homicide rate of medieval times seems to be related to another violent custom that has noticeably declined: dueling. Although there have always been isolated instances of formalized individual combat, going back to David and Goliath, if not before that, the widespread practice of dueling did not arise until the sixteenth century, beginning in Italy. The practice soon spread to France, Russia, England, most of the other European countries, and America. In France, one source notes that 4,000 men died in duels in the period

1589–1607. Another estimate, for the nine years from 1643 to 1652, was 900 deaths.[46] One incomplete tabulation of duels in England in the period 1760–1821 reported 172 deaths.[47]

Although a violent practice, dueling may well have been a method of moderating the enormous street violence of medieval times. As historian Ian Gilmour explains, "It probably cut down violence, being a partial substitute for affrays, ambushes, gang warfare, blood feuds and assassination."[48] If two men bore a grudge, it was certainly better that they fight in controlled conditions than to have a street clash involving their friends, not to mention innocent bystanders. Support for this theory comes from Cellini's autobiography, which mentions one duel in addition to all the street fights, murders, and attempted murders. After trading insults with a soldier, Cellini was about to start a sword fight, but, he reports, "we were separated" by friends on both sides, and a duel was arranged instead. As it happened, the duel never came off.[49]

In time, dueling became increasingly criticized and condemned; voluntary societies were formed to spread the word against it, and the custom died out. In the United States, the last formal duel took place in 1877.[50] In England, the custom rapidly declined after the 1840s, but in France and Germany it did not die out until after World War I. (Georges Clemenceau, prime minister of France 1917–19, fought twenty-two duels in his lifetime.)[51]

Though in historical perspective it is easy to say that the practice of dueling was doomed, this was not how it was viewed years ago. Reformers who were trying to discourage the practice were told that their efforts were futile, that "duels would continue so long as the world should endure," that they were ingrained in human nature, "a law that no power may oppose."[52] This conviction of inevitability was expressed by French scholar Camille Doucet, writing in the late nineteenth century. Though an opponent of dueling, Doucet resigned himself to it: "The effort to suppress dueling has often been made. . . . [But] all that has been accomplished toward achieving this noble purpose amounts to nothing, nor will it ever amount to more."[53]

In this respect, the decline of dueling follows the pattern seen with many other uses of force. In their heyday, they are thought to be inevitable, something no one can do anything about. Nevertheless, generations later, they have disappeared. It is likely that the same pattern still applies, and that uses of force that today seem ingrained and even essential are also destined to disappear.

13

The Decline of Slavery and Debt Bondage

Dictionaries are disappointingly vague about slavery. They say that slavery is "submission to a dominating influence." By this expansive definition, anyone who works for an employer is a slave, as is a young man in love—"a slave to love" as the songwriters like to put it —and slavery has not been abolished anywhere in the world.

The problem with this definition is that it fails to include the element of physical force, for it is this ingredient that makes slavery so different from the many other kinds of domination or control that we find in the world. The slave owner uses physical force against the slave. He can whip him, or he can lock him up in a room and not give him food. If the slave tries to run away, the owner chases after him with a gun and a rope to bring him back. Employers don't use force to keep workers or to get them to do certain tasks. Young ladies don't use force to motivate lads to swing on the porch with them.

Being based on force, slavery is the most complete and potentially the most harmful domination possible. It is, in effect, a kidnapping, but with one additional ingredient. In an ordinary kidnapping, the perpetrator acts secretly because society disapproves of this use of force. With slavery, government upholds the "kidnapping": it is legal. If the victim escapes his master, police officers and soldiers are used to hunt him down and recapture him. Let us advance a definition of *slavery* of the old-fashioned kind, what most of us have in mind when we use the term in serious discourse: *slavery is the domination of one individual by another through the use of physical force, a domination upheld by government's use of force.*

In ancient times, slavery was an everyday fixture in virtually all societies, a practice upheld by tradition, religion, and philosophy. Judaism and Christianity sanctioned slavery.[1] Both Plato and Aristotle approved of slavery as a natural and necessary institution.[2] Athens, at the height of its "democratic" glory under Pericles in 450 B.C. had approximately 115,000 slaves, or 35 percent of the entire population.[3] Some other Greek cities, including Sparta and Chios, had an even higher proportion of slaves.[4] Rome, at the end of the republic (44 B.C.), had a similarly high proportion of slaves, 33 percent.[5]

The main source of slaves in antiquity and into modern times was capture in war. For example, Julius Caesar captured approximately one million slaves during his military campaigns in Gaul from 58 to 51 B.C.[6] In general, slavery represented in these days a relatively humane treatment for prisoners of war and conquered peoples because the alternative was to be massacred. Some individuals were enslaved as a punishment for a crime, or, as discussed later, as a penalty for an unpaid debt. And, of course, the children of slaves generally became slaves themselves.

Why Slavery Declined

The demise of slavery was impelled both by economic factors and by feelings of empathy for slaves. The economic case against slavery is that it is inefficient. Being forced to work under duress, the slave tends to be a poor worker, with low productivity. At the same time, the maintenance of slaves is costly, for they must be housed, fed, guarded, and given direction for the accomplishment of every task. Therefore, if a slave is freed to work his own plot of land on a sharecropping basis, let us say, an increase in productivity will result. Working for himself, the sharecropper will be more diligent and thoughtful in carrying on production, and the owner spares all the cost of supporting, supervising, and guarding him. As a result, the owner of the land can make a greater profit than before.

Over the years, this point about productivity played a powerful role in undermining the practice of slavery and led owners to give their slaves a greater degree of freedom. In medieval Europe, the transition generally took the form of converting slaves into serfs. Although the rights and duties of serfs were quite complicated and varied from place to place, the core of the serf's obligation was to make a regular payment, a type of tax, to his lord. In most other respects, the serf was independent of the lord. He could work when he wanted, buy and sell property, come and go, even change residence.[7] There were certain restrictions if he wished to marry a serf of another lord, and he was generally required to supply temporary labor or to serve temporary military duty. But, broadly speaking, the serf was beyond the brutal and restrictive treatment meted out to slaves.

Serfdom as an alternative to slavery began to appear in Italy in the late years of the Roman Empire (A.D. 400–500) as landowners grappled with the growing problem of slaves who could easily desert and who, given the weakness of Roman military forces, could not be easily recaptured. In France, serfdom had almost entirely replaced slavery by around 1200.[8] In England, slavery rapidly disappeared after the Norman Conquest of 1066. Up until that time, slavery was common, with approximately 10 percent of the population being slaves. The Norman invaders, who considered France their home, freed slaves on the English estates they took over and made them serfs "to avoid the necessity of close supervision and management of slaves."[9] The economic pressures against slavery meant that this practice had largely died out in Europe by the late Middle Ages. It had also faded away in other places as well. In Japan, for example, it had become rare by the year 1200.[10]

It is important to note, however, that the decline in slavery in medieval times did not have a moral or legal foundation. Slavery was still legitimate and in varying degrees practiced. Europeans engaged wholeheartedly in the international slave trade, and there were some slaves in most countries. In Italy, for example, Florence and other cities of Tuscany had slavery and slave markets as late as the early 1800s.[11] Thus, in Europe, slavery became merely a disused custom, not a condemned practice, which meant that Europeans easily revived it when it became convenient in the new colonies of the West Indies and North and South America. When these colonies were formed in the seventeenth century, they faced a great shortage of labor for their sugar, rice, and tobacco plantations. At the same time, a well-established slave trade coming out of Africa provided a supply to meet the demand. The result was that slavery became widespread in these areas.

The Rise of Empathy

If economic factors were the only consideration, it seems likely that slavery would have continued in various pockets around the world until the present day. But moral and humanitarian considerations also came into play, giving rise to a campaign against slavery on the ethical level. This campaign was based on the principle of empathy. Was it right, people would ask, to subject human beings to such brutal treatment? Even the ancients were sensitive to this issue, at least as concerning slaves of their own culture and religion. Greeks were not supposed to enslave Greeks, Christians were not supposed to enslave Christians, and Muslims were not supposed to enslave Muslims. Although this principle was often transgressed in practice, its existence in ancient times reflects an early moral qualm about slavery.

Another sign of the early humanitarian concern was the practice of freeing slaves. Manumission was common in most slave societies, even in ancient times. The slave, through faithful service and prolonged personal interaction with the master, gradually became more "human" to the master, a person who deserved compassion. This compassion motivated the master to free the slave, often through a will. In some slave societies—Rome is a notable example—many leaders and distinguished citizens were former slaves or descendants of slaves.[12]

One of the earliest episodes of humanitarian political agitation in favor of slaves took place in Rome during the time of the emperor Nero. In that era, slaves were executed for crimes and misdemeanors in large numbers and in appallingly brutal ways, including being burned alive. One severely applied legal principle was that of executing all the slaves of a household where a slave had murdered the master. The theory was that this penalty would cause all slaves in a household to work actively to prevent a fellow slave from murdering the master. It was also part of the larger system of intimidation that elites believed was necessary to ensure the subjugation of the slave class. This harsh perspective was opposed by a few advanced thinkers, such as the philosopher Seneca, who argued for clemency toward slaves on the grounds that slaves were "human beings, humble friends [who] share the same roof as ourselves."[13]

The issue came to a boil when, in A.D. 61, Rome's chief of security, Pedanius Secundus, was murdered by one of his slaves, which meant that all of Pedanius's four hundred slaves, many of them women and children, had to be slain. Public opinion sided with the slaves, and furious rioting broke out in their behalf. The Senate, besieged by the mob, nevertheless ordered the mass execution on the grounds that it was necessary to uphold law and order. It was carried out by a large military force that held the crowds at bay.[14]

Though some efforts were made in ancient and medieval times to alleviate the harsh treatment of slaves, there was little opposition to the institution of slavery itself. Even in the late Middle Ages, it was not questioned. A number of countries—England in 1569, Lithuania in 1588, Russia in 1679—ended slavery on their own soil, but made no complaint of the practice as concerned other areas. The formal movement against slavery developed only in the late eighteenth century. Its founding moment was perhaps the English judicial decision of 1772 that any slave who might stand on English soil was freed, regardless of the nationality of the owner. In the following years, the Quakers and other activists in both England and Pennsylvania organized an abolitionist movement founded on the principle that "the slave trade was contrary to the laws of God and the rights of men."[15] Their agitation motivated the British government to abolish the slave trade in 1807 and led to the use of the Royal Navy to suppress that trade to both North and South America.

The nineteenth century saw the abolition of slavery in the Western world. Most Latin American countries were ahead of the United States in abolishing slavery. Chile freed its slaves in 1823, Mexico in 1829, Peru in 1854. Brazil was the last in the region to abolish slavery, which it did in 1888. In other parts of the world, abolition came later still. China ended slavery in 1910. Korea legally abolished it in 1894, but the practice did not entirely end there until the 1930s.[16]

The Muslim world, reflecting its long tradition of violence and slave trading, was the last bastion of slavery in the world—or perhaps one should say *is* the last bastion, because a certain amount of clandestine trafficking of human beings still occurs in parts of North Africa and the Arabian peninsula. However, as the 1994 *Encyclopedia Britannica* observes, "Slavery no longer exists as a legal phenomenon recognized by a political authority or government any place in the world."[17]

In historical perspective, the abolition of slavery represents an astonishingly rapid development. After all, slavery dates from the beginning of human history and persisted for thousands of years with relatively little change. Then, within just a few centuries, the custom was challenged and overthrown all over the world. To appreciate how recent this achievement is, notice that the last country to abolish slavery officially, Saudi Arabia, did so in 1962, within the lifetimes of many readers of this book.

Treatment of Debtors

The relationship between debtor and creditor resembles the relationship between slave and master. Those who have borrowed money are beholden to their creditors, and down through the ages creditors have been entitled to use force against them in various ways if they default on their obligation. A study of these practices is therefore another way to gauge the broad historical trend against the use of force.

A number of economic and moral arguments support the case for using force against delinquent debtors. First, credit is the engine of economic life. Investors lend entrepreneurs capital; workers extend their labor on credit; and sellers ship goods to buyers on credit. The health and efficiency of the economy therefore depend on the trustworthiness of borrowers. It therefore follows that the smooth functioning of the economic system requires that society have severe penalties for debtors who default on their obligations. Moral considerations also argue for severe treatment. A debtor who fails to repay a loan has broken a solemn promise, and society has an interest in upholding honesty and punishing deceit. Furthermore, a default directly hurts the creditor, whose financial affairs may be thrown into turmoil by the failure of the debtor to repay as promised.

These may be good arguments, but they are arguments for adding to the use of force in the world. A defaulting debtor may interfere with the smooth functioning of economic life, he may have broken a promise and left someone who trusted him in ruins, but whatever his transgression, he did not use force. He may have misled the lender when he asked for the money, perhaps by exaggerating his ability to repay, but he did not physically steal the money or threaten the lender with physical harm to get it. Thus, a defaulting debtor is in the same category as a religious heretic: his behavior may irritate—indeed, infuriate—others, but it does not involve violence. It is the creditor who is initiating force in the situation by using physical punishments against a misbehaving debtor. We can see, therefore, that the historical trend against the use of force was bound to work in favor of a reduction in the physical punishments against defaulting debtors.

In the earliest times, the common punishment for an insolvent debtor was to be made the slave of the creditor. In Greece, the lawgiver Dracon put this provision in his statutes in 621 B.C., thus codifying the customary practice (and giving us the adjective *draconian* to refer to a harsh policy). In other words, the penalty for not paying a debt was the same as being captured in war: slavery. The same practice prevailed among ancient Germans, Scandinavians, and Jews.[18]

In early Rome, before 326 B.C., defaulting debtors not only could be sold into slavery to foreigners, but also could be tortured on the rack, whipped, and put in fetters.[19] The early law also gave creditors unlimited power over the body of a defaulting debtor. If a debtor owed two creditors, they might, if they pleased, cut up and divide his body.[20] This theme of creditors' having full bodily possession of the defaulting debtor is echoed in Shakespeare's *Merchant of Venice,* where the moneylender Shylock claims to be entitled to cut the heart out of the defaulting Bassanio to obtain his "pound of flesh."

The rise of empathy—as well as the debtors' threat of mass violence—gradually led to a softening of the treatment of debtors. In Greece in 594 B.C., Solon decreed freedom for all those who had become slaves for debt and forbade the enslavement of debtors henceforth.[21] In early Rome, popular outrage against a creditor's harsh treatment of a young man who had assumed responsibility for a loan contracted by his deceased father inspired the *lex Poetelia* in 326 B.C. Under this measure, a debtor could not be shackled or physically punished and was given the opportunity to work off his debt while remaining in freedom. This measure was only partially and intermittently observed, however. Hundreds of years later, in 48 B.C., we note that dictator Julius Caesar "again" forbade enslavement for debt—his earlier mandate on the subject having been largely ignored.[22] As late as the time of emperor Justinian (A.D. 527–65), we can still find cases of enslavement to a creditor in the Roman Empire.[23]

In other parts of Europe, we see this same pattern of harsh penalties gradually being made somewhat lighter. In various cities in fourteenth-century Spain, including Barcelona and Majorca, defaulting bankers were condemned to death. Barcelona's practices were particularly outrageous. The city government had demanded advances from bankers, thus leaving them without resources to pay off creditors. This pushed them into default, for which crime they were executed—by the city of Barcelona! A notable example of this outrage was the beheading of Francesco Castelló in 1360. By the end of the fifteenth century, the practice of executing defaulters had been abandoned.[24]

From late medieval times to the nineteenth century, the penalty for defaulting debtors was imprisonment at the discretion of the creditor. The system was somewhat illogical, of course, because putting the debtor in prison reduced his ability to pay off his debt. However, it was felt necessary to maintain this punishment in order to threaten debtors in general to make good on their promises. In eighteenth-century England, debtors constituted the majority of the prison population and had an extremely hard time of it. Under the system prevailing at the time, prisoners of all types were expected to pay jailers for food. Being destitute, the debtors could only beg and depend on charity for their sustenance. The debtors' ward in Exeter, a city in southwest England, was known as the "shew" because inmates let down a shoe from the jail window to beg for alms. The combination of unhealthy prison conditions and near-starvation meant that imprisonment for debt was often a death sentence for the defaulter. Toward the end of the eighteenth century, Parliament made a slight effort to alleviate the plight of debtors in prison by providing that they be given four pence a day for maintenance, but it is not clear how widely this law was applied.[25]

In the United States, a correspondingly large number of debtors were found in prison. In Boston between 1820 and 1822, 3,500 people were imprisoned for debt; this number included 500 women.[26] In Baltimore County for the year 1831, a total of 959 people were imprisoned for debt; more than half for debts under $10.[27] In 1833, it was estimated that nationwide some 75,000 persons a year were sent to jail for debt.[28]

Reform of the practice of imprisoning for debt came first in the United States, where reformers mustered legal, moral, and practical arguments against it. Their case was nicely summarized in an 1832 report of a select committee of the U.S. House of Representatives. The committee argued that it was contrary to the principles of jurisprudence "to give the creditor, in any case whatever, power over the body of his debtor." In imprisonment for debt, the committee said, "the citizen is deprived of his liberty, without the accusation of a crime, without a criminal prosecution, and without a jury to decide upon his guilt; and his punishment is submitted to the sole discretion of an individual creditor." The committee also pointed to the suffering of the debtor and his family. "If all these victims of oppression were presented to our view in one congregated mass, with all the train of wives, children, and friends, involved in the same ruin, they would exhibit a spectacle at which humanity would shudder."[29]

Even as early as 1832, American reformers had a penchant for statistics and cost-benefit analysis. The House committee presented data from Baltimore County that showed that imprisonment for debt did not pay. The 1831 figures on 959 cases of imprisonment for debt showed that only 81 inmates were discharged by paying their debts. The total amount these 81 debtors paid was only $466.06, whereas the expense of boarding them in prison was $1,400. The report also noted that the community lost 7,657 workdays by imprisoning the debtors.

These arguments were sweeping the country, and in the period 1820–40 almost all the U.S. states abandoned the practice of debt imprisonment. In Europe, where governments were more protective of the interests of creditors, reform came somewhat later. Imprisonment for debt was abolished in France in 1867, England in 1869, Belgium in 1871, Switzerland and Norway in 1874, and Italy in 1877.[30]

History's Hidden Hand

In most discussions of reforms to limit the use of force, there is a tendency to view them as historical achievements over and done with. But, in truth, the transformation is a continuing evolution. We see this in the treatment of debtors. Although we have stopped putting debtors in prison, creditors and governments still use force against them in other ways. It is still the practice to seize debtor's assets in an effort to recover the amount of an unpaid debt. Although it is a lesser application of force than imprisonment, it does represent an initiation of force in response to the peaceful, if deplorable, failure of the debtor to repay his loan. (When John buys groceries on credit and later refuses to pay for them, he has not used force. If the grocer goes to court and gets the police to seize John's car or bank account, the grocer and the police are the ones who are initiating the use of force.) One would predict, then, that the use of force to seize a debtor's assets would also be a practice in decline.

As readers familiar with bankruptcy proceedings know, this is hardly a prediction but merely a summary of the recent trend in the treatment of debtors. The bankruptcy laws, which are the legal framework for dealing with the fate of insolvent debtors, have been steadily liberalized over the past 150 years. The philosophy of bankruptcy law now is not to squeeze every possible dime from the debtor and still less to punish him for his irresponsibility. The emphasis now is on giving the debtor a "fresh start," enabling him to continue a comfortable and productive life. The debtor can declare bankruptcy under the federal code's Chapter 7, and all his subsequent earnings are exempt from all past creditors. Furthermore, many of his assets are not subject to seizure by creditors. In most states, homes and homesteads, of whatever value, cannot be seized by creditors. Many states give insolvent debtors additional protection. Texas gives bankruptcy protection to an unlimited number of motor vehicles and to many other items including books, tools, and clothing, and complete protection to retirement accounts of any amount! In the United States, more than 1.4 million people a year take advantage of bankruptcy statutes to escape their debts. For many debtors, the process is little more onerous than saying, "I'm sorry."

Many feel that liberalization has gone too far, and perhaps bankruptcy statutes will be reformed to make escaping debt slightly more difficult. But the long-run trend is plain: the use of force to recover debts and to punish debtors is diminishing.

Does this mean that our economy will collapse because creditors can no longer depend on using the force of the state to collect their debts? This is the kind of dire prediction that people have been making for the past 2,000 years at each relaxation of the treatment of debtors. But the human race makes adjustments. Although punishments for default have steadily been lessening, alternative systems for dealing with the problem of financial risk have arisen. A large and growing industry provides a wide variety of protections and services that help lenders deal with credit problems without recourse to physical force. These services include systems of credit checks, loan insurance, and, of course, credits cards. All of these techniques make it easier for us to visualize how economic life can continue even in the absence of government use of force to make debtors pay their debts.

The evolution of these alternatives illustrates the remarkable way that history often works to shed force-based practices. The people who set up the first credit card businesses never supposed that they were working to reduce the use of force in human affairs. They were not idealists or philosophers who had arrived at the insight that in order to move away from a system of forcing debtors to repay, we would need an alternative system to protect creditors. Those first credit card entrepreneurs were just trying to offer a service, trying to make a buck and go home to supper with the family. Yet the unseen hand of history made them a tool in the majestic evolution against force.

We find the same pattern in just about all uses of force that have been abandoned, from human sacrifice to religious persecution. At first, people believed that life couldn't go on without these violent practices, that civilization would "collapse" if they were set aside. Yet history did set them aside—and life went on, indeed somewhat better than before because human beings have the ingenuity to devise noncoercive approaches.

14

The Changing Face of Taxation

Most of the uses of forces examined in this book are today deplored and have been discontinued, at least in the economically developed countries. Thus, those of us who live in those countries are able to take a somewhat superior attitude toward them. If *we* had been alive in times past, we say, we would have condemned human sacrifice, the torturing of criminal suspects, the slaying of religious heretics, and so on. How—we ask in disbelief—could anyone have endorsed these practices?

This attitude of superiority blinds us to the real complexity of the evolution that operates against force-based institutions. When a coercive practice is ascendant, it is not condemned. To the contrary, it is seen as essential for the health of civilization. It is endorsed by the best citizens, and its critics, if it has any, tend to be society's deviants and outsiders. Institutions based on force are deeply rooted. To understand this point, we must go beyond the discontinued uses of force that we now condemn and take a close look at contemporary coercive practices thoroughly woven into modern institutions and widely endorsed. Perhaps the best example of such a practice is taxation.

Taxation should not be confused with taxes. Everyone today complains about *taxes,* of course—about their being too high or too complicated, or about their being applied to the wrong things or collected in the wrong way. But practically no one criticizes *taxation.* It is seen as an unpleasant practice, perhaps, but one that is vitally necessary to civilization as we know it. We are quite resigned to it as an inevitable feature of collective life, its status indicated by Benjamin Franklin's often quoted aphorism that "In this world nothing is certain but death and taxes."

Although we would like to avoid questioning taxation, history will not. Taxation, after all, is a use of force. It is government's regularized taking of resources by force and by the threat of force. By taking a close look at the ways in which taxation is being challenged, modified, and eroded, we begin to gain an understanding of the subtle evolution eroding force-based practices even while national leaders endorse them and society depends on them.

The Origins of Taxation

Taxation is almost as old as the institution of war, and a practice closely bound up with war. In ancient times, the object of war—insofar as its purpose rose above revenge and blood lust—was to extract resources from the conquered peoples. After victory was achieved, the winners set up systems to ensure the continuing delivery of wealth. Taxation was thus born as a regularized system of extracting war booty from defeated enemies. Once established, however, it became a way of extracting revenue from anyone. Rulers began to realize that the same system that brought them funds from abroad could be used against their own people, or at least against unpopular or powerless subgroups. Thus, taxation became a general system of exploitation.

The history of Rome affords a useful picture of this two-stage process where taxation is applied first to foreigners, then to locals. Up until around A.D. 300, Roman taxation was directed against conquered peoples, who were forced to pay direct taxes on land as well as numerous and frequent extraordinary taxes.[1] By modern standards, these taxes were insanely oppressive, destroying the economic life and the revenue base of the colony. In Egypt, for example, land taxes were set unreasonably high and often could not be paid, especially in times of crop failure. The penalty for nonpayment included torture and whipping.[2] One way to escape from these penalties was for the landholder to turn to moneylenders to meet his tax bill. This option, however, left him open to debt bondage, which could mean slavery for him and his family.[3] The alternative, chosen by most of the destitute farmers, was to flee the land. Naturally, there were laws to prevent even this form of tax "evasion," and they meant that, in fleeing, the landowner not only lost his land, but also automatically became an outlaw.

This process of abandoning lands impaired production and gave rise to bands of robbers and rebels, as historian M. Rostovtzeff describes:

> Taxation was oppressive, the mode of collection was brutal and unfair. . . . As early as the beginning of the second century [A.D.], and even in the first, we hear repeatedly of villagers refusing to pay taxes or to perform compulsory work and resorting to the ancient Egyptian practice of striking, that is to say, leaving the villages and taking refuge in the swamps of the Delta. Little wonder that, when an opportunity offered, the fugitives were ready to raise the banner of revolt.[4]

History punished the Romans for their cruel exploitation of colonies in a perfectly fitting way: their emperors ended up inflicting this same insane tax system on them! After around A.D. 300, the Roman government was unable to raise enough revenue from colonies and provinces to fund its bureaucracy and army, so it imposed its taxes in Italy itself. It taxed land, even when it was unproductive, forcing the landowners to abandon it and thus forcing them into outlawry because this abandonment was against the law.[5] In addition to the land and poll taxes, as well as a multitude of excise taxes, the Roman government used force to extract resources in other ways. It employed wholesale conscription of military recruits—who were threatened with death if they deserted. It routinely requisitioned, at sword point, transportation services in the form of drivers, animals, and vehicles. It requisitioned food and military supplies. It quartered troops in private dwellings. And it required production from artisans—who were forbidden by law from leaving their trade.[6]

All these oppressive measures generated hoards of outlaws, an empire "full of homeless people," as Rostovtzeff puts it, "who were tracked and persecuted by the emperor's police agents, his *frumentarii* and *stationarii*. Wandering about in desperation, they formed bands of robbers and devastated the land."[7] The holocaust of Roman taxation had a further tragedy, one caused by its system of administration. Taxes were assessed through the municipal councilmen *(curia)* of the towns and cities. These individuals were given the power to collect taxes, but they were also made personally responsible for raising the full amount. When they could not, the Roman government seized their property and punished them. Thus, they were crushed between two millstones— threatened with personal ruin, on the one hand, and forced to extract their neighbors' funds through vicious means, on the other. Naturally, this situation led to a flight from these positions (often by corruptly obtained letters of nobility that exempted them from service).[8]

Taxation in the Roman Empire thus contrived the worst of all possible worlds: it severely discouraged production; it created bands of robbers and rebels that preyed on what production remained; and it destroyed the class of civic leaders who had organized all that was admirable and constructive in community life. Not surprisingly, many historians conclude that taxation caused the decline and fall of this empire.[9]

In addition to being economically irrational, taxation in olden times involved much brutal violence. Tax collectors routinely destroyed property in the process of making their inspections and collections, and methods of punishing taxpayers were often barbaric, going beyond the ordinary penalties of whipping and slaying. In Scotland, one local ruler enforced his demand for one-fifth of fishermen's catch by a "spike torture." The defaulting taxpayer was strapped to the floor on his stomach and forced to raise his head high by the placement of a spike under his chin. If he weakened during the prolonged period of confinement and let his head drop, the spike would drive through his chin to the roof of his mouth. This penalty was perfectly legal as late as 1740.[10]

The Age of Tax Revolts

One reason why ancient tax systems were so harsh and irrational was that rulers were unmindful of their human cost. Of course, revolts occurred often, but rulers were unable to see the connection between unrest and their own wrongheaded policies. There was practically no way to communicate opinions and ideas in any complete and considered fashion. Furthermore, restrictions on freedom of expression strongly discouraged such communication. Even seeming to criticize rulers was generally met with torture, exile, or execution. In this dangerous context, people avoided offering opinions about the rights and wrongs of government actions. As a result, policies, including tax policies, were developed and continued in an intellectual vacuum. Systems that caused appalling damage went on for generations, yet the policymakers had little awareness of their harm.

In late medieval times, the barriers to public discussion began to fall, at least in the more economically advanced countries of Europe. The advent of printing in the 1400s provided a means of communication, and the growing respect for human life brought about a decline in the punishments for criticizing state policies and institutions. Once this ability to criticize developed, it began to have a profound humanizing and limiting effect on taxation. The tide of public opinion, generally in the form of demonstrations, riots, and revolts, began to resist and even to overturn injurious tax policies.

In England, this opposition was strong enough to turn back most of the government's efforts to expand the tax system. In the seventeenth and eighteenth centuries, rioting and demonstrations were commonplace, and these noisy, dangerous episodes made it seem that the country was constantly on the brink of revolution. For example, when Prime Minister Robert Walpole attempted to impose an excise tax on salt and other commodities in 1733, he triggered a broad campaign of opposition. Newspaper articles and pamphlets criticized the idea; mass meetings were held; and mobs surged through London and many provincial cities, smashing windows and setting bonfires. Walpole himself had to sneak out of the Houses of Parliament to avoid the threatening crowd. This public pressure undermined Walpole's parliamentary majority and compelled him to retract the proposed tax.[11] In 1763, the same thing happened to the new tax on cider: public criticism and rioting led to its withdrawal.[12]

In Holland in 1747, mobs demanded an end to the abusive system of tax farming by burning down the houses of the leading tax collectors. As a result, the government abolished the system.[13] The United States saw the same kind of opposition. The revolution of 1776 was, to a large degree, a tax protest—beginning with the notorious antitax riot, the Boston Tea Party. The revolution established the point that rulers imposed taxes at their peril. This lesson was reinforced in 1792, when the federal government's tax on whiskey produced a revolt in western Pennsylvania. This "Whisky Rebellion" led to the tax being repealed.

In France, there was considerable public opposition to abusive taxation, but instead of leading to reform, it led to a corrupt system of tax exemptions. The tax system in France had grown up through a series of treaties and contracts between the central government and the individual towns and regions. The result was that people in different regions paid different levels of tax on the same thing and were exempt from different taxes.[14] As tax revolts occurred—and they were as numerous in France as elsewhere—they were defused on a case-by-case basis, usually by giving exemptions or tax reductions to the group causing the problem.

By the eighteenth century, this process had produced a tax system impossible to reform. The system was abusive and inefficient for the nation as a whole, but each subgroup resisted change, fearing—with reason—that they would lose their own particular exemptions. Moreover, two influential groups, the clergy and the nobility, were exempt from virtually all taxes. The overall result was a cruel, ludicrously complicated, and widely despised tax system.

The tax on salt, for example, had become a head tax: every person (not exempt) was forced to buy a huge quantity of salt from the government monopoly at a price more than twenty times the market price. Several regions, including Brittany, Navarre, Artois, and Gex, had been legally exempt from this tax and were therefore strong supporters of it, especially because it was the basis for a lucrative trade in smuggling untaxed salt to other regions.[15]

To check smuggling, the tax agency used more than 20,000 police agents with extraordinary powers to search persons and domiciles any time of day or night and to arrest anyone suspected of salt smuggling. The punishments for salt smuggling included whipping, branding, and being consigned to galleys. Resisting the salt police was regarded as treason and punishable by the torture-death of being broken on the wheel. In 1780 in the Brittany area alone, 3,439 people were convicted of salt smuggling, including 896 women and 201 children.[16]

Economists, philosophers, playwrights, and orators criticized the burdensome French tax system throughout the eighteenth century. Even the French tax court itself called the system a "tyranny which gets worse each day."[17] Finally, the pressure for reform erupted in an explosion: the revolution of 1789. Although other grievances also lay behind the movement to overthrow the regime, complaints about the tax system were the most salient.[18] During the initial uprising, many tax offices were sacked, and mobs tore down the wall that tax officials had built in Paris to prevent the flow of untaxed goods into the city.[19] In 1790 and 1791, many of the most objectionable taxes, including the salt tax, were abolished. Later, in 1794, as the revolutionaries began taking revenge against despised leaders and institutions, they executed thirty-four top officials of the tax authority.[20] These victims included Antoine Lavoisier, the brilliant chemist, who, with incredibly poor judgment, had joined the tax agency in hopes of reforming it.

The Decline in Tax Protest

In late medieval times, tax riots, tax revolts, and revolutions kept abusive taxation in check. In effect, one use of force—taxation— was restrained by another—the threatened violence of the streets. The result, achieved by the nineteenth century in most of the economically advanced democracies, was a rather limited, relatively nonintrusive tax system. By the twentieth century, however, the balance of power between tax collectors and tax protesters had shifted. For reasons not entirely clear, tax riots and revolts disappeared. In fact, tax protest ceased entirely! While all sorts of other groups—farmers, trade unionists, shopkeepers, temperance crusaders, racial and religious bigots, and so on—employed rallies, marches, and demonstrations in order to get their way, taxpayers became utterly silent.

The decline in visible opposition to taxation meant that by the twentieth century, tax administrators and government officials began to have everything their own way. Of course, harsh, punitive practices had declined, but within modern standards of criminal prosecution and punishment tax managers were granted surprising powers. They could raise taxes as they thought fit and adopt intrusive and objectionable ways of collecting and enforcing them, without having to fear blood in the streets or even an embarrassing public demonstration. The withholding of taxes from wages is an example of the kind of measure that would have led to massive riots two centuries ago. Yet twentieth-century governments have been able to adopt this practice (the United States in 1943) without a whimper of public protest. Modern tax systems stripped away banking privacy; they were allowed to ignore many civil rights, including due process, freedom of expression, freedom from illegal searches and seizures, the right to face accusers, the presumption of innocence until proven guilty, and the right against self-incrimination. Tax officials were given the authority to set up and enforce broad systems of control and surveillance, systems that force citizens to report on their financial dealings with each other and that even pay them to spy on each other. As the twentieth century progressed, the tax burden rose, with governments extracting 40, 50, and even 60 percent of national production to fund their activities.

Political diehards, comparing the almost taxless days of the nineteenth century with the present, have regretted the demise of tax revolts, and a few toy with the notion of starting one, thinking that violence is the only way to destroy a system that, from certain points of view, has become disturbingly totalitarian. But a closer look suggests that the historical trend against taxation, although it may have paused for a generation or two, is still at work. The mechanism is no longer violent protest, however, but a process of enlightenment that is exposing the real costs of taxation.

Indiana in Bondage

To understand the modern trend, we need to begin with a simple fact that anyone since the days of the pharaohs could have noticed: namely, that taking resources by force is harmful to and resented by those who are the object of the extraction. Down through the years, rulers have tended to ignore this point. Government was seen as a noble, even divine, institution. It was like God, who, practically by definition, can do no wrong. Many rulers saw taxation as a healthy tool of social discipline, a way of forcing the lower classes to work and scrimp, to prevent their succumbing to luxury and idleness.[21] Once the era of violent tax protests ended, rulers—who had no dependable way of finding out what people were thinking except through such protest—tended to overlook the resentment taxpayers were feeling. Scholars and journalists adopted the same perspective. Because the injury of taxation was not dramatically visible, they also accepted the idea that it did no real harm.

It is difficult to pinpoint when this complacency began to break down. Some of the earliest theoretical objections to taxation were laid out by eighteenth-century economists, including the French physiocrats in the 1740s and later Adam Smith in England. But their views had slight weight in the tumultuous political affairs of earlier times. Even as late as the 1930s, the prevailing assumption was that taxation did no real economic harm. The Roosevelt administration, which dearly wanted to stimulate the economy during the depression, enacted huge tax increases, including a 700 percent increase in the effective federal tax rate and new taxes on employers and workers in the form of the Social Security tax. Economists now consider these tax increases to be part of the "incredible stream of wrongheaded, harmful policy moves" that caused and deepened the depression.[22]

It wasn't until 1953 that policymakers recognized that taxation hurts the economy and that cutting taxes would help it. In that year, economist Arthur Burns guided President Eisenhower into making small tax cuts to help stimulate an economy that was sliding into recession.[23] In the 1970s, economists began to calculate the harm that taxation does to the economy by denying workers and investors some of the fruits of their labors. Their findings vary, depending on the type of tax involved and assumptions made, but all the calculations show a large effect: to raise one dollar in taxes causes a waste of between $0.24 and $1.65 in lost production.[24] So the medieval notion that taxes are harmless has rapidly been overturned. Today, it is becoming widely understood that taxation is the enemy of production and prosperity.

In recent years, scholars have also got around to studying other costs of tax systems that had been ignored in earlier times. One of these is the private-sector compliance cost—that is, the burden of keeping records, making computations, and filling out forms. The first effort to assess this burden was made in 1964 by a Montana economics professor who sent his students home with a questionnaire for their parents to fill out regarding the time it took them to prepare their individual tax returns. In 1980, the U.S. Congress became interested in the issue, and it required the Internal Revenue Service (IRS) to commission a study of the paperwork demands of the federal tax system. The study, carried out by the accounting firm of Arthur D. Little, found that in 1985 the country was devoting a total of 5.4 billion man-hours a year to tax compliance labors.[25] This was the equivalent of the entire labor force of the state of Indiana working all year long on just this activity. A decade later, a Republican senator from Indiana made this statistic the centerpiece of his campaign to reform the tax system.

Robbing Peter to Pay . . . Peter?

The welfare state philosophy has itself promoted a shift of opinion against taxation. In earlier times, the function of the state was to provide "public goods"—that is, services the individual could not purchase for himself, especially military and police forces, and public works such as roads and bridges. In this conception, it made sense that the citizen should be forced to make a sacrifice to support the state. In modern times, the defense and public-service functions of the state have become secondary. Its primary function is now to supply personal benefits to citizens: cash and items of personal consumption such as food, housing, medical care, and education—items that people can and do purchase for themselves. This shift in function tended to undermine the logic of taxation. What sense does it make, people began to ask, for the government to take away money and then give it back?

Consider farmers. Throughout most of the twentieth century, governments favored farmers with a multitude of programs designed to put money in their pockets. But at the same time, they severely taxed farmers, taking money out of their pockets. In 1985, the U.S. Department of Agriculture calculated that American farmers were paying $13.4 billion in federal, state, and local taxes. In the same year, these farmers received $13.3 billion in government income-support subsidies.[26] The same pattern has been documented for other groups the government is trying to help. A study of minimum wage workers in Portland, Oregon, undertaken in 1994, revealed that the burden of taxes on poverty-level workers lowered their effective wage from $9,786 a year to $5,881.[27] It showed, in other words, that taxation was a major reason why poor workers are poor. Today it has become a regular practice for congressional committees to publish studies of the financial harm that taxation imposes on various groups in the population.[28]

One program that is challenged by the new fiscal awareness is Social Security. Many voters are increasingly wondering why they should pay taxes for a government retirement program when the same amount of money placed in private retirement accounts will yield a pension several times as large. Today, the mysteries about government finance are dissipating, and tax-and-spend policies are more readily seen as questionable arrangements for taking money away from people and then—after considerable waste—giving it back to them.

Taxpayers Are People Too

Governments today are oriented toward relieving suffering. Let a lawmaker hear of people being treated unfairly or even made uncomfortable for a few hours, and tomorrow morning a bill to prevent it will be introduced in the legislature. Journalists spend much of their time digging up cases involving suffering, anxiety, and violations of rights. Bureaucracies document the deprivations of their clients, and the courts are brimming with cases of individuals and groups seeking redress for slights and abuses.

What, then, is a sensitive modern government to do about taxation? Taxation is necessarily harmful and vexing. It involves taking away money that people can't spare or don't think they should have to give up. It involves intimidating systems of surveillance, cumbersome processes of accounting and supervision, and stressful conflicts over enforcement. Furthermore, tax systems are based on deliberately creating anxiety, in frightening citizens into believing that, as one tax writer puts it, "given half a chance, the IRS will wipe you out and send you to jail."[29] In the past, governments ignored this suffering. Lawmakers and judges understood that tax monies are the lifeblood of government, and they took the view that taxpayers would just have to lump whatever unpleasantness came their way.

But as modern democratic government became more sensitive, it began to notice and to try to correct the hardships of taxation. This effort became especially pronounced in the 1980s. Prior to that time, critics of the tax system were largely silenced by IRS intimidation. With various "dirty tricks" at its disposal (especially harassment audits and spurious criminal prosecutions), the IRS had the power to ruin anyone's life, and the record shows that it used this power to suppress critics of the tax system.[30] In the 1980s, IRS officials lost their zeal for protecting the tax system by all means fair and foul. The result was a flood of books and articles critical of the IRS, and a rapidly rising tide of complaints and accusations. In 1987 and 1988, congressional committees held hearings in which witnesses described how inept and abusive IRS enforcement actions had destroyed their businesses and ruined their lives. One case that drew national attention was that of Alex Council, a builder in North Carolina who had been driven to suicide in 1988 by, as he explained in his suicide note, an erroneous and abusive IRS collection effort. His wife appeared before the Senate tax committee to recount the tragic case.

The wave of criticism led to the 1988 Taxpayer's Bill of Rights. This legislation in itself did not make radical changes in IRS operations, but it marked the beginning of a change in attitude in Congress, in the courts, and in the IRS itself. Before that time, the theory of tax enforcement was to be visibly harsh, to show "the bloody body going down the street" as one IRS collection officer put it, in order to intimidate other taxpayers into complying with tax laws and obeying tax officials. After 1988, this was a politically unacceptable stance.

One significant provision of the 1988 act was banning the use of collection statistics as the basis for rating the performance of employees. In the past, superiors had evaluated collection officers in terms of how much money they recovered from taxpayers and how many harsh collection actions they took—for example, seizing taxpayer assets such as homes, cars, and businesses. In Los Angeles, to motivate collection workers, an IRS group manager put up a sign outside his office that said "Seizure Fever: Catch It!" The Senate committee was appalled by this orientation. After all, modern government is supposed to be nice to people, not deliberately heartless.

In the mid-1990s, Congress revisited the tax system, with more hearings on the harsh treatment still being meted out to taxpayers in enforcement actions. Even IRS workers came forth to expose coworkers for their antitaxpayer attitudes and practices—and these whistleblowers were given congressional protection against reprisals from IRS managers. Three more laws were passed—in 1996, 1997, and 1998—that restricted the IRS and gave taxpayers more rights. A few tax officials pointed out that these reforms would endanger the IRS's ability to collect the vast sums needed by modern government, but the measures were too politically popular to be resisted, even by die-hard supporters of the welfare state. "This is a very big freight train," said a Democratic political strategist in 1997. He advised that if any liberals in Congress or the Clinton administration tried to stand in front of it, "they're just going to get run over."[31] No one did: both houses of Congress approved the reform measures virtually unanimously, and the president quickly signed the bills.

The Real Meaning of Taxpayer "Service"

This decade of reform is having a profound effect on the orientation of the IRS, as well as on that of state and local tax collection authorities. The change is perhaps best captured by the 1998 statement of IRS commissioner Charles Rossotti that the IRS must shift its focus and "think about its job from the taxpayers' point of view."[32] One measure of the shift is the decline in harsh collection actions, such as levies and liens (a *lien* is an attachment to a property, such as a home or business, which blocks its sale, and a *levy* is an extraction of money from a paycheck or bank account). Since 1990, there has been a 65 percent decline in the number of levies and an 82 percent decline in the number of liens.[33]

Another indication of the change is the growth of installment plans for paying back taxes. In the old days, the IRS refused to allow them in all but the most unusual circumstances. The theory was that the government should have its money as soon as possible and that delinquent taxpayers should be treated severely as an example to the others. Then, during the 1980s, Congress encouraged the IRS to make installment agreements a popular option, with 1.1 million taxpayers choosing to do so in 1991, and 2.9 million in 1997.[34] One tax collection officer complained to a reporter in 1999 that the installment option was undermining tax enforcement. "If you don't want to pay your taxes today," he said, "all you have to do is say two magic words: installment agreement. You just say you want one, and even if the terms you propose are ridiculous—like $10 a week when you owe tens of thousands—collection stops while your proposal goes up and down the chain of managers."[35]

One significant clause in the 1998 legislation—section 1203—provided for the dismissal of IRS agents who commit any of ten acts of harassment or taxpayer abuse, including violating a taxpayer's constitutional or civil rights. In a highly rights-sensitive society, it was inevitable that this kind of legal protection—already granted to welfare recipients, schoolchildren, and even criminal suspects—would eventually be extended to taxpayers. But notice how it weakens tax collection. A rights-oriented system leads to additional paperwork that slows things down and greatly adds to the expense of tax collection. The idea that taxpayers have rights also inhibits collection officers when they try to crack down on delinquent taxpayers. One officer told a reporter, "With this new law, if somebody says, 'I'm not paying,' then we just say 'thank you' and leave."[36]

This is the logical outcome of a system oriented toward taxpayer "service." After all, what is "the taxpayer's point of view" when IRS agents come calling? He wishes that they would go away! As the modern state becomes more sensitive to citizens' injuries and frustrations, it grows increasingly reluctant to hound them for money. This new "compassionate" approach has become embedded in the modern tax system in scores of ways. For example, the 1988 Taxpayers' Bill of Rights created a new layer of officials in the IRS called problem resolution officers, who were given the duty of blocking a collection action that would cause "significant hardship" for the taxpayer. The IRS handbook for problem resolution officers spells out a long list of conditions—loss of housing, transportation, educational opportunities, and so forth—that are to be considered a significant hardship. At the end of the list, the manual asks the officer to gauge "significant hardship" by asking, "Is the taxpayer overwhelmed by the enormity of the tax situation he or she is in, as demonstrated by crying, despair, threat of personal harm, etc.?"[37]

At first glance, it may seem comical that tax collectors should be told to cease their efforts in the event that a taxpayer sheds tears. What kind of tax system would be left, the observer wonders, if government is going to be this sensitive about putting the screws to people? This compassionate orientation follows, however, from the welfare state philosophy. To cause despair deliberately through its own tax system is illogical for a government that is giving out money to combat despair.

This is not to say that the tax system has collapsed or will collapse tomorrow. It still moves along, putting hundreds of people in jail every year and engaging in millions of enforcement actions—a number sufficient to compel the vast majority of taxpayers to obey its dictates. The important question is, What do current trends say about the strength of the tax system in the long run?

Trends in Public Attitudes

In the final analysis, the future of taxation will depend on public opinion. In our highly democratic age, with so many public officials keenly watching polls and election results, the public has the ability to overthrow a tax system simply by not liking it! To see what the future holds, therefore, it is important to look at trends in public attitudes toward the tax system.

One might suppose that the expansion of government over the past half-century would have led to growing support for the tax system. After all, a vast and growing number of people rely on government appropriations for benefits, salaries, grants, and subsidies. Government tax monies increasingly fund a vast number of activities, from schools and hospitals to train service and symphony orchestras. It would seem to follow, therefore, that people would increasingly view the tax system as a vital, valuable institution. Although it is difficult to make conclusive statements about public opinion on any subject, the available evidence suggests that something is wrong with this theory. In spite of the growing modern dependence on tax monies, support for the tax system seems to be declining.

One indication of this trend comes from public-opinion surveys that have asked various questions about the tax system. One question, which the Gallup organization first asked during World War II, is: "Do you regard the income tax which you have to pay this year as fair?" In the four surveys taken during the war, an average of 87 percent of the respondents said, "Yes." In the two surveys taken after the war, in 1946, the proportion saying taxes were fair fell to an average of 61 percent. When the question was asked in 1997, the "yes" proportion had fallen to 51 percent; and in 1999, it was 45 percent: for the first time in the history of the poll, less than a majority agreed their tax was fair.

Another question that Gallup has used quite frequently since 1947 asks respondents whether they "consider the amount of federal income tax [they] have to pay as too high, about right, or too low?" In the eight surveys conducted in 1947–53, an average of 57.0 percent said "too high." The ten surveys conducted in 1990–99 suggest that dissatisfaction has grown somewhat: an average of 60.1 percent said their taxes were "too high."

Another poll question, one reflecting taxpayers' opinion of the IRS, indicates a more dramatic shift. Since 1983, the Roper organization has been asking respondents to express their opinion toward various government agencies. The trend in the proportion of respondents with an unfavorable opinion of the IRS, shown in figure 14.1, indicates an increase in disapproval.[38] If the trend shown in the figure continues rising at the same rate, it will mean that by around the year 2030 the entire population will have a negative view of the agency.

Recent political events indicate that challenging the tax system has a strong electoral and political appeal. Perhaps the turning point in the political standing of taxpayers was marked by the 1978 campaign for Proposition 13 in California. Prior to that time, as noted earlier, taxpayers had been rather silent as administrators and politicians tightened

Figure 14.1

Trend in Negative Rating of the IRS, 1983-98

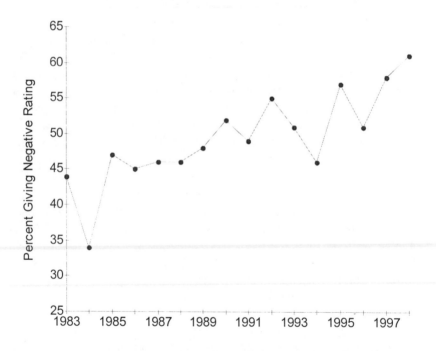

Note: Negative rating is the proportion of respondents giving "unfavorable" and "not too favorable' responses.
Source: Data courtesy of Roper Starch Worldwide.

the tax screws. The successful campaign to roll back California property taxes with Proposition 13 meant that, after more than a century and a half of silence, taxpayers were being heard as a visible, vocal political group. Since that time, tax administrators and taxpayers have waged a number of open disputes, many of them won by taxpayers with alarming—from tax administrators' viewpoint, that is—ease.

An example is the 1982–83 campaign against the withholding of interest and dividends. This withholding measure was one of the many "revenue enhancement" proposals that officials of the Reagan administration had proposed in order to extract more money, more promptly, from taxpayers. If adopted, it would have forced banks and financial institutions to withhold a portion of their customers' interest and dividend payments and send it directly to the Treasury. At the end of the year, taxpayers would have to file for a refund if the withholding had been unjustified. It resembled scores of similar "tightening" measures quietly slipped into the tax code over the preceding half-century.

But this time taxpayers did not roll over and play dead. Banks and financial institutions alerted their depositors, who contacted congressional representatives in great numbers. Once the issue had been publicized, Congress did a complete turnabout. The withholding provision, which had been passed almost unnoticed by large majorities in 1982, was overturned in 1983 by overwhelming majorities in response to the taxpayer lobbying campaign. The episode affirmed the proposition that in any open, public struggle between federal tax collectors and taxpayers, the taxpayers would win hands down. This state of affairs means that tax administrators have to be clandestine and underhanded in trying to strengthen or even maintain the tax system—not a very secure position in a democracy.

The emerging antitax climate has encouraged many politicians to be quite forward in expressing their hostility toward the tax system. An illustration is the comment that former Senate majority leader Trent Lott made in questioning IRS commissioner Charles Rossotti in 1998: "I will be honest with you. You run an agency that I don't like, and that I wish did not exist. Some call the IRS a 'necessary evil.' I know I agree with the second part of that description. I have not made my mind up about the first part."[39] Thirty years ago, anyone who publically called the government's tax collection agency "evil" would have been considered part of the lunatic fringe and probably would have been prosecuted for criminal tax evasion. Now it is a mainstream opinion.

Another straw in the wind was the 1998 House passage of the Tax Code Termination Act, a measure to abolish the entire tax code in the year 2002. The proponents did not intend to do away with taxes; they were still believers in the practice of taxation. Their theory was that setting a date for the abolition of the current system would propel the government to come up with a "better" tax system. The Washington establishment was shocked by the measure, condemning it as a danger-ous game of "Russian roulette," as one writer for the *Washington Post* put it. To a degree, it was. As such, it was a significant indicator of the trend of opinion: a majority of House members were willing to risk the collapse of the tax system! (The measure died in the Senate, so it did not become law.)

A Quiet Evolution

This review of taxation gives us a fair picture of how a force-based practice looks in its heyday. On the one hand, the practice pro-vokes a great deal of dissatisfaction and a pervasive feeling that some-thing is wrong and needs to be fixed. But, on the other, there is a virtu-ally universal belief that the practice is inevitable and necessary. We must remember, however, that people viewed religious persecution, political murder, and so forth in a similar way in their heyday: as unfortunate but vitally necessary practices.

We can also see in the story of taxation something of the con-fused and indirect process whereby a force-based practice is gradually abandoned. A coercive institution that plays a central social role is not rejected in one stroke. It weakens, it evolves, and it is displaced piece by piece by alternative, nonviolent practices. This will undoubtedly be the pattern with taxation. Congress is not going to vote to abolish taxa-tion one fine day—or if it does, it will be a largely symbolic gesture made long after taxation has ceased to be important. One can already see the main lines of this evolution in the growth of alternative methods of funding public causes, including lotteries, user fees, and philanthropic giving.

This evolution may take some time, but it is clearly coming. After all, what is this tax system that provides the funds for government's programs of social improvement? It is not an arrangement recently devised by high-minded social reformers applying rational and ethical principles. It is an oppressive scheme handed down to us by history's tyrants. It is indeed paradoxical that a system with such a disreputable background should have become the foundation of the modern welfare state. It is rather like finding a day care center set up in a medieval torture chamber. The arrangement may work for a time, but there is bound to be a growing tension between sensitive modern values and the harsh violence of the ancient technology.

So it is with taxation. The extraction of funds through force and the threat of force no longer fits in with modern values. Ethically, it clashes with our distaste for violence. Culturally, it contradicts the principle that people should be free to choose their own goals and aspirations. And politically, it transgresses the trend toward kinder, gentler government. No one is willing to face this hard truth, of course, because taxation plays such a central role in modern social and economic arrangements. But the historical drift against taxation will continue, eventually leading to the discontinuation of the practice. Then our descendants will point a finger at us and, with a grating air of superiority, ask how we could have considered this use of force to be, as Supreme Court justice Oliver Wendell Holmes put it, "the price we pay for civilization."

15

Freedom of Belief and Expression

Perhaps the most momentous development in the history of civilization has been the decline in the use of force to regulate and suppress ideas. Every advance in civilization traces, in one form or another, to new ways of thinking and doing. If century after century all new ideas had been successfully suppressed, then human beings would still remain in a savage condition.

Though it is easy for us to see how beneficial this intellectual growth has been, we generally overlook the painful side of this process. In the first place, not all new ideas are good ideas. Many have proved to be unproductive, wacky, or even horribly destructive. We can see in retrospect that if those beliefs had been suppressed, the human race would have been better off. Even ideas that are eventually judged good can cause much pain when they first emerge. People who disbelieve these ideas will be offended and scandalized. Furthermore, the advent of new beliefs is bound to threaten many people's careers and businesses. Losers in the war of ideas often pay a high price.

For these reasons, societies have traditionally practiced a great deal of intellectual repression, using force to punish the expression of deviant ideas. The regulation of thought and expression has been viewed as a necessary function of government, a duty as important as catching murderers and thieves. Even today we still hear arguments for regulating certain types of speech, and, of course, most governments still repress certain kinds of artistic and intellectual products, such as pornography. Whatever the case for regulating ideas, history's evolution against force has not heeded it. The weighty arguments for it—upholding religion, protecting public morals, defending the social order, preserving the majesty of government—in the long run have fallen before the pervasive pressure to reduce the use of force in social life.

Slaying Dreamers of Dreams

In ancient societies, the main arena of intellectual repression involved religion, a natural consequence of the central role that religion played, both politically and socially, in those times. The early chronicles of the Hebrew religion contained in the Bible are replete with episodes of religious persecution. One of the first episodes occurred, according to the book of Exodus, while the Hebrews were waiting below Mount Sinai for Moses to return with God's instructions. Some apparently became attracted by another religion and began to worship a golden calf. When Moses returned, he angrily smashed the stone tablets and ordered a massacre of those who had followed the other religion. Members of the tribe of Levi obeyed his call: "And the sons of Levi did according to the word of Moses; and there fell of the people that day about three thousand men." This bloodshed on behalf of Moses's faction earned the members of this tribe the right to become priests: "And Moses said, 'Today you have ordained yourselves for the service of the Lord'" (Exodus 32:28–29). Thus, the authority of the Hebrew priestly class was rooted not in any virtue such as wisdom or learning. Their credentials were that they had slaughtered adherents of a competing religion.

As numerous injunctions and declarations in the Old Testament confirm, this kind of slaughter was considered right and proper. For example, in the elaboration of the laws given in Deuteronomy, God, speaking through Moses, says, "If a prophet arises among you, or a dreamer of dreams . . . that prophet or that dreamer of dreams shall be put to death, because he has taught rebellion against the Lord your God . . . to make you leave the way in which the Lord your God commanded you to walk. So you shall purge the evil from the midst of you" (Deuteronomy 13:1–5).

Although doctrinal deviations represented the ultimate evil, Hebrew leaders realized that these alien ideas could gain ground only after the official religion relaxed its control of daily life and customs. Therefore, any falling off from rules of daily living was also punished by the extreme use of force. An episode described in the book of Numbers illustrates the intolerance toward even minor infractions—in this case, violating the stricture against doing work on the Sabbath:

> While the people of Israel were in the wilderness, they found a man gathering sticks on the Sabbath day. And those who found him gathering sticks brought him to Moses and Aaron, and to all the congregation. They put him in custody, because it had not been made plain what should be done to him. And the Lord said to Moses, "The man shall be put to death; all the congregation shall stone him with stones outside the camp." And all the congregation brought him outside the camp and stoned him to death with stones, as the Lord commanded Moses. (Numbers 15:32–36)

The most intolerant religions were the monotheistic ones, those that preached the existence of one true god, such as Judaism and, later, Christianity and Islam. Where polytheism prevailed, as it did in Greece and Rome, religious pluralism was more easily accommodated. The multiplicity of gods and sects prevented the development of a single priestly hierarchy that was in a position to stamp out all other beliefs. As a result, these societies had less religious persecution. But it should not be thought that the principle of freedom of religion was recognized. In Greece, although anyone was allowed to practice his own religion at home quietly, everyone was obliged to pay public respect to the gods of the town. One person who was punished for transgressing this requirement was Socrates, in 399 B.C. He was convicted of impiety ("he does not believe in the gods recognized by the city" went the charge) and forced to take poison.

The European Experience

In Europe, the main type of religious persecution was action against Christian heresies. As the Roman Catholic Church grew fat with political power in the Middle Ages, rulers and church leaders embraced doctrines that called for the violent suppression of religious deviants. Innocent III, who came to the papacy in 1198, laid out the theology of violent persecution. Heretics, he believed, were "ministers of diabolical error who are ensnaring the souls of the simple." He therefore urged bishops to "destroy all these heresies, and repel from your diocese all who are polluted by them. If necessary, you may cause the princes and people to suppress them with the sword."[1] This was his justification for inaugurating the twenty-year Albigensian Crusade, a campaign of war and massacre against the Christian Catharist heresy in Languedoc, France.

The same logic justified the papal Inquisition, which began in 1227. The Inquisition was a regularized system for identifying heretics, forcing them to confess and to testify against other heretics, and then punishing them, often by burning them at the stake. One of the common tortures of the inquisitors was to hang the accused by his wrists tied behind his back and thus gradually dislocate his shoulders. The Catholic theologians of the day defended these violent practices as necessary to save souls. Thomas Aquinas, for example, pronounced the torture and murder of the Inquisition as a necessary application of Christian "charity," born of concern for one's fellow man.[2]

The early Protestant reformers also endorsed using the force of the state to command religious obedience. In sixteenth-century Geneva, John Calvin established a tightly controlled regime that enforced a multitude of church regulations. Church attendance was compulsory; jewelry and long hair were prohibited; and tailors had to get official permission to introduce a new style of clothing. Deviations in doctrine were punished by death. Calvin had the devout Michael Servetus—his former friend—burned at the stake for espousing an unacceptable doctrine of the Trinity.

Like Aquinas, Calvin was an enthusiastic supporter of government. Its primary function, he said, is "to prevent the true religion, which is contained in the law of God, from being with impunity openly violated and polluted by public blasphemy." The function of suppressing heresy was so important to Calvin that he put those who did it—government officials—on a high pedestal: "Wherefore no man can doubt that civil authority is, in the sight of God, not only sacred and lawful, but the most sacred, and by far the most honorable, of all stations in mortal life."[3]

By the seventeenth century, the intellectual steam had gone out of doctrines of religious persecution in Europe. Most rulers began to realize that persecuting religious sects merely inflamed the civil strife that endangered their regimes. They began to see the political expediency of toleration. Many Christian leaders were also growing increasingly uneasy about using violence to enforce church doctrine. One of the most outspoken leaders of the movement for religious toleration was Roger Williams, the founder of Rhode Island. His tract, *The Bloudy Tenent of Persecution for Cause of Conscience,* written in 1644, began by noting "the blood of so many hundred thousand soules of Protestants and Papists, spilt in the Wars of present and former Ages." Williams went on to make the moral and practical case for toleration: "God requireth not an uniformity of Religion to be inacted and inforced in any civill State; which inforced uniformity (sooner or later) is the greatest occasion of civill Warre, ravishing of conscience, persecution of Christ Jesus in his servants, and of the hypocrisie and destruction of millions of souls."

Taming the Mobs

Elite opinion may have shifted against religious persecution, but this shift removed only one source of the problem. Persecution also grew out of the superstitions and hatreds of common people. More often than not, religious persecution was an act of mob violence akin to and sometimes indistinguishable from communal fighting along racial or ethnic lines. Religious and political leaders might associate themselves with this mass action, but the initiative came from the common people, folk surprisingly ready to act out their primitive hatreds by taking life and risking their own lives.

One of the earliest recorded instances of mob action in religious persecution took place in 530 B.C. The Greek philosopher Pythagoras (expounder of the well-known Pythagorean theorem) established a religion in the Italian town of Croton. Not surprisingly, his religion held that everything in the world, spiritual and material, could be explained by mathematics. At first, the doctrine was quite popular and spread to many surrounding towns. Unfortunately, the Pythagoreans identified themselves with one political faction, and when that faction fell out of power, mobs attacked and killed Pythagoreans throughout Italy.[4]

In medieval Europe, most of the persecutions of the Jews grew out of mob action. In the fourteenth century, during the time of the great plague, Jews were massacred under the suspicion that they had caused the plague by poisoning the wells. Mobs slaughtered the entire Jewish population in Brussels. In Cologne, town councilors tried to point out the folly of blaming Jews for the plague because Jews were also dying of it, but the proletarian mob ignored their logic and stormed the Jewish quarter. In Mainz, Jews defended themselves, killing two hundred of the attacking mob before being overpowered and slaughtered. Pope Clement VI denounced the hysteria (in 1348) and urged local clergy to take Jews under their protection, but his words had little effect. From Basle to Antwerp, excitable mobs rose up in violence.[5]

The religious violence that shook Europe in the sixteenth century was promoted to a large extent by mob violence. The split between Catholics and Protestants brought about by the Reformation left government authorities in a difficult position. Following the principle that religion must be enforced by the state, they first tried persecution: Catholics in power burned out-of-power Protestants, and Protestants in power slew out-of-power Catholics. Rulers eventually realized that this bloodshed inflamed tensions, and they moved toward the principle of toleration: the force of the state should not be used to uphold any religion. Unfortunately, the common people could not be made to see the wisdom of this idea. They still wanted to oppress those of a different creed.

In France, for example, by around 1560 many political and religious leaders had come to see the wisdom—or at least the necessity—of practicing a live-and-let-live approach. The government, led by Michel de L'Hopital as chancellor, announced a policy of religious toleration and lifted restrictions against the Protestant Huguenots (then approximately 20 percent of the population). But people in the towns and villages failed to honor the idea of toleration, and the previously persecuted Huguenots were perhaps the worst offenders. In areas where they were strong, mobs of them sacked and occupied Catholic churches and convents, and slew or expelled Catholic priests. In areas where the balance of power went the other way, Catholic mobs did the same to the Protestant Huguenots. In 1562, a mob of unarmed Huguenots clashed with the armed followers of a Catholic leader: twenty-three Huguenots were slain in this "Massacre of Vassy," an event that inflamed the Protestants and led directly to the First Religious War. France was to see seven more such wars in the following thirty years.[6]

In England, too, it was the mob that kept religious persecution alive long after the political elite had opted for toleration. In 1709, a demagogic High Church clergyman, Dr. Henry Sacheverell, attacked the idea of religious toleration and accused the Whig government of betraying the Church of England to an independent Protestant sect known as the Dissenters. Although the political elite considered Sacheverell's points nonsense, they felt they had to punish such a direct challenge to their governmental authority, so they put Sacheverell on trial for sedition. Mobs favoring the High Church thereafter sacked Dissenters' meeting houses in London. Perhaps the worst civil violence in London's history was the anti-Catholic rioting of 1780, when mobs rampaged for days, attacking Catholic chapels and schools. The cause of the rioting was the government's proposal to reduce the official oppression of Catholics by dropping the punishment of life imprisonment for teaching in a Catholic school. The mob violence caused subsequent governments to go slow in giving Catholics other rights.

In the United States, the first settlers copied Europe's practices of religious persecution. Though fleeing religious oppression themselves, the Puritans were quick to oppress those not of their sect. The Quakers suffered the most from this intolerance. Beginning in 1656, when the first Quakers appeared in Boston, members of this peaceful sect were whipped, branded, maimed, and pilloried. In four instances, Quakers were hung.[7] These punishments were merely an outgrowth of the Puritan leaders' broad policy of forcing religious conformity on everyone. It was, for example, against the law not to attend church.[8]

By the time of the writing of the Constitution in the late eighteenth century, practices of official persecution had faded in the United States, and the idea of religious tolerance was implanted in the nation's legal structure. The first article of the Bill of Rights (1791) declared, "Congress shall make no law respecting an establishment of religion, or prohibiting the free exercise thereof." The mobs, however, lagged behind the law. The nineteenth century saw a great deal of communal violence directed against religious minorities. Among numerous riots against Catholics in the Northeast, one included the sacking and burning of a Catholic girls' school in Charlestown, Massachusetts, in 1834.[9] New and unusual sects met considerable hostility. Mobs attacked the Shakers in Massachusetts and the Perfectionists in Vermont. The Mormons, established in 1830, moved from New York and then again from Ohio in response to hostile mobs. In Nauvoo, Illinois, a mob lynched Mormon founder Joseph Smith and his brother, prompting the migration of the sect to Utah.[10]

By the twentieth century, most antireligious mob violence had died away, a consequence of the general lessening of mob violence discussed in chapters 8 and 12. As a result, one could say that a genuine freedom of religious thought and belief was finally established, in practice as well as in legal theory. This is not to say that this freedom is complete. Small-scale criminal violence, such as vandalism and arson, still occurs against church groups. And government officials have occasionally used their powers to persecute deviant sects. One recent case involved the imprisonment of the Reverend Sun Myung Moon of the Unification Church on trumped-up charges of federal tax evasion in 1982.[11] The abuse of Moon and his church, though reprehensible, was mild, however. In an earlier day, the alarming emergence of such a seemingly threatening foreign religious movement would have touched off an inquisition or massacres. That only two men (Moon and an assistant) had to spend a few not-too-uncomfortable months in a minimum security federal prison to appease the mass—and mass media—hysteria documents the remarkably pacific tenor of our times.

Beyond the staggering bloodshed it has caused, religious persecution has left its mark on the shape of religion itself. From the time of Moses, the Western tradition of religion has been a dogmatic one, emphasizing one right way in matters of theology, worship, and church organization. This dogmatism was possible only because force could be used to uphold one religious view against others. Modern religions still tend to function in this dogmatic pattern, even though the coercive mechanisms for sustaining uniformity have passed away. Dogmatic creeds are repeated by rote, and religious texts, especially the Bible, are held up as exclusive sources of religious and moral truth.

This dogmatic orientation seems likely to fade now that we have agreed not to use force to uphold one religious tenet over another, so that religious communities are unavoidably compelled to recognize a plurality of beliefs and doctrines.

Freedom of the Press

The development of printing in the fifteenth century represented a quantum leap in humans' ability to disseminate ideas. Governments were quick to appreciate the disruptive power of printing and moved to repress it with extremely harsh punishments. One reaction was to institute a blanket prohibition, banning all printing. The Muslim world followed this practice until the nineteenth century. Other countries followed it for a time. In 1535, the French monarch, Francis I, banned all printing under penalty of death by hanging. Many countries—including Austria, Germany, France, Spain, and England—saw the execution of printers and authors. Records show that at least six English booksellers and authors were executed in 1530–33. In the Swiss canton of Zurich, seventy-four writers were sentenced to death in the period from 1500 to 1700. Their offenses included "attacks on authority" and "sneering at matrimony."[12]

Most governments eventually came to appreciate the positive value of printing and worked out ways of regulating publications. Written material was submitted to prepublication screening—that is, censorship—and those books found offensive were denied licenses for publication. One of the first of these censorship agencies was set up by the city government of Frankfort, Germany, in 1485; its first edict was to ban the printing of vernacular translations of the Bible.[13] In eighteenth-century France, some three thousand edicts were issued to regulate the censorship system. By 1789, the French government had 178 censors, saying yea or nay to what could be printed. Apparently regretting his career, the head of the French censorship office in the mid–eighteenth century wrote in his memoirs that "A man who had only read those books approved by the government, as prescribed by law, would have been almost a century behind his contemporaries."[14]

In his *Aeropagitica,* published in 1644, John Milton eloquently stated the intellectual case against censorship. His theory was that although freedom might be used to publish lies and distortions, the truth would also be free to appear, if government did not censor publications. With falsehood and truth appearing side by side, truth would win because "she needs no policies, nor strategies, nor licensings to make her victorious." In practice, however, it was not the intellectual or moral arguments that broke down censorship. Even those who preached freedom of the press were not ready to practice it whenever it served their political purposes to censor others. These inconsistent theorists included Milton himself, who, after he joined the English Puritan regime in 1649, worked to suppress publications of critics of the government.[15]

What undermined censorship, in the first instance, was an unwillingness to clamp down forcefully on illegal publications. Just because a government says something must not be printed, it does not mean that everyone will obey. There will be some individuals who, out of idealism or the desire to make money, will print and distribute unauthorized books anyway. A government has to be extremely violent in punishing transgressors—using torture and execution freely, for example—if it wants to succeed in stamping out the illegal traffic. If, being too sensitive to restraints on the use of force, it cannot act ruthlessly, then prohibitions are failures, and sooner or later rulers give them up.

This was clearly the pattern with censorship in England. By the latter half of the seventeenth century, a considerable industry of illegal publications had grown up, fostered by government's growing leniency toward violators. Instead of burning the transgressing printers, the government merely burned the offending books. Furthermore, prosecution was spotty, for the government was unwilling to establish the enormous police force that would have been necessary to track down all the illegal publishers. The result was that when Parliament abandoned the censorship and licensing system in 1695, it was, to a large degree, merely ratifying the status quo.

Other issues of a practical nature worked in favor of liberalization. The 1695 decision to drop censorship, which seems so momentous to the modern eye, was at the time almost unnoticed, hidden in legislation concerning the renewal of a number of minor measures. The debate over this issue, as the nineteenth-century British historian Thomas Babington Macaulay reported, was not about fundamental principles, not about human rights or the role of intellectual freedom in furthering civilization. Instead, members of Parliament were concerned about "petty grievances," especially the waste and delay caused by inept administration of the censorship system. One complaint was that books from abroad would mildew in storage at the London docks before the censor came to inspect and approve them. "Such were the arguments which did what Milton's *Areopagitica* had failed to do," commented Macaulay.[16]

Just two years after censorship was done away with, legislation was proposed to reinstate it, but mundane considerations, not intellectual arguments, again won the day. Those who wanted to bring back censorship had a good case. Using freedom of the press, a swindler had published false information about a financial bond issue to beat down its price. But after two years of press freedom, the terms of debate had changed. For one thing, the country had learned that religion and morality did not collapse with a free press. In fact, the legally free press was more responsible and "more prudish" (Macaulay's words) than the previously illegal and anonymous publications had been. Furthermore, the demise of censorship created vested interests. Newspapers sprang up and provided the literate classes with a source of information and entertainment. The parliamentarians themselves had come to enjoy having London newspapers to read with their morning coffee, according to

Macaulay, which made them reluctant to close down the industry.[17] So the bill to reintroduce censorship was defeated.

Most of the other European countries lagged considerably behind England in abandoning censorship, although a certain degree of de facto freedom existed long before the censorship laws were set aside. France and Norway officially dropped censorship in 1814, Belgium in 1830, Denmark in 1849. Zurich was the first canton in Switzerland to drop censorship, in 1830. By 1905, all the European democracies had rejected the idea of prior censorship and licensing.

A Movement on Many Fronts

The end of censorship was only one step in the campaign for press freedom, however, for governments still continued to engage in many actions of control and repression. In England, governments frequently carried out postpublication actions against writers and printers in the years following the abolition of censorship in 1695. For example, in 1775 a Mr. John Tooke was fined two hundred pounds and sentenced to a year in prison for criticizing the British killings at Lexington and Concord.[18] In the period 1816–34, there were 183 prosecutions for seditious and blasphemous libel, or defamation of the king and his ministers.[19]

As in the case of religious persecution, mass sentiments played an important role in continuing to restrict freedom. In early-nineteenth-century England, a number of popular associations were dedicated to prosecuting seditious libels and punishing obscene libels, including the Proclamation Society, the Society for the Suppression of Vice, and the Constitutional Association.[20] It was only after these organizations lost members and enthusiasm—after around 1830—that prosecutions of writers and printers largely ended.

Another method that governments in many European countries used to repress publications, especially newspapers, was the imposition of special taxes on them. The idea behind such taxes was to put pamphlets and newspapers out of reach of the poorer classes. In England, in 1836, three different taxes on newspapers made them four times as expensive as they would have been without tax. During this period, hundreds of publishers and news vendors were prosecuted for violating press taxes. Punitive press taxes were repealed in England in 1855, in Holland in 1869, in Germany in 1874, and in Austria in 1899.[21]

The rest of the world has followed the trend toward press freedom set in Europe, as data compiled by Freedom House show. This organization makes a yearly survey of 186 countries, rating them according to the degree of government restriction on the media. In its survey for 2002, Western Europe had the highest number of free countries, with 20 of its 21 countries rated "free" (Turkey, included in this group, was "partly free"). The area with the poorest showing was the Middle East, with only one of the 14 countries rated "free." Overall, the survey placed 75 countries in the "free" category, 50 in the "partly free" category, and 61 in the "not free" category.[22]

The evolution against the use of force to control and punish writers, printers, and publishers has been a long and complex process. Even though the trend began many centuries ago, most of the economically advanced countries did not achieve a full degree of press freedom until the twentieth century. And, of course, perfect freedom is not yet recognized anywhere. All governments claim the right to use force to suppress the publication of materials offensive to morality or public decency. As the deplorable state of public entertainment testifies, however, this power is very lightly used today, certainly in comparison with the restrictions applied in earlier times.

The breadth and depth of this evolution suggest that it is a universal pattern and that countries that today practice a considerable degree of repression will eventually move to more liberal practices. It would also appear that there is no turning back from this pattern. Even if freedom of expression endangers a cherished political or social institution, it is probably that institution, and not freedom of expression, that will have to suffer. It's a point to keep in mind as we trace out, in the next chapter, how freedom of expression has worked to undermine the prestige and credibility of government itself.

16

Government in the Age of Disrespect

In using force to restrict expression, government has suppressed critics of many kinds: critics of established religion, critics of social customs, critics of the prevailing scientific views, and so on. From a government official's point of view, however, the most annoying nonconformists are those who criticize *him,* those who challenge his authority and undermine his prestige. Aside from the desire of vain rulers to protect their reputations, there are valid political reasons for silencing critics. If criticism is allowed to build, it can set the stage for riots and even a violent revolution. Rulers concerned with maintaining domestic peace and preserving the established order have often found it wise, even imperative, to suppress those who would stir up partisan hatreds.

However great the interests of rulers and regimes in repressing dissent, these needs have not, in the long run, prevailed. The evolution against the use of force has pushed them aside, leaving governments increasingly open to criticism. In the developed countries, opposition is not just permitted, but encouraged and facilitated. The freedom to criticize rulers and oppose policies is now taken to be an essential feature of modern democratic government. Without it, say the political scientists, democracy cannot function properly. This may well be true, but it is not the complete story. It is not clear whether, in the long run, democracy can function *with* this freedom, either.

Freedom of political opposition is the last of the liberties to emerge in the West from the process of taming the social violence of medieval days. Prior to 1700, rulers in all countries reacted to overt opposition with stern measures. Criticizing rulers or demonstrating against them was generally treated as treason, an attempt to overthrow the regime by force. Therefore, such critics were readily executed—usually in horrible ways to deter others from engaging in similar acts. For example, in 1668 the apprentices of London went on a "morality riot," attacking houses of prostitution. The king's ministers saw anti-government overtones in the melee and convicted four of the riot leaders of treason. These four were hanged, drawn, and quartered. A few years later, a Nonconformist preacher who likened King Charles II to the evil Hebrew king Jeroboam was convicted of treason.[1]

In colonial Massachusetts in 1631, we find the General Court in Boston ordering that a certain Philip Ratcliffe "shall be whipped, have his ears cutt off, fined 40 pounds, and banished out of the limits of this jurisdiction, for uttering malicious and scandalous speeches against the government."[2] A few years later, in 1634, Governor John Winthrop's prestige was upheld by a similar order, which declared that "John Lee shall be whipt and fyned for speaking reproachfully of the Governor, saying hee was but a lawyer's clerk, and what understanding hadd hee more than himself."[3]

With the passage of time—in the countries moving toward a decrease in the use of force—the punishment of political critics gradually grew less severe. Governments became less willing to use the death penalty against critics, and they began to respect the judicial rights of the writers and orators they were trying to punish. This milder climate, in turn, made it possible to organize masses of people in opposition to the government when conflicts over freedom of expression arose. If governments tried to arrest and punish an upstart printer or orator, they could face a tide of sentiment reflected in newspapers, public demonstrations, and mobs. Rulers found out the hard way that once this "public opinion" had been aroused in support of a particular case of free expression, trying to silence critics was often ineffective and brought embarrassment to the rulers who attempted it.

In England, the changing climate was manifested during the notorious Sacheverell affair of 1709. In an attempt to punish a Tory clergyman—Dr. Henry Sacheverell—for making remarks hostile to the government, the government brought charges against him. His clever defense delayed the trial, giving mobs a chance to organize in his support. These mobs provided an "escort" for Sacheverell and rampaged through London on the third night of his trial. The intimidation of the mob and the unpopularity of the prosecution prompted the Whig government to let Sacheverell off with a slap on the wrist: he was barred from the pulpit for three years. He emerged from the dispute a hero, and the Whig government was overwhelmingly defeated in the election that followed.[4]

This episode represented only a first step toward establishing the freedom to criticize the government, however. Throughout the eighteenth century, British governments repeatedly arrested and imprisoned journalists for making critical observations about government policies and personnel. But when public opinion was mobilized in their defense, the journalists usually won. In 1763, government agents were sent to arrest forty-nine people associated with producing a pamphlet highly critical of King George III and his ministers. The defendants included John Wilkes, a skilled orator and popular political leader in London. At his trial, great crowds gathered at the courthouse in his defense. With a brilliant speech about "whether English liberty shall be a reality or a shadow," Wilkes achieved the dismissal of the case. He and the printers sued for and won damages for legal transgressions made during the arrests, thus further humiliating the government.[5]

A few years later, in 1771, the House of Commons tried to arrest and punish printers for publishing reports on its parliamentary debates. (Prior to that time, the House had prohibited the reporting of its debates.) Mass demonstrations formed in support of the printers, and the House, confused on legal grounds and intimidated by the mobs, let the case drop, thus establishing de facto the freedom to publish and comment on parliamentary debates.

Although Britain may have been the first country in Europe to recognize the freedom to criticize government, the real leader in this movement has been the United States. Even before it was a nation, rulers were especially reluctant to apply severe punishments against journalists, and, as a result, press freedom flourished. An early example of the pattern involved Benjamin Franklin and his elder brother James Franklin in 1722. In his Boston newspaper the *New England Courant,* James had criticized the colonial government for its ineffective effort to eliminate pirates preying on shipping outside Boston harbor. The government arrested James and put him in jail for a month. In the meantime, his brother Ben continued to put out the paper.

When James was released, he went back to his criticisms, whereupon the General Court passed an order that he must have prior approval before publishing anything. He ignored the order, was arrested, and then was sent before a grand jury to be indicted for contempt. The jury refused to indict, the case was dropped, and the government was thus denied the power of prior censorship.[6] What stands out in this episode is the lack of violence employed by government to make its will prevail. James Franklin wasn't whipped or tortured or drawn and quartered. His printing press wasn't smashed, and not a finger was laid on his brother, who continued to put out the offending publication. Many legal niceties were observed, including the use of juries of local inhabitants sympathetic to Franklin. And, finally, the governor was willing to accept defeat gracefully. Imagine the same scenario played out in an earlier age of bloodthirsty tyrants. The result would not have been a blow for freedom of the press, but simply two dead printers.

The well-known Zenger case of 1735 provides another illustration of how mildly critics were treated in America. John Peter Zenger's *New York Weekly Journal* had been attacking the royal governor, William Cosby, and his administration for favoritism and corruption. Cosby was upset and tried to get a grand jury to indict Zenger on charges of seditious libel. But Zenger and his publication were popular, and the jury refused to indict him. Then the governor had Zenger arrested for sedition. While Zenger was held in jail awaiting trial, his wife and friends continued to put out the *Journal,* building up popular support. Cosby was furious, but was unwilling to attempt drastic measures to suppress the paper. When the trial was held, the courtroom was packed with Zenger's supporters, who cheered when the jury acquitted him. The presiding judge could have overruled the decision to acquit, but, intimidated by the crowd, he let the decision stand.[7]

The Zenger trial set an interesting precedent on permissible criticism of government. Up until that time, law and constitutional theory held that any comment or report that fostered "an ill opinion of the government" was criminally libelous. This definition included even perfectly correct observations, such as a true statement that a governor had taken a bribe. Indeed, a factually based criticism was especially deserving of punishment because people were more likely to believe it and act on the basis of it—that is, to rise up in revolt against the government. Following this logic, the prosecutor at the Zenger trial asserted that the truth of Zenger's criticisms only aggravated his crime. Zenger's defense lawyer disagreed and argued that Zenger's writings could not be considered seditious if they were factually correct. The judge ruled this argument to be out of order, but the jury heard it and acted on it. In this way, the principle was established that a person could criticize government in the United States if what he or she said was factually correct. (The same point wasn't accepted in England until nearly a century later.)[8]

The Zenger case marks but one step in the long evolution of the freedom to criticize government and its officials. It is a history of progress and reverses, including many efforts at repression, some of which were temporarily successful. But the overall trend has clearly been toward a decline in government's ability to use force against its critics. This evolution continues in our own time. For example, in 1964 the country saw an interesting echo of the Zenger case in the Supreme Court's decision in a lawsuit brought against the *New York Times* by the city of Montgomery, Alabama. During the civil rights disturbances in Montgomery in 1960, the *Times* had published a full-page advertisement, paid for by the civil rights lobby, which protested a "wave of terror" in Montgomery and made certain false and inflammatory allegations about how the city police had mistreated protesters. For example, it falsely said that the police had padlocked the dining hall at a local black college with the aim of starving the students by keeping them from getting their meals. The city of Montgomery, in the person of its commissioner of public affairs, L. B. Sullivan, sued the *Times* for libel. The Supreme Court found against Sullivan, concluding that public officials did not have the right to sue for libel even when the accusations against them were untrue and recklessly made.[9] As a result, journalists now have the freedom to say derogatory things about government officials whether they are true or false.

When Children Ridicule Rulers

The erosion of government's ability to repress critics is more than an interesting instance of the general decline in the use of force. It has important political implications. It may indeed be true that a functioning democracy needs to allow the freedom to criticize government, but there is a drawback to this freedom that few commentators have paused to notice. *Criticism lowers respect for public officials and the political process.* As it becomes increasingly safe to complain about rulers and to point out flaws in their policies, the volume of antigovernment criticism grows, giving the public an increasingly cynical view of government. We have now entered the age of disrespect, an era when people roll their eyes when you ask them what they think of their rulers.

Several years ago in my hometown of Sandpoint, Idaho, an episode occurred that illustrates the vulnerable condition of government today. A volunteer group called the Sandpoint Mural Society, to which I belonged, was promoting the painting of a landscape mural on a downtown building. After we had obtained the approval and support of the building's owner, chosen the artists, and raised the money, we found our project blocked by city hall. The members of the town's planning commission briefly considered our project in a closed meeting one night and decided to ban all murals, including ours, from the town.

What happened next was so typical of modern political life that it hardly merits reporting, but by the standards of centuries ago it was astonishing. At the time this dispute took place, I was reading sixteenth-century English history, keeping a close eye on the uses of force practiced in those days. I was particularly struck by the case of John Stubbs, a Puritan journalist who had written a pamphlet arguing that it would be inadvisable for Queen Elizabeth to contract a marriage with the French prince Alençon. Stubbs thought this marriage would shift the loyalty of the crown toward the Catholic Church. For daring to give public advice to the monarch, Stubbs had his right hand cut off by the executioner—before an eager crowd that had gathered to watch the gristly spectacle.

Perhaps even more appalling, after the deed was done, Stubbs is reported to have raised the bloody stump of his arm and cried, "Long live the Queen!" Today, we wonder what could have motivated him to make that remark; to our way of thinking, the natural response in the circumstances would be to utter a curse. In order to make sense of his salute to the queen, we need to understand the context of the times.

This bloody punishment was not an accident, a deplorable departure from the way the institutions of government operated. In the days of Queen Elizabeth, official violence was everywhere. The mutilation or execution of critics and detractors was government's stock in trade—and the practice was universally accepted. Remember, Elizabeth's father was Henry VIII, most famous for getting rid of two of his six wives—Anne Boleyn and Catherine Howard—by chopping off their heads. It is less well known that Henry butchered many other people in his paranoiac anger, from loyal subordinates such as Thomas Cromwell to scores of innocent noblemen—adults and children—who in some distant way might be heirs to the crown.

Against this backdrop of ready violence, anyone who had his hand chopped off for criticizing a queen was getting off lightly. A day later, Elizabeth and her ministers might have changed their minds and wanted John Stubbs's head. It was to dissuade them from such a change of heart, I suspect, that Stubbs was prompted to announce his loyalty to the vicious government that cut off his writing hand.

This glimpse of politics in yesteryear puts the battle of the Sandpoint Mural Society in perspective. In broad outlines, the conflict paralleled the Stubbs episode: citizens were making a challenge to government authority. But this was America of the 1990s, where no one takes no for an answer. Our group protested the commission's decision and demanded a rehearing. The local newspaper interviewed us and reported our side of the dispute. Well-wishers wrote letters to the editor supporting our position. One of the local art teachers brought the issue to the attention of her eighth-grade students, who wrote letters to the planning commission criticizing the decision and urging it to allow the mural. The packet of charming, handwritten letters eventually came into my hands. "Dear City Planning Commission," began one, "I think you should let them do whatever they want to do to their building."

Another said, "Dear City Planning Commission, I think what you are saying is really dumb."

How far we have come! Four hundred years ago, an adult who published a considered opinion questioning a state decision had his hand cut off and was forced to plead for his neck. Today, children criticize government officials to their faces without the slightest trace of fear.

This difference in openness has an enormous effect on how government operates, of course, and the mural society conflict bears this out. As a result of the public agitation against the planning commission, another hearing was held. It was an open hearing this time, and we were able to make a full presentation of our case. Moved by our arguments and feeling the personal pressure of our supporters in the council chambers, the commission reversed itself and voted unanimously to approve the mural!

The first reaction we may have to this outcome is one of pride. The bad old days were indeed bad, we say. Thank goodness we're more civilized; thank goodness we respect freedom of expression. However, consider the implications of this episode for the prestige of the commissioners and the city government they represented, They lost from every point of view. First, they angered a group of citizens by blocking their project. Then they were publicly criticized for having "wrong" ideas. Then they reversed themselves, publicly demonstrating that they didn't know what they were doing in the first place.

Could this disgrace have been avoided by having better commissioners? I doubt it. The Sandpoint commissioners were upstanding, well-intentioned local citizens. In intellect and character, they were probably above the average of the inhabitants of the area. No, the muddle can't be blamed on shortcomings in personnel. The problem is, first, that commissioners are wielding the coercive power of government—which is bound to anger the citizens against whom it is used. Second, the commissioners are overloaded with too many complex decisions. They can't possibly look into all the dozens of land-use issues that come before them each year. They don't have time to listen to the hundreds of people with opinions on each of these cases or make detailed studies about the long-run implications of each possible decision.

The result is that inevitably they make superficial decisions, decisions that often are revealed later as shallow and have to be reversed when more facts and opinions are included.

You can't fix either of these problems with political reforms. If you do away with government's use of force, you haven't got government. The planning commission would become some kind of civic advisory body that could influence landowners only through persuasion and moral power. And if you try to subdivide authority to make it possible for policymakers to know what they are doing, then you lose the main selling point of government—namely, its ability to function as an overarching authority. If people on every block have their own neighborhood planning commission, then there can't be an overall land-use policy for the entire town.

So government is imbued with fatal flaws—flaws that characterize even the smallest units. Sandpoint is a village of four thousand, and yet there is considerable resentment against local officials. Time and again, city fathers and mothers have made questionable decisions. Time and again, they sought to use official force—fines, taxing power, police, jails—to "cram their decisions down our throats," as opponents put it. Sometimes those who protest these decisions are successful in having them overturned, sometimes they are not. But win or lose, the protest and criticism cost government in terms of prestige and credibility. The result is that most people are cynical about this small town's government. During the mural dispute, one of the leaders of the local Lions Club, a group active in local volunteer projects, commiserated with me. "We get that kind of obstructionism from the city all the time," he confided. I even received a personal note from one of the city's own employees congratulating the Mural Society. "See, you *can* beat city hall!" she wrote.

To understand the malaise of modern government, we need to look beyond the imperfections of its personnel and the flaws in its operations. They always have been a part of government. What is new is the robustness and openness of the system of complaint, as government loses the power to intimidate its detractors.

Sex and Lies

One reason we have tended to overlook this corrosive pattern of political criticism is that it did not appear particularly troublesome in earlier times. Democracies thrived for many years while allowing freedom of expression, so it seemed that government could withstand criticism. This supposition, it is now beginning to appear, was premature. When it first emerges, democratic government benefits from a lag in attitudes. The restrictive practices and the patterns of deference established in more repressive times will persist, limiting the depth and intensity of the opposition. The corrosive criticism that is the natural condition in a fully developed democracy is held back by the shadow cast by the sword of earlier times. Only generations later, when that shadow fades, is the full impact of freedom felt.

Consider, for example, the quite remarkable immunity that the press used to give politicians concerning personal vices. It was an unwritten rule for major publications not to report political leaders' scandalous personal behavior—such as alcohol and drug abuse or promiscuous sexual behavior—even when it was thoroughly documented. Thus, the voting public was never allowed to suspect that its admired lawmakers were incorrigible drunks or deplorable womanizers. Only in recent times has this taboo been broken down, in both the United States and most other developed democracies. In the United States, the floodgates opened in 1987, when newspapers published pictures of Democratic presidential candidate Gary Hart relaxing with his mistress on a yacht in Bimini, while his wife languished nobly at home in Colorado. The publicity immediately destroyed his candidacy. Since that time, politicians have developed greater staying power against public revelations of their deplorable personal behavior, but the political class has not benefited from this stubbornness. The public has simply accepted the fact that it has a low caliber of rulers. When the defense of a president's bald-faced lying is the observation that "they all do it," surely the enterprise of government is on shaky ground.

One factor that accounts for the flowering of the freedom to criticize politicians is the development of open, impersonal systems of justice and administration. Until quite recent times, lawmakers and administrators were above the law, despite what democratic constitutional theory said. They held secret meetings, they kept information to themselves, and they manipulated agencies of law enforcement, taxation, and regulation to protect their reputations and careers. They were able, in many cases, to intimidate reporters, publishers, and scholars who might reveal their transgressions or scandals in the programs and agencies they headed. This process of intimidation and cover-up took place at all levels of government—local, state, and federal.

In just the past few decades, however, the biased and sometimes corrupt systems that protected government officials and their programs from public scrutiny have been dramatically dismantled. The Freedom of Information Act, now the fulcrum of many exposés, was passed in 1966, but it did not become effective until amendments approved in 1974 and 1976. In 1970, Congress adopted open meeting regulations that required policymaking to take place in public view, and these regulations spread to state and local governments thereafter. Another recent development is the idea that government employees who reveal scandals and corruption in their agency deserve protection. The first whistleblower protection statute was approved in 1989. Of course, it is not yet fully effective, but it represents a considerable improvement in the freedom to criticize. In earlier times, employees who revealed embarrassing truths about their agencies and programs were not just harassed or fired. They could even be jailed under trumped up criminal charges arranged with complaisant prosecutors.

Another aspect of the new impartiality has been the use of the judicial apparatus against top officials. In olden times, the police and the courts worked for the ruling class. People spoke of "the king's justice," meaning the apparatus the king deployed *against* his enemies and enemies of his realm. The idea that this institution should be turned against the king was unthinkable. In modern times, it has become not just thinkable, but routine. The judiciary and agencies of law enforcement are becoming increasingly independent of lawmakers and administrators, and are exposing their failings with shocking regularity. An early example of this development was the Federal Bureau of Investigation (FBI) sting operation mounted against members of the

Congress in 1979. Being aware that members of Congress were taking payoffs, FBI officials devised a scheme to trap the worst offenders. An FBI agent posing as an alien needing citizenship clearance gave the lawmakers $50,000 to see whether they would quietly take it or right-eously refuse it. Eight of the legislators approached took the cash and were prosecuted for bribery.

Another illustration of the new independence and assertiveness of the judicial branch has been the Independent Counsel Act, passed in 1978. This act provided for the creation of investigators with sweeping powers to investigate wrongdoings of presidents and other high ad-ministration officials. The twenty investigations conducted under the act have dug up acres of dirt about the executive branch, including the Iran-Contra, Whitewater, and Monica Lewinsky scandals. It has been true dirt, information the American people are entitled to know about their highest officials, but its release has inevitably lowered the prestige of presidents and the presidency. Although the Independent Counsel Act was allowed to expire in 1999, it seems clear that similar mecha-nisms for investigating top officials will still be available. The country will no longer allow its highest leaders to remain above the law.

Another change that brings politicians into disrepute is the de-velopment of modern media. A century ago, barriers in communication and transportation meant that few citizens had any direct contact with high national officials. To them, presidents and senators were abstrac-tions. Therefore, the public could have a rosy, or at least neutral, view of them. Today, everyone sees politicians on the glass screens in their living rooms. Unfortunately, what they see is not at all appealing. In order to avoid giving offense and damaging their electoral prospects, politicians adopt an evasive style. They dodge embarrassing questions. They pretend to take stands, but avoid really doing so. They make promises they can't keep or don't intend to keep, and they change posi-tions to curry favor with different constituencies. This behavior is probably compelled by the logic of the mass-popularity contests that elections have become, but regardless of its cause, it is unflattering to the politicians involved.

The Declining Trust in Government

The newfound freedom to criticize government and government officials is not a politically neutral development. The growth of criticism has the obvious effect of causing a remarkable—and, for some observers, worrisome—decline in popular confidence in government. Opinion poll data reveal that today the distrust of government is higher than at any time since polling began. In the late 1950s, polls showed that more than three-quarters of Americans looked to the federal government "to do what is right all or most of the time." Today, only approximately one-quarter will give this answer.[10] Responses to another question about the perceived honesty of public officials indicate the same trend. When people were asked in 1958 how many "of the people running government are crooked," only 24 percent said "quite a few." By 1994, a majority, 51 percent, said that "quite a few" of the people running government were crooked.[11]

Another sign of declining enthusiasm is falling participation in elections. In overall terms, voter turnout is a function of two factors: (1) the restrictions and limitations on registering and voting, and (2) the voters' level of interest and commitment. Over the past two centuries, the restrictions on voting have steadily been relaxed: more people have been permitted to vote, and it has become increasingly easier to register and vote. As a result of this trend, the proportion of the adult population participating in elections increased—until around 1960. Then, even though additional reforms have made voting still easier, the proportion of adults turning out to vote has trended downward: an obvious sign that voters have become increasingly distanced from the political process.

In U.S. presidential elections, the peak was reached in 1960, when 63 percent of the adult population (population age eighteen and older) voted. This figure has fallen to approximately 50 percent in recent elections. In the 1996 election, for example, the figure hit a new low of 48.8 percent. The same pattern is seen in congressional off-year elections. The relaxation of restrictions on voting led to increased participation, until it reached a high of 45 percent in 1966. Since that time, this figure has declined, falling to a low of 32.9 percent in the 1998 off-year elections. The decline in primary elections, where the nominations of party candidates are made, has been even steeper. Half a century ago, more than 50 percent of the adult population voted in primaries. Today, that figure is approaching the vanishing point: in the 1998 primary elections, only 17.4 percent voted—another record-breaking low.[12] These numbers mean that, in one sense, we do not have a democracy in this country any longer. A majority of citizens are not even participating in, let alone endorsing, the selection of government officials.

This pattern of declining approval is not unique to the United States. It appears to be the general condition of mature democratic government. The European democracies used to pride themselves on their high voter turnout in elections, which was said to demonstrate the high level of support that citizens had for their regimes. Under this interpretation, support is declining, for voter turnout has been going down in these countries in recent years.[13] Public-opinion surveys from a number of democracies show a pattern of declining confidence in political institutions.[14] A good illustration is Sweden. From a distance, Sweden would appear to be a well-governed country with a broad cradle-to-grave welfare system, a system that goes further than any in the world to banish worry and suffering. One would assume, therefore, that the Swedes would be grateful to the politicians who have brought about this achievement. The opposite proves to be the case. Data from opinion polls beginning in 1968 show that, as one Swedish political scientist reported, "trust in politicians has been plummeting more or less constantly for the past thirty years in Sweden."[15]

It is difficult to imagine any solution to the increasing negativity. The problem does not seem amenable to political reforms. The past half-century has seen the passage of numerous reforms designed to check corruption and restore citizen confidence in political leadership, including sunshine laws, sunset laws, and campaign finance reforms: they obviously haven't reversed the slide in opinion. The political class might attempt to restore its credit by reimposing some form of censorship, thereby suppressing critical comment. But there is great doubt whether it could succeed in this course for long, even if it had the desire to. The evidence, spanning several hundred years and scores of countries, strongly indicates that the freedom to criticize government has become an ingrained feature of modern civilization. It seems likely, therefore, that criticism of government and the resulting cynicism about rulers will continue.

Is "None of the Above" the Politician of the Future?

No one quite knows what to make of the striking decline in public support for government and government officials in the Western democracies. In some ways, it doesn't seem particularly alarming, for in this more pacific and contented age, the political alienation is not leading to violent movements of rebellion or revolution. But from the standpoint of constitutional theory, it is deeply unsettling. The justification for the vast and intrusive apparatus of coercion known as the welfare state is that the populace wants it. Indeed, that is the only available justification today, for rulers can no longer say (even if they still believe it) that they know what is best for us and are entitled to impose it on us against our will. As the evidence increasingly pours in from opinion polls and the ballot box that the public is skeptical about the modern political system, it leaves the enterprise of big government without a coherent rationale.

In recent years, some pundits have suggested, half-jokingly, that printed ballots should include, in addition to the names of the candidates, the option "none of the above." At first glance, this proposal doesn't seem radical. Indeed, it is consistent with democratic theory. However, if you suggest this idea to any member of the political class, you will get a surprisingly hostile reaction. At root, the anxiety comes from the suspicion that "none of the above" might win! Such an outcome would have devastating moral implications for democratic government. A victory of "none of the above" would reveal that the candidate who got the most votes could not be said to represent "the will of the people." If he took office, he would be in a weak and embarrassing position. If he did not take office and the election were held again with new candidates—the logical way to proceed following democratic theory—the result might be even more distressing: "none of the above" might win again—and again! In this way, the voting public would end up crippling government by denying it personnel.

Because of this worrisome possibility, it is unlikely that politicians will adopt this particular election reform. We no doubt shall go on using elections that make voters choose between candidates, even undesirable ones, thus maintaining the pretense that the victors have public support. But in the long run, growing apathy and political dissatisfaction seem bound to have an effect, in one form or another, in undermining government's vitality, scope, and importance.

17
Swimming in History's Tide:
Lessons for Voluntarists

The study of history is generally thought to be a restful under-taking, one that removes the student from the troubles of the day and immerses him safely in the dead past. Armies march to and fro, but only in the mind's eye, not into our living rooms. A study of the history of force, however, does not afford this degree of detachment. The examination of the violent practices of the past reveals a trend, and a trend is a living, moving thing. It is a finger pointing at historians and their generation, challenging them to declare their loyalties and to announce their intentions.

On this subject, however, our loyalties are divided and our intentions confused. On the one hand, we know that for thousands of years, humankind has been struggling to emancipate itself from the curse of force. And we know that it has been succeeding, with coercive practices being gradually abandoned century by century. Our attitudes and values on the subject are also changing: we are becoming increasingly skeptical about force. Few people today would boldly proclaim, "Force is a sound and proper basis for human institutions." We know that the path of the future and of future achievement lies in moving away from the use of force.

But we also notice many ways that force is still widely used. Judging from some of our practices, we do indeed appear to believe that force is a sound and proper basis for human institutions. The modern welfare state with all its taxation and regulation utterly depends on it.

The upshot is that we are uncertain how to proceed. It is unrealistic, and in some instances counterproductive, to strive to eliminate all use of force. Those who adopt this stance will be viewed as irresponsible cranks. Yet it is also unrealistic to embrace the use of force as a fixed and necessary element of civilization. This stance ignores the real and powerful historical trend against force. The human race is indeed turning away from the use of force, and this movement has accelerated in modern times. Those who say that coercive practices such as war or taxation are an immutable part of the human condition are going to be as wrong as past observers who said the same thing about slavery, dueling, or religious persecution.

We need a middle position, then, one that accomodates force-based institutions in the current stage of social evolution, but also recognizes the historical trend away from them. I have taken to calling this position *voluntarism.* Voluntarism holds that all uses of force, even those that seem most necessary and unavoidable today, are slated for eventual displacement. Therefore, none should be clung to as inevitable or indispensable. Yet the elimination of force-based institutions is an achievement that lies largely over the horizon, beyond our ability to accomplish in our generation. To some degree, it is beyond our ability even to imagine how many of today's coercive practices will be displaced. It will be up to history, subtly altering attitudes and institutions, to take uses of force that today seem essential and turn them into practices that are considered unthinkable. Because this alteration has already happened in many, many instances, we can be rather confident that it will continue to happen.

Voluntarists, then, do not strive to make history or to change the course of history. Theirs is the more modest project of trying to place themselves on history's side, finding ways to support the evolution against force in the context of their time and place. This is by no means an easy assignment because history does not follow a simple linear path. Sometimes the attempt to eliminate a use of force produces a backlash that prolongs that use of force. One thinks, for example, of the 1960s attempt by the U.S. judicial establishment to eliminate capital punishment before the public was ready for the change. In contriving the demise of coercive practices, history has been amazingly subtle and indirect. As we contemplate joining with this evolution, then, we need to appreciate the complexity of the task.

The Limits of Nonviolence

The first issue that reformers need to face is the problem of violent aggressors. Down through the years, many idealists have preached the doctrine of nonviolence, but none of them have come up with a satisfactory answer to the problem of aggressors. A good example of this failing is seen in the case of Leo Tolstoy, the great Russian philosopher and novelist. Tolstoy analyzed the ills of the czarist regime and found, at bottom, that they stemmed from its reliance on physical coercion. In *The Kingdom of God Is Within You,* written in 1899, he condemned the many uses of force prevalent in his day, including wars of conquest, military conscription, taxation, the violent punishment of criminals, the flogging of peasants, the expropriation of lands, persecution to uphold the Russian Orthodox Church, and state censorship of reformist writings (including his own). He eloquently argued that government's use of force impeded progress: "Violence, which men regard as an instrument for the support of Christian life, on the contrary, prevents the social system from reaching its full and perfect development." He believed that under the influence of a public opinion inspired by Christian teachings, "violence is diminishing and clearly tending to disappear." Tolstoy's solution for hastening the day of nonviolence was to implement the principle of Christian love and follow the commandment to "resist not evil by violence."[1]

Although appealing at first glance, the idea of rejecting all use of force proves to be untenable because it does not address the problem of violent aggressors. Even if the principle of nonviolence were widely accepted, there are bound to be some people disposed to employ force to accomplish their ends. If you refuse to use force to resist them, two bad consequences follow. First, the aggressors accomplish their ends, demonstrating that force is an effective tactic—and thereby making it more appealing. Second, they may well overrun and destroy *you,* the advocate of nonviolence. This is more than a theoretical possibility. As shown in the review of the history of war and conquest (chapter 6), societies less prone to use force than their neighbors often were overrun, and their more peaceful philosophies obliterated.

What is true among nations also applies to individuals. Advocates of strict nonviolence have never had a solution to the problem of violent crime. Tolstoy, in making the argument that government's use of force wasn't necessary, simply denied the existence of violent aggressors:

> Who are these evil men from whose violence and attacks the government and the army saves us? If such men existed three or four centuries ago, when men prided themselves on their military skill and strength of arm, when a man proved his valor by killing his fellow-men, we find none such at the present time. Men of our time neither use nor carry weapons, and, believing in the precepts of humanity and pity for their neighbors, they are desirous for peace and a quiet life as we are ourselves. Hence this extraordinary class of marauders, against whom the State might defend us, no longer exists.[2]

As my review of homicide (chapter 12) suggested, Tolstoy was probably right in thinking that the proportion of violent individuals is gradually declining over time, but it is unrealistic to expect that violent aggressors would ever entirely disappear. The problem of individual violence will always be with us in some degree as long as human beings have free will and the ability to act physically against others.

Most people are fearful about violent aggressors. It seems obvious to them that force has to be used to deter and restrain them, and they will not listen to any philosophy that suggests that they are to submit to being killed in their beds until murderers tire of the sport. This is probably why Tolstoy's views on nonviolence—farsighted and sound in so many ways—have been ignored.

But if we say that the use of force against aggressors is acceptable and necessary, how far should this idea extend? The danger—and history has seen countless examples—is that in response to the threat of aggression, one becomes an aggressor. To meet the dangers of foreign attack, one builds up armaments that threaten opponents. Or a nation may start a preemptive war, attacking another country to upstage a possible attack on itself. The same problem arises domestically. To counter violent criminals, the police are given authority to use force energetically and end up behaving like criminals themselves. In an effort to check crime, draconian punishments are adopted, punishments that brutalize society and provoke retaliation. The policy of matching threat for threat and violence for violence can lead to a continuation, even an escalation, of violence. So it does not reduce the use of force in the world.

There is no simple solution to this difficult dilemma. However, one useful perspective in grappling with it is the *principle of moderated response:* aggression should be met with a response, but with less force than the original provocation. According to this principle, the proper treatment of an aggressor is neither to try to get even following the idea of "an eye for an eye," nor to turn the other cheek, ignoring the aggression altogether. Instead, the rule should be something like "half an eye for an eye." This approach may calm a possible action-reaction cycle and lead the way to a less violent world.

The principle of moderated response is no more than a general perspective. It does not decree any particular policy for responding to the aggressive use of force in specific cases. About the only thing one can say for certain is that, paradoxical as it seems, the goal of reducing the use of force cannot be achieved by applying the principle of never using force!

Who Is to Blame for Force?

When force is used to check violent aggressors, it may be called a *reactive* use of force. The aggressor is the one who initiates the use of force, and agents of society are only reacting to this initiative. This reactive force is not the only socially approved use of force, however. Societies also undertake the *assertive* use of force. That is, they initiate force against peaceful individuals in order to try to solve social or economic problems or as a way of punishing behavior that, though not violent, is considered undesirable.

For example, in bygone days, a person who disagreed with a

tenet of the official religion was not being violent in his disbelief. He was not striking anyone or breaking into houses or blowing up buildings. He simply declined to make certain religious declarations—for example, that God consisted of a trinity of Father, Son, and Holy Ghost. But because this refusal to endorse the prevailing doctrine was offensive, government officials would initiate force against him to discourage other people from doing the same thing. Burning people at the stake for their religious beliefs is an example of the assertive use of force.

Today we have moved beyond persecution for religious beliefs, but the general practice of initiating force to address social problems still persists. In thousands of ways, governments initiate force against peaceful individuals to punish them for nonviolent actions that are considered wrong and even to punish them for inactions—that is, for failing to do what the government expected them to do. A person who fails to buckle his automobile safety belt, for example, is not in any sense an aggressor. But he may end up in jail for failing to do it. Taxation is another example of the assertive use of force: government agents initiate force or the threat of force to compel peaceful individuals to give up their money.

Most people endorse this idea of using force assertively in order to improve behavior and accomplish social goals. Many embrace it wholeheartedly, and many others, although not enthusiastic, are resigned to it as an inevitable feature of society. The voluntarist would not be content with the practice, however, and would seek to move society away from it.

One is at first tempted to assume that because government applies the assertive use of force, government is the cause of the problem. All the regulation and other intrusions, one might say, are the doing of arrogant kings and ambitious senators who, throughout history, have sought to impose their wishes on the rest of the world. To check the assertive use of force we just need to reign in government officials. A closer look reveals, however, that the pressure for regulation is much more broadly based.

We see the pattern in religious persecution. Governments did not invent the idea of using force against religious deviants. The practice generally started with ordinary people who were scandalized and frightened by the alien religion. They formed mobs that attacked and killed the deviants and destroyed their places of worship. From the persecution of the Pythagoreans in the sixth century B.C. to French persecution of Huguenots in the seventeenth century to English persecution of Catholics in the eighteenth century: in each case, intolerant mobs initiated the violence. A government that attempted to practice religious tolerance would have placed itself in peril. To survive, government officials had to go along with popular demands and formalize the policy of persecution.

Another illustration of the same point is the regulation of markets. For thousands of years, governments around the world have attempted to set the prices and control supplies of basic foodstuffs, especially grain and bread. This regulation involves an assertive use of force. When a farmer brings a sack of grain to market and sells it for a certain price, he has not used force against anyone. He is engaging in a voluntary transaction with the buyer. If a government official fines him or puts him in jail because this price is different than the set price, it is the official who is initiating the use of force. The reformer would say, Why not ask government officials to avoid this practice?

But rulers did not take up regulation because they were bored and needed something to do. In most cases, government officials were responding to and attempting to deflect the violence that members of the public were prepared to employ. In earlier times, mass violence in connection with food supplies was common. Crop failures or disruptions in transportation created a shortage of grain. The shortage drove prices up and made it difficult for many people to afford food. Aggrieved consumers formed mobs that attacked stores and warehouses and seized grain. The violence put the government in a difficult situation. If it did nothing, mob action would probably escalate. The rioting might even touch off a destructive civil war—as bread riots did, in fact, spark the French Revolution. Seeing this danger, rulers stepped in to regulate the price of foodstuffs. They sometimes even seized and distributed the stockpiles held by farmers and merchants. In this way, the government defused the riots. In such a situation, it's no good telling rulers that "force is wrong," and it doesn't help to point out that these measures of regulation will aggravate the food shortage. If government fails to act when there are riots in the streets, the violence will escalate. A hands-off policy would be likely to lead to more bloodshed, a result that both rulers and philosophers of peace want to avoid.

The fact is most people are prepared to use force or willing to countenance the use of force to implement their anger, their intolerance, or their selfishness. Government's force-based systems of subsidy and regulation are for the most part merely a reflection of this human reality. Take the case of tariffs, a policy condemned by so many economic theorists as inimical to prosperity. Policies developed to restrict imports did not begin with theory. They had their roots in the violence of the workers whose products were being displaced by imports. Through riots and attacks on ships and barges, workers imposed de facto import prohibitions. To calm the violent scene, government legislated various types of import restrictions. Often, the violence of workers was quite personal. In London in the early eighteenth century, rioting silk weavers roamed the streets attacking women who were wearing Indian calico dresses, stripping the garments off them. A government law limiting the importation of calicoes calmed the disturbances.

Today, all countries have some type of progressive taxation— that is, a system that purports to take from the rich in order to give to the poor. Some academic philosophers may praise these schemes, but the schemes did not begin in academia. They were compelled by street violence. For thousands of years, human societies have been wracked by costly, violent struggles caused by the have-nots attempting to seize the wealth of the haves. The have-nots never have benefited in any permanent way from all this violence, but that fact has not prevented the upheavals. Therefore, rulers seeking domestic peace have been prompted to engage in some show of redistribution of wealth as a way of heading off civil war. Even as late as the 1930s, most of the economically advanced countries saw violent mass movements that sought to overthrow the rich in the name of the poor. Policies of progressive taxation and redistribution, such as the New Deal in the United States, were undertaken in part to defuse this threatened explosion. These programs may have been foolish and counterproductive in economic terms, but who can say that, from the standpoint of promoting social peace, they were not needed?

The source of government's use of assertive force, then, lies in the disposition of ordinary people to use force to act out their grievances. They don't like the style of their neighbor's house, or they think it wrong that he pays low wages to his workers or sells a drug they disapprove of or declines to contribute to the local school, and they are willing to resort to violence to make him behave "better." Government's use of force is, in most cases, simply an orderly substitute for the use of force by gangs and mobs.

Attitudes do change, however. As my explorations have shown, people have become less willing to use force themselves and more upset about the prospect of its being used by others. As we saw in the discussion of mob violence (chapter 12), a remarkable reduction has occurred in most kinds of collective, politically oriented violence in the developed world over the past century, which has made possible a decline in government involvement in a number of areas. For example, in most of the economically developed countries, food rioting is a thing of the past—which means that their governments can afford to be less involved in setting food prices. The threat of a violent revolution by the have-nots has also subsided, which, in turn, has made policies of income redistribution less imperative.

Humans haven't become angels, of course. Even in developed countries, workers and farmers on occasion resort to physical blockades to prevent the entrance of lower-priced foreign goods such as lumber (from Canada into the United States) or beef (from Britain into France). The complete abandonment of all tariffs and import restrictions would probably lead to an increase in this type of violence. Government programs are a substitute for citizen violence in many other areas as well. Today there are some "environmentalists" who resort to blockades and the destruction of property to express their anger against what they feel are threats to the natural world. Drug regulation is another volatile area. If government entirely ceased hounding those who sell drugs such as heroin, it is probable that we would see vigilante mobs using violence of their own against drug dealers. Quite a number of parents feel that drug use will destroy or has destroyed the lives of their children, and they are prepared to attack those who appear to be responsible for an obvious social curse. Government's drug war, misguided as it may be, is a war that many citizens want fought—and would be willing to fight themselves if government declined to do it.

Knowledge and the Use of Force

One factor working to reduce the reliance on the assertive use of force is the growth of knowledge. The use of force always involves harmful side effects. Many times these side effects are so severe that they outweigh the good that was supposed to be accomplished by using force. A war that was supposed to end an international dispute simply leads to another war. An attempt to ban alcoholic beverages leads to a thriving bootleg industry. A program to seize farmland to give to poor peasants leads to mass starvation of those same peasants. Time and again humans have reached for force to solve a problem—only to learn, perhaps generations later, that they only made the problem worse.

In ancient times, when the human race had little ability to ana-lyze social relationships or to recall the effects of past policies, the most absurd policies of taxation and regulation were repeatedly undertaken on nothing more than impulse. Rulers would see a problem and assume that a simple ban or regulation would solve it. One recalls, for example, the Roman emperor Diocletian's sweeping price-control edict that at-tempted to control inflation (caused by his own debasement of coin-age). He killed many people trying to enforce it, but only succeeded in further wrecking the Roman economy. As knowledge about cause and effect in social and economic life has expanded, nations have become better able to avoid those uses of force that are harmful in the long run.

The changing perspective on government regulation of food prices illustrates this kind of development. In olden days, food rioters and government officials may have supposed that they were solving a problem through their use of force, but they were only adding to it. When mobs or the government seized food or forced vendors to sell it at low prices, they discouraged farmers and merchants outside the area from shipping food into the stricken region. Furthermore, the threat of seizures and price control deterred farmers and middlemen from increasing supplies in future years. They were reluctant to plant crops and invest in means of transportation and storage because they feared that the government might seize their supplies or force them to sell below cost. The conclusion is that when force is used, either by mobs or by government acting on behalf of mobs, it aggravates the problem of food shortages.

In ancient times, this problem wasn't recognized. Even if a few people noticed the connection, they didn't have the means of communication to share their insight with others and with future rulers. So mobs and kings would go on with their violent policies of seizure and regulation, wrecking the agricultural economy generation after generation. In modern times, the growth of scholarship and communication has made it possible to bring knowledge to bear on decisions about whether to use force. In England, for example, the development of economic theory by theorists such as Adam Smith in the late eighteenth century began to make rulers somewhat sensitive to the harm caused by attempting to regulate prices. Many came to understand that refraining from using force to regulate commerce was a constructive approach. This policy of laissez-faire was implemented —political conditions permitting—and accounted in no small degree for England's prosperity.

Another example of the role of analysis concerns the treatment of criminals. In olden days, the aim in the treatment of criminals was to cause suffering, to make the wrongdoer feel pain. This was the logic behind punishments of mutilation and painful, degrading incarceration. In more recent times, reformers and scholars began to examine the theory of punishment and to trace out its implications. They began to notice a connection that had been previously ignored: by inflicting physical suffering on a wrongdoer, they degraded and demoralized him, thus making him a burden to society and a menace to his neighbors after the punishment was completed. This analysis is gradually leading societies to reduce the use of physical force in the treatment of criminals.

In broad terms, then, knowledge promotes the evolution away from force. One way to join this historical movement, therefore, is to help develop the understanding of cause and effect in social life.

Voluntary Alternatives

In this book, I have described social evolution in negative terms. I have said that there is a historical trend *against* force. But a movement away from something can also be described as a movement *toward* something else. One way that reformers can find creative opportunities for assisting history's design is by looking at the positive side of this evolutionary process.

Suppose a community needs a school. Currently, this kind of need is filled through the assertive use of force. A government entity imposes a tax, forcing inhabitants to pay for the school under the threat of being taken to jail or having their property seized. The money collected is then turned over to a bureaucracy to establish and operate a school. This is the prevailing system for funding schools almost everywhere today. It is accepted because even though it involves a use of force, people feel that force is being used for a "good" purpose—and also because many can see no other practical way to accomplish the task.

Voluntarists would like to move away from such coercion-based practices. But how should they proceed? If they think in terms of working *against* force, they will expend their energies in a campaign against the existing force-based school system. This is a negative stance that puts them in the unpopular position of working to destroy schools, dismiss teachers, and deprive children of education.

Tactics and perspectives change entirely if reformers start by focusing on the positive view of history's trend. If history is moving away from force, what is it, necessarily, turning toward? The answer is *voluntary alternatives,* methods of accomplishing social purposes that do not involve threatening friends and neighbors with harm to body or property.

One such alternative is commercial activity—that is, producing, buying, and selling on the basis of economic exchange. We may criticize entrepreneurs' motives, and we may decry the harmful side effects of trade and industry, but neither of these complaints alters the fact that market activities are voluntary: no one uses guns to get people to make things or sell things or buy things. That is the meaning behind the term *free market:* the exchanges are free of force and the threat of force. Sometimes we are so busy criticizing entrepreneurs that we overlook the fact that they do meet human needs. Commercial establishments—restaurants, dental clinics, hardware stores, computer makers—are, literally, community service agencies. They just happen to operate on the principle of economic exchange between suppliers and customers.

Returning to my school example, then, voluntarists do not need to expend their energies in a negative and unpopular campaign against existing force-based schools. They can take the positive route of creating a school that operates on a voluntary basis. They can set up their school as a business that meets its expenses through the fees that parents pay to send children to the school. Such private schools may be expected to attract growing numbers of students as the frustrations and inefficiencies of the coercion-based school system become increasingly apparent. Thus, the reformers will have promoted a turning away from the use of force by providing a superior alternative.

Philanthropy

As time goes on, the reformers will probably find that this school, although a useful and constructive institution, does not meet all the educational needs of the community. For example, some poor families may not be able to afford to send their children there. When most people notice this kind of gap, their first impulse is to look to coercion to address the problem. Capitalism, they say, needs to be controlled and supplemented through the action of government. In the case of schools, they say, we have to force people to pay for them so that poor children can attend.

It is true that systems based on economic exchange cannot address all aspects of all social problems. It does not follow, however, that force is the only way to fill the remaining gaps. Voluntary approaches can meet needs not served by commercial arrangements. One important alternative is philanthropy, the giving of wealth without the expectation of a material personal benefit in return. Generosity is a natural and surprisingly strong human motive, one that often impels people to devote their time and wealth to improving their community. Virtually all of the helpful community institutions we have today— universities, hospitals, libraries, and so on—were originally developed and promoted by philanthropists. Philanthropists built roads and bridges, funded artists and composers, and created endowments for the promotion of every imaginable aim, from medical research to candles for the poor.

Philanthropy takes many forms. There are inventor-philanthropists who develop ideas and products for human benefit—such as Ben Franklin, who gave his famous stove for the benefit of all. There are entrepreneur-philanthropists, individuals who develop a business partly or mainly with the aim of social improvement and are willing to lose money in the process. Such civic-minded entrepreneurs played an important indirect role in winding down the violence of food riots, for example. Applying their interest in scientific agriculture, they established "model farms" to develop and demonstrate agricultural techniques, spurring the English Agricultural Revolution of the eighteenth century.

Education is a community function that philanthropy has widely supported. The United States had, by the early nineteenth century, an extensive educational system rooted in philanthropy, with funds being supplied by wealthy donors, church members, and local merchants. The tradition continues today. Virtually every private school in the country has a scholarship system to support students unable to pay the fees, and philanthropists in dozens of cities have established voucher systems to help inner-city children attend private schools. A reformer who finds a gap in the provision of education by private, fee-paying schools, then, does not need to turn to the coercion of the tax system for a remedy. All he has to do is open his own wallet—and convince his friends to do the same.

Shaping Behavior through Persuasion

Philanthropy may be able to supply funds for community services such as libraries, art museums, hospitals, and schools, but there are many problems that money can't solve. These problems are rooted in the behavior—or rather, the misbehavior—of human beings. For example, the best-funded school system in the world might be a failure if parents don't send their children to it. Traditionally, it has been assumed that government's assertive use of force should be used to correct problems of this kind. To promote school attendance, for example, government threatens parents with fines or even jail for failing to send their children to school, and children found playing hooky are dragged to school or to jail.

But force isn't the only way to get people to do the right thing. Many voluntary methods exist for pursuing the same aim, including advertising, nagging, persuading, offering personal example, shaming, and shunning. To get parents to send their children to school, voluntary reformers might employ billboards and radio ads, or they might visit parents and remind them about the importance of sending children to school, or they might publish a list of parents who fail to send their children to school. Another voluntary technique to promote good behavior is the use of rewards and payoffs. Parents might be paid to send their children to school, for example, or prizes might be awarded for families with good attendance.

Voluntary methods of social improvement often can be made more effective if reformers band together in a formal organization that enhances their resources and authority. Although one can find examples of voluntary organizations in ancient times, the service-oriented voluntary organization is a rather modern development. Beginning in the eighteenth century, people began to realize that they could address problems by joining with like-minded friends to form a society funded by voluntary donations and sustained with voluntary labor. In the 1830s, the French observer Alexis de Tocqueville noted the "vast number" of private associations in the United States. "Americans," he reported, "make associations to give entertainments, to found seminaries, to build inns, to construct churches, to diffuse books, to send missionaries to the antipodes."[3] Today, the United States has approximately one million voluntary groups. They are numerous in other countries as well. Britain has approximately half a million, Germany 250,000, Spain 110,000. As government comes to be seen as an inappropriate or ineffective method for providing community services, these groups can perform virtually all of the same tasks by relying on voluntary methods of fund-raising and influence.

Limits on the Voluntary Sector

In surveying the voluntary sector today, we should keep in mind that it does not exist in pure form. Voluntary institutions are still tied to and often dominated by the prevailing force-based system. Commercial enterprises are impaired and distorted by government's assertive use of force in the form of taxation, tax subsidies, licensing arrangements, tariffs, regulations, and liability lawsuits. Modern philanthropy is also debilitated by government. The tax system has made philanthropy into something of a tax dodge and fostered the creation of self-serving, self-perpetuating foundations. Furthermore, the looming importance of government has deprived philanthropy of its vision, with the result that many philanthropists and foundations direct their funds to supporting government agencies and government programs.

Government and its readily available systems of coercion also undermine the healthy systems of social persuasion. Those who campaign against bad habits—smoking, drinking, using drugs—do not confine themselves to voluntary methods, but appeal to government to force people to abandon these habits. Those leading efforts to promote tolerance and goodwill toward minority groups have often turned to government to try to force their neighbors to change their prejudiced ways. Not surprisingly, these reformers have generated a backlash of resentment.

Government also weakens and perverts voluntary organizations. Its taxation drains resources from them, its subsidies deflect them into unproductive and self-serving modes of behavior, and its programs of regulation and liability lawsuits block innovation and creativity. Furthermore, government undermines them psychologically. "With its vast resources and powers, government is supposed to handle everything," say prospective donors and volunteers. "Why should we rise from our couches?"

The evolution against force still has a long way to run. In our thinking and practices, we shall continue for many years to look to force-based government to deal with social problems, even as we deplore its institutions and disparage the people who operate them. Beyond the hubbub and cynicism of politics, however, voluntary systems of improvement, systems that do not rely on force to accomplish their ends, are growing.

To be sure, these voluntary approaches lack the flair and drama of government. Coercion always promises sweeping reforms, "comprehensive" measures that purport to solve problems once and for all. Voluntarism, on the other hand, is a humble, piecemeal approach. It does not intoxicate with power, inviting one person or one party to "change the course of history." But at least voluntary methods always work some good. The problem with grand crusades directed at promoting government action is that they often fail, and in failing they waste untold amounts of time, energy, and idealism. Reformers who associate themselves with voluntary efforts are on a more secure path to progress. They directly improve the world through their business enterprises and voluntary organizations, and they have the satisfaction of knowing that, whatever their level of accomplishment, they are working in harmony with history's larger design.

Notes

Chapter 2, The History We Can't Believe

1. Christopher Hibbert, *The Roots of Evil: A Social History of Crime and Punishment* (Boston: Little, Brown, 1963), p. 17.

2. Evan Luard, *War in International Society* (New Haven, Conn.: Yale University Press, 1987), pp. 23, 394.

3. Luard gives an example of this kind of blanket statement: "the total number killed in war in this century is far greater, both absolutely and as a proportion of population, even for European and North American states, than in *all* earlier times" (*War in International Society,* p. 394, italics added). This seems a rather clear example of the fallacy of presentism because Luard makes no effort to compile any data on the historical costs of war. As regards Europe and North America, it is easy to falsify the allegation merely by pointing to the staggering death rates of known conflicts of the past three or four hundred years. For example, the English civil war of the mid–seventeenth century cost approximately half a million lives, which, as historian Simon Schama points out, yields a British death rate higher than that of World War I (*A History of Britain: The Wars of the British 1603–1776* [New York: Hyperion, 2001], p. 13). As discussed in chapter 6, studies that have attempted to assemble the relevant figures for the past two centuries find no overall increase in the costs of war. Indeed, as I explain, when properly interpreted, these studies strongly suggest a diminution in the death rate owing to war.

Another instance of this greatest-in-history fallacy is found in the final report of the Carnegie Commission on Preventing Deadly Conflict. It makes the claim that "the twentieth century proved to be the most violent and destructive in all human history." The report contains no evidence to support this claim, not even an effort to collect such evidence. It is especially disappointing to find this error in a work that purports to be authoritative. The commission consisted of sixteen "international leaders and scholars with long experience and path-breaking accomplishments in conflict prevention and conflict resolution" as well as an advisory council of forty-two "eminent practitioners and scholars," and a staff of fourteen. Carnegie Commission on Preventing Deadly Conflict, *Preventing Deadly Conflict: Final Report* (Washington, D.C.: Carnegie Commission on Preventing Deadly Conflict, 1997), p. 11.

4. *Bonner County Daily Bee,* June 17, 1999, p. 6.

5. Margareta Sollenberg, Peter Wallensteen, and Andres Jato, "Major Armed Conflicts," in *SIPRI Yearbook 1999,* edited by Adam Daniel Rotfeld (Oxford: Oxford University Press, 1999), p. 18.

6. For a discussion of irresponsible exaggerations of the level of U.S. military spending, see James L. Payne, "Wrong Numbers: Lies and Distortions about Defense Spending," *The National Interest* 14 (winter 1988–89): 60–71.

7. David McKittrick, Seamus Kelters, Brian Feeney, and Chris Thornton, *Lost Lives* (Edinburgh: Mainstream, 1999).

8. Lewis F. Richardson, *Statistics of Deadly Quarrels,* edited by Quincy Wright and C. C. Lienau (Pittsburgh: Boxwood Press, 1960), pp. 112, 128.

9. Jean Chesneaux, *Peasant Revolts in China 1840–1949* (London: Thames and Hudson, 1973), p. 40.

10. SIPRI lists twenty-three ongoing wars in the year 2000, with estimates for the number of dead given for eighteen of these wars: 29,575. Adding in a prorated estimate for the five wars with unknown casualty figures gives a total of 37,790. This number probably understates the figure of war deaths around the world that one might obtain if a perfectly complete tabulation were made. However, it should be remembered that the figure for war deaths in the 1900–1924 period also involves undercounting—and to a much greater degree than tabulations for the modern period. Scores of military clashes and massacres in that earlier period probably went unrecorded. Compiled from data given at the FIRST/SIPRI web site: http://first.sipri.org/index.php?.

11. Robert S. McNamara and James G. Blight, *Wilson's Ghost: Reducing the Risk of Conflict, Killing, and Catastrophe in the 21st Century* (New York: Public Affairs, 2001), p. 17.

12. Will Durant, *The Reformation* (New York: Simon and Schuster, 1957), p. 576.

Chapter 3, What History Is Up To

1. The generalized disapproval of the use of force appears to be a relatively modern position. Of course, many ancient religions and philosophies stressed the idea of kindness to others, but, as noted earlier, these creeds made no distinction between harmful acts of force and the many other ways humans might harm each other. And specific uses of force, such as war, human sacrifice, and so on, have been criticized since ancient times.

A generalized focus on force perhaps first appeared with the Anabaptists of the sixteenth century, who disapproved of the use of force by those in authority. The Anabaptists unfortunately also became embroiled in a disappointingly large amount of violence themselves. The Mennonites, an offshoot of the Anabaptists, were more consistent about avoiding the use of force, as were the English Quakers.

In the nineteenth century, anarchists such as Pierre Proudhon and Mikhail Bakunin disapproved of the state's use of force, but they were prepared to use force to destroy the state. Members of William Lloyd Garrison's Christian "nonresistance" movement in the United States were consistently opposed to the use of force. Leo Tolstoy echoed their views. In England, Auberon Herbert made an impassioned (and unheeded) plea for "Voluntaryism," a doctrine that focused on avoiding the use of force.

In modern times, skepticism about the use of force has been a central theme for the many libertarian thinkers who emerged around the mid–twentieth century, including Leonard Read, Ayn Rand, and Murray Rothbard, as well as for near-libertarians such as Friedrich Hayek and Ludwig von Mises. In general, libertarians make a clear distinction between the *initiation of force,* which they almost always consider wrong, and the *defensive use of force,* which they generally endorse.

Chapter 4, Overcoming Human Sacrifice

1. "Tacitus, Germania," in *Voyages and Travels Ancient and Modern,* edited by Charles W. Eliot, vol. 33 of *The Harvard Classics* (New York: P. F. Collier, 1910), pp. 100, 101, 110, 114.

2. Nancy Jay, *Throughout Your Generations Forever: Sacrifice, Religion, and Paternity* (Chicago: University of Chicago Press, 1992), p. 66.

3. Nigel Davies, *Human Sacrifice in History and Today* (New York: William Morrow, 1981), pp. 28, 37, 265.

4. Hyam Maccoby, *The Sacred Executioner: Human Sacrifice and the Legacy of Guilt* (New York: Thames and Hudson, 1982), pp. 76–77.

5. Edward Westermarck, *The Origin and Development of the Moral Ideas* (London: MacMillan, 1906–8), cited in Davies, *Human Sacrifice,* p. 22.

6. Davies, *Human Sacrifice,* p. 22.

7. Martin S. Bergmann, *In the Shadow of Moloch: The Sacrifice of Children and Its Impact on Western Religions* (New York: Columbia University Press, 1992), p. 3.

8. In 2 Chronicles 33:6, child sacrifice in the same valley of the son of Hinnom is reported to have been performed by Manaseh, one of the Hebrew kings and predecessor of Josiah.

9. Bergmann, *In the Shadow of Moloch,* p. 4.

10. Will Durant, *Caesar and Christ: A History of Roman Civilization and of Christianity from Their Beginnings to A.D. 325* (New York: Simon and Schuster, 1944), p. 42.

11. Bergmann, *In the Shadow of Moloch,* p. 23.

12. J. B. Bury, *A History of Greece to the Death of Alexander the Great* (New York: Modern Library, 1913), p. 728.

13. Durant, *Caesar and Christ,* pp. 47, 51.

14. Ibid., p. 64.

15. Thomas Cahill, *How the Irish Saved Civilization* (New York: Anchor, 1995), pp. 136, 140. Cahill also reviews the archeological evidence for human sacrifice in Britain and Denmark, pp. 138–40.

16. Davies, *Human Sacrifice,* pp. 207–17.

17. Patrick Tierney, *The Highest Altar: Unveiling the Mystery of Human Sacrifice* (New York: Penguin, 1989), pp. 24–41.

18. Davies, *Human Sacrifice,* pp. 78–82.

19. Dennis D. Hughes, *Human Sacrifice in Ancient Greece* (London: Routledge, 1991); Will Durant, *The Life of Greece* (New York: Simon and Schuster, 1939), pp. 193–94.

20. Davies, *Human Sacrifice,* p. 40.

21. John Goddard, *Kayaks down the Nile* (Provo, Utah: Brigham Young University Press, 1979), p. 142.

22. Davies, *Human Sacrifice,* p. 40.

23. Ibid., p. 63.

24. Ibid., p. 86.

25. Durant, *The Life of Greece,* p. 194.

Chapter 5, The Changing View of Genocide

1. Barbara Harff, "Recognizing Genocides and Politicides," in *Genocide Watch,* edited by Helen Fein (New Haven, Conn.: Yale University Press, 1992), pp. 32–36.
2. Samuel Totten, William S. Parsons, and Israel W. Chamy, eds., *Century of Genocide: Eyewitness Accounts and Critical Views* (New York: Garland, 1997); Neil Jeffrey Kressel, *Mass Hate: The Global Rise of Genocide and Terror* (New York: Plenum Press, 1996).
3. Charles M. Laymon, ed., *The Interpreter's One-Volume Commentary on the Bible* (Nashville, Tenn.: Abingdon Press, 1971), p. 124.
4. Will Durant, *Our Oriental Heritage* (New York: Simon and Schuster, 1954), pp. 460–61.
5. R. J. Rummel, *Death by Government* (New Brunswick, N.J.: Transaction, 1994), pp. 51–52.
6. *Bhagavad-Gita As It Is* (Los Angeles: Bhaktivedanta Book Trust, 1983), pp. 56, 59.
7. Ibid., pp. 74, 115.
8. Ibid., pp. 87, 106.
9. Kurt Jonassohn with Karin Solveig Bjornson, *Genocide and Gross Human Rights Violations in Comparative Perspective* (New Brunswick, N.J.: Transaction, 1998), pp. 18–20.
10. Quoted in Seumas MacManus, *The Story of the Irish Race,* rev. ed. (Old Greenwich, Conn.: Devin-Adair, 1983), p. 425.
11. Quoted in ibid.
12. Quoted in Norman Davies, *Europe: A History* (New York: HarperCollins, 1998), pp. 705, 706.
13. Rummel, *Death by Government,* pp. 57–58.
14. *Colonial Overlords* (Alexandria, Va.: Time-Life, 1990), pp. 25–26.
15. Quoted in MacManus, *The Story of the Irish Race,* p. 708.

Chapter 6, New Ideas about Empire, War, and Military Forces

1. Niccolo Machiavelli, *The Prince and the Discourses* (New York: Modern Library, 1950), p. 53.
2. Colin Wilson, *A Criminal History of Mankind* (London: Grafton, 1985), p. 269.
3. Norman Davies, *Europe: A History* (New York: HarperCollins, 1998), p. 615.
4. Ibid., pp. 624–28.
5. Ibid., p. 725.
6. Ibid., p. 744.
7. Esther Forbes, *Paul Revere and the World He Lived In* (Boston: Houghton Mifflin, 1942), pp. 4, 59.

8. Barbara W. Tuchman, *The Proud Tower: A Portrait of the World Before the War, 1890–1914* (New York: Bantam, 1967), p. 156.

9. Stephen E. Ambrose, *Undaunted Courage: Meriwether Lewis, Thomas Jefferson, and the Opening of the American West* (New York: Touchstone, 1996), p. 288.

10. Arthur Herman, *How the Scots Invented the Modern World* (New York: Crown, 2001), p. 108.

11. Will Durant, *Caesar and Christ: A History of Roman Civilization and of Christianity from Their Beginnings to A.D. 325* (New York: Simon and Schuster, 1944), pp. 44–45, 50–51.

12. Ibid., p. 54.

13. Will Durant, *Our Oriental Heritage* (New York: Simon and Schuster, 1954), p. 430.

14. Ibid., p. 421.

15. Ibid., p. 461.

16. John Mueller, *Retreat from Doomsday; The Obsolescence of Major War* (New York: Basic, 1989), pp. 54–55.

17. Paul Johnson, "Another 50 Years of Peace?" *Wall Street Journal,* May 9, 1995, p. A20.

18. Mueller, *Retreat from Doomsday,* pp. 3–4.

19. In one remarkable case of fabrication, writer and editor Norman Cousins advanced entirely fictitious figures about war and the incidence of war since 3600 B.C., figures he openly described as "fanciful." Nevertheless, his numbers—which showed an increase in violence in modern times—made their way into many publications, including the *New York Times* and *Time* magazine, as real data. This "hoax" is cited in J. David Singer and Melvin Small, *The Wages of War 1816–1965: A Statistical Handbook* (New York: John Wiley, 1972), pp. 10–11.

20. Quincy Wright, *A Study of War* (Chicago: University of Chicago Press, 1942), vol. 1, pp. 641–46.

21. Ibid., pp. 236–37.

22. Lewis F. Richardson, *Statistics of Deadly Quarrels,* edited by Quincy Wright and C. C. Lienau (Pittsburgh: Boxwood Press, 1960), p. 167; Singer and Small, *The Wages of War,* p. 201.

23. Richardson, *Statistics,* p. 112.

24. Compiled from Michael Clodfelter, *Warfare and Armed Conflicts,* vol. 1 (Jefferson, N.C.: McFarland, 1992).

25. Ibid.

26. The preferred measure of a nation's emphasis on military forces is its defense burden—that is, the proportion of gross national product (GNP) devoted to defense. Unfortunately, it is difficult to obtain valid measures of defense budgets and GNP for many countries, so valid defense burden statistics cannot be compiled for them. As it happens, the force ratio (individuals under arms per one thousand population) is a good alternative measure for a nation's emphasis on military forces, and it can be calculated for almost all countries. For an elaboration of this point, see James L. Payne, *Why Nations Arm* (Oxford: Basil Blackwell, 1989), chapter 2.

27. U.S. Arms Control and Disarmament Agency, *World Military Expenditures 1971* (Washington, D.C.: Government Printing Office, 1972), author's calculation

from data given on pp. 10–13; U.S. Department of State, Bureau of Verification and Compliance, *World Military Expenditures and Arms Transfers 1999–2000* (Washington, D.C.: Government Printing Office, 2002), p. 51.

28. Payne, *Why Nations Arm,* p. 221.

29. Peter Taylor and Hermann Rebel, "Hessian Peasant Women, Their Families, and the Draft: A Social-historical Interpretation of Four Tales from the Grimm Collection," *Journal of Family History* (winter 1981), p. 368.

30. Barbara W. Tuchman, *The First Salute* (New York: Knopf, 1988), pp. 46–47.

31. Devi Prasad and Tony Smythe, *Conscription: A World Survey* (London: War Resisters' International, 1968), pp. 14, 40–41, 139.

32. Of the sixty-three long-established countries used in figure 6.1, fifteen were not covered in the compilations of the International Institute of Strategic Studies because they were too small to be of interest. Therefore, this tabulation is based on forty-eight countries.

33. Lawrence H. Keeley, *War Before Civilization* (New York: Oxford University Press, 1996).

34. Ibid., p. 14

35. Ibid., pp. 18–19.

36. Ibid., pp. 18, 91.

37. Napoleon A. Chagnon, *Yanomamo: The Fierce People* (New York: Holt, Rinehart and Winston, 1968), p. 20, note 2.

38. Keeley, pp. 196-97.

39. Ibid., p. 88.

40. *The Statesman's Year-Book, 1891* (London: MacMillan, 1891), p. 186.

41. Evelyn Colbert, *The Pacific Islands: Paths to the Present* (Boulder, Colo.: Westview Press, 1997), p. 6.

42. Marlita A. Reddy, ed., *Statistical Record of Native North Americans,* 2d ed. (New York: Gale Research, 1995), p. 9; William C. Sturtevant, ed., *Handbook of North American Indians* (Washington, D.C.: Smithsonian Institution, 1978), p. 1.

43. Carol R. Ember, "Myths about Hunter-Gatherers," *Ethnology* 17 (1978): pp. 439–48, cited in Raymond C. Kelly, *Warless Societies and the Origin of War* (Ann Arbor, University of Michigan Press: 2000), p. 2.

44. Margareta Sollenberg, Peter Wallensteen, and Andres Jato, "Global Patterns of Major Armed Conflicts," in *SIPRI Yearbook 1999,* edited by Adam Daniel Rotfeld (Oxford: Oxford University Press, 1999), p. 18.

45. Nils Petter Gleditsch, Peter Wallensteen, Mikael Eriksson, Magareta Sollenberg, and Havard Strand, "Armed Conflict 1946–2001: A New Dataset," *Journal of Peace Research* 39, no. 5, (2002): 615–37.

Chapter 7, Beyond Political Murder

1. Chester G. Starr, *A History of the Ancient World,* 4th ed. (New York: Oxford University Press, 1991), p. 544.

2. An illustration of this error is Franklin Ford's comprehensive *Political Murder from Tyrannicide to Terrorism* (Cambridge, Mass.: Harvard University Press,

1985). Ford lumps all killings of high officials together, making no distinction between, say, the slaying of Julius Caesar by other senators and the killing of John F. Kennedy by an outsider and stranger. Assassinations (killings by outsiders) have actually increased in modern times owing to the development of firearms and explosives which enable assassins to act from a greater distance, and to the development of the mass media, which allows a wider circle of potential assassins to know about, and have reasons for hating, political leaders. Political murders—socially acceptable murder by insiders—have declined dramatically. If one combines the two kinds of killing into one category, as Ford does, no overall trend will be apparent.

3. Compiled from data given in Chris Scarre, *Chronicle of the Roman Emperors* (New York: Thames and Hudson, 1995).

4. Will Durant, *Caesar and Christ: A History of Roman Civilization and of Christianity from Their Beginnings to A.D. 325* (New York: Simon and Schuster, 1944), p. 194.

5. Michael Grant, *Nero: Emperor in Revolt* (New York: American Heritage Press, 1970), p. 77.

6. Scarre, *Chronicle,* pp. 139–42.

7. Quoted in Will Durant, *The Reformation* (New York: Simon and Schuster, 1957), p. 711.

8. C. M. Bowra, *Classical Greece* (New York: Time-Life, 1965), p. 25.

9. Durant, *Caesar and Christ,* p. 23.

10. Michael Grant, *History of Rome* (New York: Charles Scribner's Sons, 1978), pp. 96, 171, 176.

11. John Addington Symonds, *The Age of the Despots* (New York: G. P. Putnam's Sons, 1960), pp. 84–85, 97.

12. Will Durant and Ariel Durant, *The Age of Reason Begins* (New York: Simon and Schuster, 1961), pp. 157–58.

13. Ibid., pp. 204, 216–20.

14. Will Durant and Ariel Durant, *The Age of Louis XIV* (New York: Simon and Schuster, 1963), p. 202.

15. The impulse to political murder lingered for many decades, however. Oliver Cromwell, Charles II, and James II were the target of numerous attempted murders arranged by high officials. The assassination plot against Charles II by the Council of Six is a clear example; see Durant and Durant, *The Age of Louis XIV,* pp. 285–86. Historian Ian Gilmour notes that the last person to be killed by a parliamentary act of attainder was John Fenwick in 1697. Fenwick had been involved in an assassination plot; see *Riot, Risings, and Revolution: Governance and Violence in Eighteenth-Century England* (London: Hutchinson, 1992), p. 41.

16. Quoted in Durant and Durant, *The Age of Louis XIV,* p. 245.

17. I think political science would have more luck unraveling the confusions surrounding *democracy* if this arrangement were defined simply as a political system where force is not employed to obtain and retain leadership posts. This suggestion follows John Mueller's insightful observations in *Quiet Cataclysm: Reflections on the Recent Transformation of World Politics* (New York: HarperCollins, 1995), pp. 156–59.

18. *The Columbia Viking Desk Encyclopedia,* 3rd ed. (1968), p. 237.

19. Durant and Durant, *The Age of Louis XIV,* pp. 19, 81–84.

20. Norman Davies, *Europe: A History* (New York: HarperCollins, 1998), p. 709; Robert Cole, *A Traveller's History of France,* 3rd ed. (New York: Interlink, 1995), p. 114.

21. Cole, *A Traveller's History,* p. 118.

22. J. M. Thompson, *Louis Napoleon and the Second Empire* (New York: Norton, 1967), pp. 43, 72.

23. Ian Grey, *The Romanovs: The Rise and Fall of a Dynasty* (Garden City, N.Y.: Doubleday, 1970), pp. 300, 271.

24. Durant and Durant, *The Age of Louis XIV,* pp. 407–8.

25. Will Durant and Ariel Durant, *Rousseau and Revolution* (New York: Simon and Schuster, 1967), pp. 440–43.

26. Grey, *The Romanovs,* p. 229.

27. K. C. Tessendorf, *Kill the Tsar! Youth and Terrorism in Old Russia* (New York: Atheneum, 1986), p. 110.

28. Dmitri Volkogonov, *Lenin: A New Biography,* translated by Harold Shukman (New York: Free Press, 1994), p. 214.

29. Ibid., p. 232.

30. *The New Encyclopaedia Britannica,* 15th ed. (1994), vol. 28, p. 183.

31. Ibid., vol. 7, p. 733, and vol. 8, p. 237.

32. David Remnick, "Gorbachev's Last Hurrah," *The New Yorker,* March 11, 1996, p. 68.

33. Daniel Tretiak, "Political Assassinations in China, 1600–1968," in *Assassination and Political Violence,* a report to the National Commission on the Causes and Prevention of Violence (New York: Praeger, 1970), p. 636.

34. Tretiak, "Political Assassinations," pp. 637–55.

Chapter 8, Whatever Happened to Revolution?

1. Michael I. Rostovtzeff, *The Social and Economic History of the Roman Empire,* 2d ed. (1926; Oxford: Clarendon Press, 1957), p. 2.

2. Will Durant, *The Life of Greece* (New York: Simon and Schuster, 1939), p. 250.

3. Will Durant, *The Reformation* (New York: Simon and Schuster, 1957), pp. 110–11.

4. Ibid., pp. 565–66, 581–82.

5. Will Durant and Ariel Durant, *The Age of Louis XIV* (New York: Simon and Schuster, 1963), p. 290.

6. Norman Davies, *Europe: A History* (New York: HarperCollins, 1998), p. 627.

7. Robin Briggs, *Communities of Belief: Cultural and Social Tensions in Early Modern France* (Oxford: Clarendon Press, 1989), p. 110.

8. Davies, *Europe,* p. 805.

9. George Sansom, *A History of Japan 1334–1615* (Stanford, Calif.: Stanford University Press, 1961), p. 208.

10. John Whitney Hall, *Japan from Prehistory to Modern Times* (New York:

Dell, 1970), p. 127.

    11. Ibid., p. 144.

    12. Ibid., p. 284.

    13. Margareta Sollenberg, Peter Wallensteen, and Andres Jato, "Global Patterns of Major Armed Conflicts," in *SIPRI Yearbook 1999,* edited by Adam Daniel Rotfeld (Oxford: Oxford University Press, 1999), p. 20.

    14. Charles Edmond Akers, *A History of South America* (1904; reprint, New York: E. P. Dutton, 1920), p. 207.

    15. Quoted in Sue Anne Pressley, "Cyber-savvy 'Texians' Are Papered into a Corner of the Southwest," *Washington Post,* March 12, 1997, p. A3.

    16. David B. Kopel and Paul H. Blackman, *No More Wacos: What's Wrong with Federal Law Enforcement and How to Fix It* (Amherst, N.Y.: Prometheus, 1997), pp. 50, 409–11.

    17. Charles Tilly, *The Contentious French* (Cambridge, Mass.: Harvard University Press, 1986), p. 383.

    18. Arturo Bray, *Militares y civiles* (Buenos Aires: n.p., 1958), pp. 138–39.

    19. Data for 1972 supplied to the author by Freedom House. Data for 2001 found in Adrian Karatnycky, ed., *Freedom in the World: The Annual Survey of Political Rights and Civil Liberties 2001–2002* (New York: Freedom House, 2002).

Chapter 9, The Evolution of Criminal Punishment

    1. Alice Morse Earle, *Curious Punishments of Bygone Days* (1896; reprint, Bedford, Mass.: Applewood, 1995), pp. 74–77; Edwin Powers, *Crime and Punishment in Early Massachusetts 1620–1692* (Boston: Beacon Press, 1966), pp. 163–64.

    2. Brian Innes, *The History of Torture* (New York: St. Martin's Press, 1998), p. 96.

    3. Earle, *Curious Punishments,* p. 55.

    4. Ibid., p. 52.

    5. Innes, *The History of Torture,* p. 59.

    6. Earle, *Curious Punishments,* p. 140.

    7. Pieter Spierenburg, "The Body and the State," in *The Oxford History of the Prison,* edited by Norval Morris and David J. Rothman (New York: Oxford University Press, 1995), p. 53.

    8. Innes, *The History of Torture,* p. 56–57.

    9. Torsten Eriksson, *The Reformers: An Historical Survey of Pioneer Experiments in the Treatment of Criminals,* translated by Catherine Djurklou (New York: Elsevier, 1976), p. 1; Guido Ruggiero, *Violence in Early Renaissance Venice* (New Brunswick, N.J.: Rutgers University Press, 1980), p. 41.

    10. Eriksson, *The Reformers,* p. 2.

    11. J. B. Bury, *A History of Greece to the Death of Alexander the Great* (New York: Modern Library, 1913), p. 172.

    12. John Laurence Pritchard, *A History of Capital Punishment* (1932; reprint, Port Washington, N.Y.: Kennikat Press, 1971), pp. 13–14.

    13. *The New Encyclopaedia Britannica,* 15th ed. (1994) vol. 16, p. 813.

    14. Pritchard, *A History of Capital Punishment,* p. 19.

15. E. J. Burford and Sandra Shulman, *Of Bridles and Burnings: The Punishment of Women* (New York: St. Martin's Press, 1992), pp. 46–47, 78–79.

16. Ian Gilmour, *Riot, Risings, and Revolution: Governance and Violence in Eighteenth-Century England* (London: Hutchinson, 1992), p. 150.

17. Randall McGowen, "The Well-Ordered Prison," in *The Oxford History of the Prison,* edited by Morris and Rothman, p. 80.

18. Barbara W. Tuchman, *A Distant Mirror: The Calamitous 14th Century* (New York: Ballantine, 1978), p. 135.

19. Ericksson, *The Reformers,* pp. 11–12.

20. Spierenburg, "The Body and the State," pp. 73–74.

21. Sean McConville, "The Victorian Prison," in *The Oxford History of the Prison,* edited by Morris and Rothman, p. 133.

22. Christopher Hibbert, *The Roots of Evil: A Social History of Crime and Punishment* (Boston: Little, Brown, 1963), pp. 133–34.

23. Spierenburg, "The Body and the State," p. 70.

24. McGowen, "The Well-Ordered Prison," p. 83.

25. Hibbert, *The Roots of Evil,* p. 137

26. Ibid., pp.138–39.

27. Ibid., pp. 147–49.

28. *Encyclopedia of American Prisons* (New York: Garland, 1996), p. 155.

29. "Law Briefing," *Insight,* June 20, 1988, p. 58.

30. This figure is the average cost for federal and state prisons for the year 2000, calculated from data given in *Federal and State Prisons: Inmate Populations, Costs, and Projection Models* (Washington, D.C.: U.S. General Accounting Office, 1996), pp. 24–25, 30–31. The figure includes both operating and capital costs.

31. Quoted in Marc Mauer, *Race to Incarcerate* (New York: New Press, 1999), p. 189.

32. Mauer, *Race to Incarcerate,* pp. 21–22.

33. Norman Davies, *Europe: A History* (New York: HarperCollins, 1998), p. 543.

34. Robert M. Baird and Stuart E. Rosenbaum, eds., *Punishment and the Death Penalty* (Amherst, N.Y.: Prometheus Books, 1995), p. 110.

35. George Ryley Scott, *The History of Torture Throughout the Ages* (London: Torchstream, 1949), pp. 135–36.

36. Amnesty International, *The Death Penalty List of Abolitionist and Retentionist Countries* (London: Amnesty International, 1999); Pritchard, *A History of Capital Punishment,* pp. 20–21.

37. Hugo Adam Bedau, *The Death Penalty in America: Current Controversies* (New York: Oxford University Press, 1997), p. 17.

Chapter 10, Terrorism in the Modern World

1. Alex P. Schmid, "Terrorism and Related Concepts: Definition," in Alex P. Schmid and Albert J. Jongman, *Political Terrorism,* 2d ed. (New Brunswick, N.J.: Transaction, 1988), pp. 1–38.

2. Bruce Hoffman, *Inside Terrorism* (New York: Columbia University Press,

1998), p. 43.

3. Sidney Lens, *The Labor Wars: From the Molly Maguires to the Sitdowns* (New York: Doubleday, 1973), pp. 17–29.

4. John L. Scherer, *Terrorism: An Annual Survey,* vol. 2 (Minneapolis: J. L. Scherer, 1983), p. 103; Brent L. Smith, *Terrorism in America: Pipe Bombs and Pipe Dreams* (Albany: State University of New York Press, 1994), pp. 17–21; Federal Bureau of Investigation, *Terrorism in the United States, 1998* (Washington, D.C.: Government Printing Office, 1998), pp. 23–34.

5. Cited in George Gerbner, "Rethinking Media Violence," available at www.mediaed.org/videos/CommercialismGlobalizationAndMedia (April 12, 2002). This statistic does raise the question of why, if viewers disapprove of violence, television programming includes so much of it. There are several answers, but perhaps the most important is the power of morbid fascination. Huge traffic jams are caused at the scene of an accident by passing motorists straining to see what happened. None of these motorists approve of accidents, but they cannot suppress a basic human impulse to watch mayhem. A second explanation for violent television shows—advanced by Gerbner—is that these programs are the only ones that translate well for sale in foreign cultures. Even though they are less desired and less watched in the United States, producers make them because they yield the highest income worldwide.

6. Craig Rosebraugh, quoted in Brandon Bosworth, "America's Homegrown Terrorists," *The American Enterprise* (April–May 2002), p. 49.

Chapter 11, Islam and Global Terrorism

1. Data on force ratios taken from U.S. Department of State, Bureau of Verification and Compliance, *World Military Expenditures and Arms Transfers 1999–2000* (Washington, D.C.: Government Printing Office, 2001). Data for the year 1999. In this data set, there are 46 Muslim countries and 118 non-Muslim countries. To identify countries with a majority Muslim population, I have used the listing in Gilles Kepel, *Jihad: The Trail of Political Islam* (Cambridge, Mass.: Harvard University Press, 2002), pp. 434–35.

2. Data taken from the SIPRI Web site: http://first.sipri.org/index.php? (March 6, 2002). In this data set, there are 48 Muslim countries, 11 of which were involved in wars, and 118 non-Muslim countries, 13 of which were involved in wars.

3. Data given at the National Defense Council Foundation Web site: http://ndcf.org/Conflict_list/World2001/NDCFWorldConflictCount2001.htm (July 16, 2002). In this data set, there are 49 Muslim countries and 119 non-Muslim countries.

4. Compiled from Freedom House, *Freedom in the World: The Annual Survey of Political Rights and Civil Liberties 2001–2002* (Piscataway, N.J.: Transaction, 2002). In this data set, there are 50 Muslim countries and 142 non-Muslim countries.

5. U.S. Department of State, *Victims of Trafficking and Violence Protection Act 2000, Trafficking in Persons Report* (Washington, D.C.: Government Printing Office, June 2002).

6. Data taken from the Amnesty International Web site at www.amnesty.org/rmp/dpli (April 12, 2002). This data set includes 195 countries, 51 Muslim and 144 non-Muslim.

7. Compiled from a table in Kanan Makiya, *Republic of Fear: The Politics of Modern Iraq,* updated ed. (Berkeley and Los Angeles: University of California Press, 1989), pp. 292–95.

8. U.S. Department of State, *Patterns of Global Terrorism—2001* (Washington, D.C.: Government Printing Office, May 2002), appendix B.

9. Will Durant, *The Age of Faith* (New York: Simon and Schuster, 1950), pp. 168–69.

10. Ibid., pp. 233–37.

11. Ibid., p. 170.

12. Ibid.

13. Robin Wright, *Sacred Rage: The Wrath of Militant Islam* (New York: Simon and Schuster, 1986), pp. 146–55.

14. *The Complaint of Peace by Erasmus* (1517; New York: Scholars' Facsimiles and Reprints, 1946), p. 36.

15. Sharon La Franiere, "Rebel Action Seen Likely to Prolong Chechnya War," *Washington Post,* October 28, 2002, p. A16.

16. Lawrence Wright, "The Man Behind Bin Laden," *The New Yorker,* September 16, 2002, p. 78.

17. Kepel, *Jihad,* p. 297.

18. Rajiv Chandrasekaran, "Concerned by Indonesia's Voice of Caution," *Washington Post,* May 14, 2002, p. A17.

19. Kepel, *Jihad,* passim.

Chapter 12, Violence in the Streets

1. Will Durant and Ariel Durant, *Rousseau and Revolution* (New York: Simon and Schuster, 1967), pp. 933–34.

2. Ibid., pp. 954–63.

3. Ibid., p. 962.

4. Ian Gilmour, *Riot, Risings, and Revolution: Governance and Violence in Eighteenth-Century England* (London: Hutchinson, 1992), pp. 23–33.

5. Ibid., pp. 345–72.

6. Ibid., p. 312.

7. John Stevenson, *Popular Disturbances in England 1700–1870* (London: Longman, 1979), p. 237.

8. Cited in ibid., p. 306.

9. Ibid., p. 306.

10. Ibid., p. 298.

11. Ibid., p. 283.

12. Manfred Gailus, "Food Riots in Germany in the Late 1840s," *Past and Present* 145 (November 1994), p. 162.

13. Ibid.

14. Charles Tilly, *The Contentious French* (Cambridge, Mass.: Harvard University Press, 1986), p. 384.

15. Paul E. W. Roberts, "Caravats and Shanavests: Whiteboyism and Faction Fighting in East Munster, 1802–11," in *Irish Peasants: Violence and Political Unrest*

1780–1914, edited by Samuel Clark and James S. Donnelly Jr. (Manchester: Manchester University Press, 1983), pp. 85–88.

16. Samuel Clark and James S. Donnelly Jr., "The Unreaped Harvest," in *Irish Peasants,* edited by Clark and Donnelly, p. 421.

17. Ruth Delany, *The Grand Canal of Ireland* (Dublin: Lilliput Press, 1995), passim, especially pp. 77–85.

18. Richard Maxwell Brown, "Historical Patterns of Violence in America," in *Violence in America: Historical and Comparative Perspectives,* 2 vols., a report to the National Commission on the Causes and Prevention of Violence (Washington, D.C.: Government Printing Office, July 1969), vol. 1, p. 40.

19. Philip Taft and Philip Ross, "American Labor Violence: Its Causes, Character, and Outcome," in *Violence in America,* vol. 1, pp. 226–27. The total killed in the 1877 episode was estimated to be "hundreds" by the 1967 President's Commission on Law Enforcement and Administration of Justice, quoted in Fred P. Graham, "A Contemporary History of American Crime," in *Violence in America,* vol. 2, p. 374.

20. Taft and Ross, "American Labor Violence," p. 233.

21. Ibid., pp. 237–38, 253–54.

22. Paul M. Angle, *Resort to Violence: A Chapter in American Lawlessness* (London: Bodley Head, 1954), p. 19.

23. Taft and Ross, "American Labor Violence," pp. 269, 274, 292.

24. Brown, "Historical Patterns of Violence," p. 39.

25. Gilmour, *Riot,* p. 299; Robin Brooks, "Domestic Violence and America's Wars: An Historical Interpretation," in *Violence in America,* vol. 2, p. 411.

26. Richard Hofstadter and Michael Wallace, *American Violence: A Documentary History* (New York: Vintage, 1971), pp. 218, 223–24, 230.

27. Ibid., pp. 241, 246, 250; "The Long Hot Summer of 1919," *Washington Post,* March 1, 1999, p. A6; "The Chicago Race Riot of 1919," *Encyclopaedia Britannica Online* (http://graphics.nytimes.com/images).

28. Hofstadter and Wallace, *American Violence,* p. 263; Morris Janowitz, "Patterns of Collective Racial Violence," in *Violence in America,* vol. 2, p. 323.

29. Hofstadter and Wallace, *American Violence,* pp. 47–48.

30. Sheldon G. Levy, "A 150-Year Study of Political Violence in the United States," in *Violence in America,* vol. 1, p. 70. Other measures of violence in the Levy study, such as injuries, do not show the modern period as the period with the lowest number of occurrences of political violence, but this is probably accounted for by the overreporting bias of modern news systems.

31. House Report No. 754, 52d Cong., quoted in William H. Riker, *Soldiers of the States: The Role of the National Guard in American Democracy* (Washington, D.C.: Public Affairs Press, 1957), p. 52.

32. Roger Allen Brown, William Fedorochko Jr., and John F. Schank, *Assessing the State and Federal Missions of the National Guard* (Santa Monica, Calif.: Rand Corporation, 1995), pp. 38–52.

33. James Buchanan Given, *Society and Homicide in Thirteenth-Century England* (Stanford, Calif.: Stanford University Press, 1977), p. 36 (incorporating corrections for the county of Warwick noted in the *Errata*).

34. Historian Lawrence Stone further reinforces this point, claiming that any

recorded decline in homicides "underestimates the true scale of the shift, since record-keeping and preservation have indisputably improved rather than decayed over the centuries." See "Interpersonal Violence in English Society 1300–1980," *Past and Present* 101 (November 1985), p. 24.

35. Ted Robert Gurr, "Historical Trends in Violent Crime," in *Crime and Justice: An Annual Review of Research,* vol. 3, edited by Michael Tonry and Norval Morris (Chicago: University of Chicago Press, 1981), pp. 303–15.

36. Ibid., p. 306.

37. Ibid., p. 313.

38. Quoted in Stone, "Interpersonal Violence," p. 28.

39. For a comprehensive discussion of the difficulties in discerning the long-term trend in the murder rate for the United States, see Roger Lane, *Murder in America* (Columbus: Ohio State University Press, 1997), especially pp. 307–12. See also Gurr, "Historical Trends," pp. 324–40.

40. Gurr, "Historical Trends," p. 326.

41. Given, *Society and Homicide,* pp. 33–34.

42. Barbara W. Tuchman, *A Distant Mirror: The Calamitous 14th Century* (New York: Ballantine, 1978), p. 9.

43. Alex De Jonge, *Fire and Water: A Life of Peter the Great* (New York: Coward, McCann and Geogehegan, 1980), p. 20.

44. Gilmour, *Riot,* p. 156.

45. Benvenuto Cellini, *The Autobiography of Benvenuto Cellini,* translated by George Bull (New York: Penguin, 1956), pp. 96, 100, 135.

46. Will Durant and Ariel Durant, *The Age of Louis XIV* (New York: Simon and Schuster, 1963), p. 16.

47. Gilmour, *Riot,* p. 277.

48. Ibid., p. 264.

49. Cellini, *Autobiography,* p. 51.

50. J. C. Furnas, *The Americans: A Social History of the United States 1587–1914* (New York: G. P. Putnam's Sons, 1969), p. 531.

51. Gilmour, *Riot,* p. 279.

52. Ibid., pp. 269, 272.

53. From a letter to the editor of the *Revue des Revues,* reproduced in Leo Tolstoy, *The Kingdom of God Is Within You* (New York: Charles Scribner's Sons, 1925), p. 147.

Chapter 13, The Decline of Slavery and Debt Bondage

1. Marc Bloch, *Slavery and Serfdom in the Middle Ages,* translated by William R. Beer (Berkeley and Los Angeles: University of California Press, 1975), pp. 10–14.

2. Will Durant, *The Life of Greece* (New York: Simon and Schuster, 1939), p. 280.

3. Ibid., pp. 254, 278.

4. Rachael Louisa Sargent, *The Size of the Slave Population at Athens during the Fifth and Fourth Centuries Before Christ* (Urbana: University of Illinois, 1924;

reprint, Boulder, Colo.: Greenwood Press, 1973), p. 128.

5. William D. Phillips Jr., *Slavery from Roman Times to the Early Transatlantic Trade* (Minneapolis: University of Minnesota Press, 1985), p. 18.

6. Ibid., p. 18.

7. Bloch, *Slavery and Serfdom,* p. 49.

8. Ibid., p. 34.

9. Phillips, *Slavery from Roman Times,* p. 59

10. George Sansom, *A History of Japan 1334–1615* (Stanford, Calif.: Stanford University Press, 1961), p. 206.

11. Milton Meltzer, *Slavery: A World History,* updated ed. (New York: Da Capo Press, 1993), p. 239.

12. Michael Grant, *Nero: Emperor in Revolt* (New York: American Heritage Press, 1970), p. 110.

13. Ibid., p. 109.

14. Ibid., p. 111.

15. Language used by David Hartley in the British House of Commons in 1776, quoted in "Slavery," in *The Encyclopaedia Britannica,* 11th ed. (1911), vol. 25, p. 222.

16. "Slavery," in The New *Encyclopaedia Britannica,* 15th ed. (1994), vol. 27, p. 293.

17. Ibid.

18. "Roman Law," in *The Encyclopaedia Britannica,* 11th ed. (1911), vol. 23, p. 546.

19. Will Durant, *Caesar and Christ: A History of Roman Civilization and of Christianity from Their Beginnings to A.D. 325* (New York: Simon and Schuster, 1944), p. 130; "Roman Law," p. 551.

20. "Roman Law," p. 551.

21. J. B. Bury, *A History of Greece to the Death of Alexander the Great* (New York: Modern Library, 1913), pp. 174–75.

22. Durant, *Caesar and Christ,* p. 184.

23. Ibid., p. 400.

24. Manuel Riu, "Late Medieval and Early Modern Aragon," in *The Dawn of Modern Banking,* compiled by the Center for Medieval Studies, University of California, Los Angeles (New Haven, Conn.: Yale University Press, 1979), pp. 140–55.

25. Christopher Hibbert, *The Roots of Evil: A Social History of Crime and Punishment* (Boston: Little, Brown, 1963), pp. 132, 133, 138.

26. Henry Bamford Parkes, *The United States of America: A History,* 2d ed. (New York: Alfred A. Knopf, 1967), p. 265.

27. "Report of the Visiters and Governors of the Jail of Baltimore County," in U.S. House of Representatives, 22d Cong., 2d sess. (1832), *Report No. 5 (Abolish Imprisonment for Debt),* p. 11.

28. S. E. Forman, *Our Republic: A Brief History of the American People,* rev. ed. (New York: Century Company, 1922), p. 313.

29. "Report of Visiters," pp. 1, 2, 11.

30. *Encyclopaedia Britannica,* 11th ed. (1911), vol. 10, p. 62; vol. 7, p. 906.

Chapter 14, The Changing Face of Taxation

1. M. Rostovtzeff, *The Social and Economic History of the Roman Empire,* 2d ed., vol. 1 (Oxford: Clarendon Press, 1957), p. 515.

2. Ibid., p. 487.

3. Ramsay MacMullen, *Corruption and the Decline of Rome* (New Haven, Conn.: Yale University Press, 1988), p. 43.

4. Rostovtzeff, *Social and Economic History,* p. 348.

5. Ibid., p. 519.

6. Ibid., pp. 486, 522–24.

7. Ibid., p. 411.

8. MacMullen, *Corruption,* pp. 44–47.

9. Ibid., p. 44.

10. Arthur Herman, *How the Scots Invented the Modern World* (New York: Crown, 2001), pp. 105–6.

11. Ian Gilmour, *Riot, Risings, and Revolution: Governance and Violence in Eighteenth-Century England* (London: Hutchinson, 1992), pp. 84–89; John Stevenson, *Popular Disturbances in England 1700–1870* (London: Longman, 1979), p. 60.

12. Gilmour, *Riot,* p. 305.

13. Charles Adams, *For Good and Evil: The Impact of Taxes on the Course of Civilization* (Lanham, Md.: Madison, 1993), p. 268.

14. Joseph R. Strayer and Charles H. Taylor, *Studies in Early French Taxation* (Cambridge, Mass.: Harvard University Press, 1939), pp. 21–23, 88–91. Louis R. Gottschalk, *The Era of the French Revolution (1715–1815)* (Boston: Houghton Mifflin, 1929), pp. 22–27.

15. George T. Matthews, *The Royal General Farms in Eighteenth-Century France* (New York: Columbia University Press, 1958), pp. 106–8.

16. Ibid., pp. 109–13.

17. Ibid., p. 276.

18. Gilbert Shapiro, "What Were the Grievances of France in 1789?" in *Revolutionary Demands: A Content Analysis of the Cahiers de Doléances of 1789,* Gilbert Shapiro and John Markoff (Stanford, Calif.: Stanford University Press, 1998), pp. 253–79.

19. Adams, *For Good and Evil,* p. 220.

20. Matthews, *The Royal General Farms,* pp. 278–82.

21. Gilmour, *Riot,* p. 82.

22. John H. Makin and Norman J. Ornstein, *Debt and Taxes* (New York: Random House, 1994), pp. 94–95.

23. Ibid., p. 113.

24. James L. Payne, *Costly Returns: The Burdens of the Federal Tax System* (San Francisco: ICS Press, 1993), pp. 87–101; Martin Feldstein, "How Big Should Government Be?" *National Tax Journal* 50, no. 2 (June 1997), p. 211.

25. Payne, *Costly Returns,* pp. 18–21.

26. James L. Payne, "Where Have All the Dollars Gone?" *Reason* (February 1994), p. 17.

27. Martin L. Buchanan, *Unintended Consequences: How Government Poli-*

cies Hurt Oregon's Poor, working paper (Portland, Oreg.: Cascade Policy Institute, 1996), pp. 6–7.

28. Examples include many publications of the House-Senate Joint Economic Committee, such as *The Impact of the Welfare State on the American Family* (September 1996) and *The Economics of the Estate Tax* (December 1998).

29. Paul N. Strassels and Robert Wool, *All You Need to Know about the IRS: A Taxpayer's Guide* (New York: Random House, 1981), p. 3. Strassels, a former IRS official, claims that "nothing is more central to the IRS strategy of tax collection than scaring you, the taxpayer, and keeping you that way."

30. David Burnham, *A Law unto Itself: Power, Politics, and the IRS* (New York: Random House, 1989), chapters 4, 7, 9–12; George Hansen, *To Harass Our People: The IRS and Government Abuse of Power* (Washington, D.C.: Positive, 1984), pp. 92–104.

31. Mark Mellman, quoted in Albert B. Crenshaw and Clay Chandler, "Archer Would Shift Tax Suit Burden," *Washington Post,* October 21, 1997, p. C3.

32. Associated Press, "When Taxpayers' Tears Flow, Even IRS Workers Can Have a Bad Day," *Coeur d'Alene Press,* March 1, 1998, p. A11.

33. In 1990, 2.6 million levies were issued; in 1999, the number was 0.9 million. In 1990, 1.1 million liens were filed; in 1999, the figure was 0.2 million. The source for 1990 figures is the IRS *Data Book.* Data for 1999 are taken from Albert B. Crenshaw and Stephen Barr, "New Commitment to 'Service' May be Taxing IRS," *Washington Post,* May 19, 1999, p. A21. The 1999 figures are full-year projections from first half of year data.

34. *Wall Street Journal,* May 3, 1995, p. 1; U.S. General Accounting Office, *Increasing EFT Usage for Installment Agreements Could Benefit IRS* (Washington, D.C.: Government Printing Office, June 1998), p. 3.

35. David Cay Johnston, "Job Fears Push I.R.S. to Relax Effort," *New York Times,* May 18, 1999, p. 1.

36. Ibid.

37. Section (10)(30)(5)(k).

38. The Roper question gives respondents four choices in rating the agency: highly favorable, moderately favorable, not too favorable, and unfavorable. The "unfavorable" percentage shown in figure 14.1 is the sum of the respondents answering the last two categories. Data for 1997 taken from Princeton Survey Research Associates survey in September–October 1997 for the Pew Research Center for the People and the Press.

39. Albert B. Crenshaw, "Rossotti Promises Reorganized IRS," *Washington Post,* January 29, 1998, p. A4.

Chapter 15, Freedom of Belief and Expression

1. Quoted in Will Durant, *The Age of Faith* (New York: Simon and Schuster, 1950), pp. 774–75.

2. Ibid., p. 974; Robert S. Hoyt, *Europe in the Middle Ages* (New York: Harcourt, Brace, 1957), pp. 363–64.

3. Francis William Coker, ed., *Readings in Political Philosophy* (New York:

284 *Notes*

MacMillan, 1938), p. 337.

    4. J. B. Bury, *A History of Greece to the Death of Alexander the Great* (New York: Modern Library, 1913), pp. 302–3.

    5. Barbara W. Tuchman, *A Distant Mirror: The Calamitous 14th Century* (New York: Ballantine, 1978), pp. 113–14.

    6. Will Durant and Ariel Durant, *The Age of Reason Begins* (New York: Simon and Schuster, 1961), pp. 339–42; Norman Davies, *Europe: A History* (New York: HarperCollins, 1998), p. 506.

    7. Alice Morse Earle, *Curious Punishments of Bygone Days* (1896; reprint, Bedford, Mass.: Applewood, 1995), pp. 138–41.

    8. Ibid., p. 35.

    9. J. C. Furnas, *The Americans: A Social History of the United States 1587–1914* (New York: G. P. Putnam's Sons, 1969), p. 526.

    10. Ibid., p. 522.

    11. For a full account of this shabby episode, see Carlton Sherwood, *Inquisition: The Persecution and Prosecution of the Reverend Sun Myung Moon* (Washington, D.C.: Regnery Gateway, 1991).

    12. Robert Justin Goldstein, *Political Censorship of the Arts and the Press in Nineteenth-Century Europe* (New York: St. Martin's Press, 1989), p. 35.

    13. Davies, *Europe,* p. 445.

    14. Quoted in Goldstein, *Political Censorship,* p. 36.

    15. Will Durant and Ariel Durant, *The Age of Louis XIV* (New York: Simon and Schuster, 1963), p. 227.

    16. Lord Macaulay, *History of England to the Death of William III* (London: Heron, 1967), vol. 4, p. 125.

    17. Ibid., pp. 174–75, 300–301.

    18. Louis Edward Ingelhart, *Press Freedoms* (New York: Greenwood Press, 1987), p. 116.

    19. Data from E. L. Woodward, *The Age of Reform 1815–1870* (Oxford: Clarendon Press, 1939), quoted in Robinson Blann, *Throwing the Scabbard Away: Byron's Battle Against the Censors of Don Juan* (New York: Peter Lang, 1991), p. 19.

    20. Blann, *Throwing the Scabbard Away,* pp. 21–31.

    21. Goldstein, *Political Censorship,* p. 54.

    22. Leonard R. Sussman and Karin Deutsch Karlekar, eds., *The Annual Survey of Press Freedom 2002* (New York: Freedom House, 2002), p. 8.

Chapter 16, Government in the Age of Disrespect

    1. Ian Gilmour, *Riot, Risings, and Revolution: Governance and Violence in Eighteenth-Century England* (London: Hutchinson, 1992), p. 24.

    2. Alice Morse Earle, *Curious Punishments of Bygone Days* (1896; reprint, Bedford, Mass.: Applewood, 1995), p. 73.

    3. Ibid., p. 76.

    4. Gilmour, *Riot,* pp. 42–54.

    5. Ibid., pp. 307–8

    6. Nat Hentoff, *The First Freedom: The Tumultuous History of Free Speech*

in America (New York: Delacorte Press, 1980), pp. 62–63.

7. Ibid., pp. 63–67.

8. Paul Johnson, *A History of the American People* (New York: Harper-Collins, 1997), p. 98.

9. Hentoff, *The First Freedom,* pp. 242–49.

10. Robert J. Blendon, John M. Benson, Richard Morin, Drew E. Altman, Mollyann Brodie, Mario Brossard, and Matt James, "Changing Attitudes in America," in *Why People Don't Trust Government,* edited by Joseph S. Nye, Jr., Philip D. Zelikow, and David C. King (Cambridge, Mass.: Harvard University Press, 1997), p. 206.

11. Ronald Inglehart, "Postmaterialist Values and the Erosion of Institutional Authority," in *Why People Don't Trust Government,* edited by Nye, Zelikow, and King, p. 217.

12. Gerald F. Seib, "Capital Journal," *Wall Street Journal,* October 7, 1998, p. A24.

13. Pippa Norris, ed., *Critical Citizens* (Oxford: Oxford University Press, 1999), p. 258.

14. Russell J. Dalton, "Political Support in Advanced Democracies," in *Critical Citizens,* edited by Norris, pp. 63–64, 69.

15. Soren Holmberg, "Down and Down We Go: Political Trust in Sweden," in *Critical Citizens,* edited by Norris, p. 105.

Chapter 17, Lessons for Voluntarists

1. Leo Tolstoy, *The Kingdom of God Is Within You* (New York: Charles Scribner's Sons, 1925), pp. 18, 239. Tolstoy attributes the dictum "Resist not evil by violence" to the nineteenth-century American pacifist Adin Ballou.

2. Ibid., p. 166.

3. Alexis de Tocqueville, *Democracy in America,* edited by Phillips Bradley (New York: Vintage, 1945), vol. 2, p. 114.

Index